EMPOWERMENT OF RURAL WOMEN
The Deterrents and Determinants

By the same Author

— Corruptions at the Grassroots: The Shades and Shadows
— Participatory Rural Appraisal: The Experience of NGOs in South India

---

ABOUT THE AUTHOR

M.P. BORAIAN is a Reader in Extension Education and Director of Employment Bureau at the Gandhigram Rural University. He obtained his Doctoral degree in rural development from Gandhigram Rural University and pre-doctoral degree in rural development from National Institute of Rural Development. He was a recipient of Fellowship from the United Nations' International Labour Organization. He has appraised, monitored and evaluated over 40 rural projects. He was associated with Research Projects sponsored by UNICEF, ILO, SIDA, SAREC, Planning Commission and ICSSR. He has published more than 60 research papers in professional journals of national and international repute.

EMPOWERMENT OF RURAL WOMEN

The Deterrents and Determinants

M.P. BORAIAN

CONCEPT PUBLISHING COMPANY, NEW DELHI-110059

Cataloging in Publication Data—DK
Courtesy: D.K. Agencies (P) Ltd. <docinfo@dkagencies.com>

Boraian, M. P.
Empowerment of rural women : the deterrents and determinants / M.P. Boraian.
p. cm.
Study conducted at Dindigul District of Tamil Nadu, India.
Includes bibliographical references (p.)
Includes index.
ISBN 13: 9788180695261
ISBN 10: 8180695263

1. Rural women—India—Dindigul (District)—Social conditions. 2. Rural women—India—Dindigul (District)—Economic conditions. 3. Rural women—Government policy—India—Dindigul (District). I. Title.

DDC 305.409 548 2 22

This book is published with partial grant provided under UGC's Unassigned Grant through Gandhigram Rural University.
The project on which the present report is based was funded by the Indian Council of Social Science Research. However, the responsibility for the facts stated, opinions expressed, and conclusions reached is entirely that of the author and not of the Indian Council of Social Science Research.

ISBN- 13: 978-81-8069-526-1
ISBN- 10: 81-8069-526-3

First Published 2008

Published and Printed by
Concept Publishing Company
A/15-16, Commercial Block, Mohan Garden
New Delhi-110059 (INDIA)
Phone : 25351460, 25351794
Fax : 091-11-25357103
Email : publishing@conceptpub.com

Foreword

M.P. Borain's study is a holistic approach to the question to rural women's empowerment with special reference to the women of Dindigul district. It is sensitive and well researched assessment of levels of empowerment and the factors that account for the position of women in the district. The reality bytes of questionnaires focus on relevant issues and problems and point towards possible solutions. Women's life has thus been on the threshold of transition from one phase of life to another phase, from mere welfare and development to that of mobilization and empowerment.

Research of this kind is the need of the hour, especially when one half of society hitherto neglected is involved. This approach may be recommended and implemented in other districts as well and will contribute immensely to the uplift of rural women in the State.

K.M. Ramathal
Chairperson

Preface

Perhaps no other species on the earth, than women, command deification and glorification at one end, and confront subjugation and suppression at the other end. Cutting across the major religions in India, women dominate the divine world as goddesses with reverence and restraint by the humanity. As mothers in the mundane world, they command respect and regard from the society. But then, as women in the family and community, they face hardship and humiliation from not only men but the women too! Bearing the blessings on the one side and burdens on the other side, women continue to march forward with a firm resolve to be an inevitable partner in society.

Change which has been affecting both the environment and society in varying degrees, has certainly been benefiting the women, but perhaps at a much slower pace, than it affects men. Education of girls, emergence of drudgery-reducing technologies, evolving of women-friendly policies, formation of self-help groups, generation of employment and income, enhanced awareness about social legislations, increasing mobility, more freedom than before and greater exposure to the world outside their hamlets or villages—all these developments have brought about a tremendous change in the lives of women.

Changes in a series of spheres – technological spheres, economic sectors, social structure, legal safeguards, political policies, community based women's groupings, and an array of associated fields have made the women to remove their ignorance, reduce their fear and raise their status. The pace of progress in their lives is slow but steady and sustaining. Most of these developments have contributed to the growing independence of women and their contribution to their own self, their family, group and the community. Over a period, they have been getting enabled, enlightened, energized and enthused, so as to be more 'on their' own and wherever possible, 'develop, but not depend on others'.

The women of today, have therefore, reached a new stage – the "take-off stage", towards greater independence from the traditional dependence stage. Greater nuclearization has given the women an added advantage of becoming a near equal social partner. Employment of women has further fortified their economic partnership. Political space given to women in the local bodies has scaled up their political participation. Self-Help Groups have given them a collective personality, mobilized the totality of their strength, and raised their community partnership. Women are thus gradually becoming equal partners in all sectors of economic and social life.

An increasing partnership status of women is not casting its impact on all sections of the women uniformly. Women play an upper hand in some families, equal in others, secondary in some others and face servitude in a few families. The life style of women in towns, cities, educated, economically well off and broad minded families, presents an advanced and modern profile. Whereas in the countryside, among peasants and the poor, their life style is largely traditional, gradually changing though. However, in both the urban and rural systems, the rich and poor families, the continuum of dominance ranges from male-controlled to female-controlled. The magnitude of families remaining on the extremes of the continuum and in the middle, depends upon a multitude of factors.

A small segment of women with all features of empowerment are already part of the society – be it is rural or urban, rich or poor, literate or illiterate—absolutely without any external intervention but completely with inherited qualities, added with an environmental build up, of course. Such self- empowered women could be seen in society like scattered stars, recognized largely by the local community. A few among them emerge stronger by significant contributions and leave their imprints beyond their villages, districts or states or even countries. Such category of women is a reality and they stake their claim from the men in every thing that is due to them, and much more too. These women enjoy not merely equal status but also over power the male domination and make them to listen, but never dictate. Examples of such women are abound in every sphere—in politics, social work, corporate, micro enterprises, panchayat institutions, academic world, grassroot activism, down to the domestic front.

Cutting across geographic boundaries, classes, castes and cultures, families could be classified into four broad categories viz., male dominant, female dominant, equal (or near equal) partner, and suppressed families. Therefore, though our Indian society is basically patriarchal, the marks of matriarchy could be seen in every community, industry, polity and society. Existing socio-cultural and community-based organizational developments have contributed to a spurt in their number, with signs of its ascendance.

Households with such self empowered women are practically female dominant. Added to this group of women with innate qualities of empowerment, duly fortified by their opportunities and environment, we witness a new genre of women cropping up in the countryside through the movement of self-help groups. They have been providing the rural households with a new class of emerging leaders, who are fast rising to be equal to men in every measurable aspect of gender equality.

In the context of the above, it is sought to highlight the status of women in the rural belts of a backward district in Tamil Nadu state. The study highlights the status of women, the process empowerment of rural women, and spells out what constitutes empowerment, what factors contribute to empowerment and what are the constraints which hamper the process of empowerment. Towards the end, the study advocates a series of interventions in the social, health, educational, skill training, economic, political, legal, organizational and developmental spheres which affect the process of empowerment of rural women. The researcher welcomes comments and contributions from the readers on the methods and outcome of the study.

Acknowledgements

I express my heartfelt gratitude to the *Indian Council of Social Science Research (ICSSR),* New Delhi for sponsoring the present study on "Empowering Rural Women - Locating the Deterrents and Determinants."

I am deeply thankful to our former Vice Chancellors *Dr. Ms. G. Pankajam* and *Dr. T. Karunakaran* for providing encouragement, and support in all our research endeavours.

I express my sincere gratitude to *Dr. M. Sundaravadivelu*, Registrar, Gandhigram Rural University and *Dr. N. Narayanasamy,* Professor and Head, Department of Extension Education for their motivation and cooperation in this research pursuit.

I am thankful to *Dr. M.A. Sudhir,* Professor and Head, and *Dr. S. Gunasekaran,* Reader in Statistics, Department of Applied Research, GRU, for their support in the research methodological and statistical components of the study.

I also thank the Research Assistants Ms. T. Kavitha and Ms. Roopa, and the Investigators Ms. Kasturi and Ms. Sumathy who helped in collecting data, consolidation and processing.

I thank the computer and secretarial team Ms. B. Vani, Messrs. R. Saravanan, P. Sellachamy and P. Maruthupandi for their painstaking effort in shaping up this report.

Gandhigram
2nd October 2007

M.P. BORAIAN

Contents

Foreword by ***Dr. K.M. Ramathal*** v

Preface vii

Acknowledgements xi

List of Tables xv

List of Figures xviii

Acronyms and Abbreviations xix

1. Status of Women 1
2. Review of Literature 23
3. Design of the Study 41
4. Response of the Rural Women 54
5. Opinion of Experts on Women Empowerment 125
6. Indicators of Women Empowerment 147
7. Perception of Men about Women Empowerment 157
8. Summary of Findings and Conclusion 169
9. Policy Options for Empowerment Intervention 188
10. Case Studies on Select Rural Women 198

Bibliography 209

Index 223

List of Tables

1.1	Sex Ratio (1901—2001)	6
1.2	Literacy in Tamil Nadu	7
1.3	Work Participation in Tamil Nadu	8
3.1	List of Study Villages	48
3.2	Population details of Study Villages	49
4.1	Religion and Community particulars of the Respondents	55
4.2	Family Type and Pattern of Family of the Respondents	57
4.3	Age, Birth Order and Place of Birth of the Respondents	57
4.4	Marital Status, Age at Marriage and Type of Marriage of the Respondents	59
4.5	Educational Status of the Respondents and their Spouses	60
4.6	Maternity details and Adoption of Birth Control Measures by the Respondents	62
4.7	Basic Amenities available in the Respondent Households	65
4.8	Occupation of Respondents and their Spouses—Before and After Marriage	66
4.9	Vocational and Leadership Skills of the Respondents and their Benefits	67
4.10	Occupation, Household Income and Annual Income of the Respondents	68
4.11	Domestic Expenditure of Respondent Households	70
4.12	Savings Position of Respondent Households	70
4.13	Liabilities of Respondents according to their Sources	71
4.14	Sharing of Domestic Responsibilities in the Respondent Households	72
4.15	Members Making Domestic-Related Decisions in the Respondent Households	74
4.16	Access and control of the Respondents Over Productive Resources	76

4.17 Awareness of the Respondents about Social Legislations 78
4.18 Opinion of Respondents on the Changes in Social Customs and Relaxation in Social Restrictions 79
4.19 Perception of Respondents on Men's Rating of Women's Status 80
4.20 Major Problems Faced by the Respondents, Girl Children and other Women 82
4.21 Sources of Women's Problems and Proposed Methods of Overcoming 83
4.22 Views of Respondents on the Concept of Empowerment 86
4.23 Ideal Characteristics of Empowered Women as stated by the Respondents 87
4.24 Views of Respondents on the Obstacles to Women Empowerment and Methods of Overcoming 89
4.25 Freedom of Women as an Indicator of Empowerment 90
4.26 Participation in Community Activities as an Indicator of Empowerment 91
4.27 Gender Discrimination as an Indicator of Empowerment 92
4.28 Violence Against Women as an Indicator of Empowerment 93
4.29 Acquisition of Power and Influence as an Indicator of Empowerment 94
4.30 Yardsticks used in Assessing Women Empowerment as reported by the Respondents 95
4.31 Level of Freedom among the Respondents 99
4.33 Level of Gender Discrimination among the Respondents 105
4.34 Level of Violence against Women among the Respondents 111
4.35 Level of Power and Influence among the Respondents 116
4.36 Level of Overall Empowerment among the Respondents 121
5.1 Birth Order of Respondents 125
5.2 Religion, Community, Education and Vocational and Life Skills of Respondents 126
5.3 Marital Status, Type of Marriage, Education and Occupation of the Respondents and Spouses 128
5.4 Dominating Member in the Present and their Parents' Families 129

5.5 Sources of Problems, Status of Women, and Men's Response to Women Empowerment 130
5.6 Concept and Assessment of Women Empowerment at Various Levels 133
5.7 Dimensions of Women Empowerment and their Constituents 136
5.8 Strategies and Barriers to Women Empowerment 139
5.9 Role of the Government, NGOs and Panchayats in Women Empowerment 140
5.10 Socio-Demographic Factors Influencing Women Empowerment 143
6.1 Relevance of Basic Needs as an Indicator of Women Empowerment 149
6.2 Opinion of Respondents on the Relevance of Resources as an Indicator of Women Empowerment 149
6.3 Opinion of Respondents on the Relevance of Health Care as an Indicator of Women Empowerment 150
6.4 Opinion on the Relevance of Education as an Indicator of Women Empowerment 151
6.5 Opinion of Respondents on the Relevance of Decision Making as an Indicator of Women Empowerment 151
6.6 Opinion of Respondents on the Relevance of Economic Freedom as an Indicator of Women Empowerment 152
6.7 Opinion of Respondents on the Relevance of Public Participation as an Indicator of Women Empowerment 152
6.8 Opinion of Respondents on the Relevance of Freedom of Mobility as an Indicator of Women Empowerment 153
6.9 Opinion of Respondents on the Relevance of Psychological Qualities as an Indicator of Women Empowerment 154
6.10 Opinion of Respondents on the Relevance of Government Support as an Indicator of Women Empowerment 154
6.11 Score Values of Factors relevant to Women Empowerment 155

List of Figures

1. Map of Dindigul District 47
2. Religion and Community of the Respondents 56
3. Age, Birth Order and Place of Birth of Respondents 58
4. Education of the Respondents and Spouses 61
5. Ante-natal and Post-natal Care by the Respondents 63
6. Adoption of Birth Control Measure by the Respondents 64
7. Annual Income of the Households and Respondents 69
8. Liabilities of Respondents according to their Sources 72
9. Decision-Making by Family Members 75
10. Access and Control of Respondents over Productive Resources 77
11. Perception of Women on Men's Rating of Women 81
12. Sources of Women's Problems and Present Status of Rural Women 84
13. Views of Respondents on the Concept of Empowerment 86
14. Ideal Characteristics of Empowered Women 88
15. Yardsticks used in Assessing Women Empowerment 96
16. Comparative Status of Women and Response of Men to Women Empowerment 131
17. Dimensions of Women Empowerment 136
18. Score Values of Factors Relevant to Women Empowerment 156

ACRONYMS AND ABBREVIATIONS

AGPRP	:	Awareness Generation Project for Rural Poor Women
APCWD	:	Asian and Pacific Centre for Women and Development
BC	:	Backward Caste
BLCC	:	Block Level Coordination Committee
CBOs	:	Community Based Organizations
CCE & VT	:	Condensed Courses of Education & Vocational Training for Adult Women
CEDAW	:	Convention on the Elimination of All Forms of Discrimination Against Women
CSWB	:	Central Social Welfare Board
EDP	:	Entrepreneurship Development Programme
GBS	:	Gross Budgetary Support
GDI	:	Gender-related Development Index
GDP	:	Gross Domestic Product
GEM	:	Gender Empowerment Measure
GER	:	Gross Enrollment Ratio
HDI	:	Human Development Index
HDR	:	Human Development Report
HIV	:	Human Infectious Virus
AIDS	:	Acquired Immuno Deficiency Syndrome
HWW	:	Hostels for Working Women
IAS	:	Indian Administrative Service
IAY	:	Indira Awas Yojana
IMR	:	Infant Mortality Rate
IMRY	:	Indira Mahila Rozgar Yojana
ITI	:	Industrial Training Institute
JGSY	:	Jawahar Gram Samriddhi Yojana
M.Phil.	:	Master of Philosophy

MAVIM	:	Mahila Arthik Vikas Mahamandal
MMR	:	Maternal Mortality Rate
MRCP	:	Maharashtra Rural Credit Programme
NABARD	:	National Bank for Agricultural and Rural Development
NCW	:	National Commission for Women
NGO	:	Non-Governmental Organization
NORAD	:	Norwegian Agency for Development and Cooperation
NSHG	:	Non-Self-Help Group
PG	:	Post Graduate
Ph.D.	:	Doctor of Philosophy
PHC	:	Primary Health Centre
PRI	:	Panchayati Raj Institution
RMK	:	Rashtriya Mahila Kosh
RSVY	:	Rashtriya Sam Vikas Yojana
SAARC	:	South Asian Association for Rural Reconstruction
SC	:	Schedule Caste
ST	:	Schedule Tribe
SEP	:	Socio-Economic Programme
SGSY	:	Swarnajayanti Gram Swarozgar Yojana
SHG	:	Self-Help Group
SSH	:	Short Stay Homes
STEP	:	Support for Training and Employment Programme
TH	:	The Hindu
TN	:	Tamil Nadu
UG	:	Under Graduate
UN	:	United Nations
UNDP	:	United Nations Development Programme
UNIFEM	:	United Nations Development Fund for Women
UT	:	Union Territory

Chapter 1

Status of Women

> *"Woman is the companion of man, gifted with equal mental capacities. She has the right to participate in the minutest details of the activities of man and she has the same right of freedom and liberty as he. She is entitled to a supreme place in her own sphere of activity as man is in his".*
>
> *–Mahatma Gandhi*

1.1 India's Gender Ranking

India occupies 126th position in respect of Human Development Index (HDI) among the 177 countries ranked by the UNDP (2006). Women held only 9.3 per cent of parliamentary seats, and their ratio of income to male was 0.38. (HD Report 2005). In respect of Gender-related Development Index (GDI), India was placed in the 98th position (among 140 countries) with a GDI value of 0.586. Norway (0.960), Australia (0.954) and Iceland (0.953) stood in the first three slots while Niger (0.271), Sierra Leone (0.279) and Burkina Faso (0.311) were placed the last. Females had a higher life expectancy (65.0) than males (61.8) but lower adult literacy (47.8 as against 3.4 for males) and gross enrollment ratio for primary, secondary and tertiary schools (56 as against 64 for males) (HDR, 2005).

Not giving birth to girls is marked in many regions across the country by what the Nobel prize winning economist, Amartya Sen, calls "high-tech sexism"—determining a foetus' sex and aborting the foetus if it happened to be a female. Inadequate nurturing results from giving girls a subordinate claim over the family's food, educational and medical care resources, compared with boys.

Currently, the national figure stands at 933 women to 1000 men, but what is most disturbing is that the number of girls per 1000 boys in the 0-6 age group has fallen from 945 in 1991 census to 927 in 2001 census. If the German ratio of 94.8 to 100 can be used as the cut-off point, below which we should suspect any anti-female intervention.

Professor Sen has called attention to the "remarkable geographical split" of India—the entire North and West are below benchmark and the whole East and South (with the exception of Tamil Nadu) are above it. In an attempt to understand why there is such a trend towards elimination of female foetuses and infants, let us examine the status of women across the countries and in India.

1.2. Status of Women—Global Scenario

- *Economic Status*: At present, one in every four households in the world is headed by a woman. When compared to men, the majority of women earn, on an average, about three-fourths of the pay of males for the same work outside of the agricultural sector, in both developed and developing countries. In most countries, women work approximately twice the unpaid time men do. Women make up 31 per cent of the official labour force in developing countries and 46.7 per cent worldwide. Rural women produce more than 55 per cent of all food grown in developing countries. The value of women's unpaid housework and community work is estimated between 10-35 per cent of GDP worldwide, amounting to $11 trillion in 1993. Women hold 35.1 per cent of professional posts in the United Nations Secretariat, including 17.9 per cent in senior management.
- *Educational Status*: There is inequality in the opportunity given to girls for their formal school education worldwide. Of the world's nearly one billion illiterate adults, two-thirds are women. Two-thirds of the 130 million children worldwide, who are not in school, are girls. During the past two decades, the combined primary and secondary enrollment ratio for girls in developing countries increased from 38 per cent to 78 per cent.

- *Political Status*: United Nations observed that, despite the recent election of women heads of state in Chile, Liberia, and Germany, women are making scant progress around the world in getting into leadership positions in business, government and academia. Even in wealthy nations, the pace is still too slow, said the report prepared by UN Secretary General Kofi Annan to mark the International Women's day (2006). 'Serious obstacles remain that hinder women's effective participation', said the report, which called for increased participation to be translated into influence in the decision making process. (The Hindu, March 9, 2006, p.14) The first country to grant women the right to vote was New Zealand in 1893. Only 24 women have been elected heads of state or government in the century. Women hold 10.5 per cent of the seats in the world's parliaments. In early 1995, Sweden formed the world's first cabinet to have equal number of men and women. Of the 185 highest-ranking diplomats in the United Nations, seven are women. The percentage of female cabinet ministers worldwide has doubled in the last decade, from 3.4 in 1987 to 6.8 per cent in 1996.
- *Health Status*: Women outlive men in almost every country. There are slightly fewer women than men in the world 98.6 women for every 100 men. The life expectancy of women has gone up. In 1992, the average woman lived for 62.9 years in developing countries compared to 53.7 years in 1970. In industrialized countries, women's average life expectancy in 1992 was 79.4 years, up from 74.2 in 1970. Women are becoming increasingly affected by HIV. Today, about 42 per cent of estimated cases are women, and the number of infected women is expected to reach 15 million by the year 2010. An estimated 20 million unsafe abortions are performed worldwide every year, resulting in the deaths of 70,000 women. Approximately, 585,000 women die every year, over 1,600 every day from causes related to pregnancy and child birth. In sub-Saharan Africa, 1 in 13 women die from pregnancy or child birth related causes, compared to 1 in 3,300 women in the United States. Globally, 43 per cent of

all women and 51 per cent of pregnant women suffer from iron-deficiency anaemia.

- *Violence Against Women*: Every year, an estimated two million girls suffer the practice of female genital mutilation. Worldwide, 20 to 50 per cent of women experience some degree of domestic violence during marriage. The primary victims of today's armed conflicts are civilian women and their children, not soldiers. The use of rape as a weapon of war has become more evident. In Rwanda, from April 1994 to April 1995, estimates of the number of women and girls raped range from 15,700 to over 250,000.

1.3. Status of Women in India

Launching the nation-wide campaign to reverse the alarming decline in the ratio of women in the population in the country, Minister for Women and Child Development, Government of India said: "It is a tragedy that every year, half million girl children are being killed and prevented from being born, ironically with the help of modern tools of science and technology leading to the decline in the ratio of women in the population. It is shocking that the declining sex ratio has already led to a situation where brothers shared a wife and in some cases, even fathers and sons shared a wife in several parts of the country". My Ministry would therefore, observe the next 10 years as the decade of the Survival of Girl Child. (*The Hindu*, March 9, 2006 p.13)

Contemporary Status: Women who number 498.7 million according to 2001 Census represented 48.2 per cent of country's population of 1,027.01 crores. The sex ratio of 933 women per 1000 men as revealed by the Census Report 2001 shows the misuse of the prenatal diagnostic technique to do away with female foetus. Health-wise, high rates of infant and maternal deaths and severe anaemia in over half of all married women in India are some of the indicators of the low priority accorded to women's health in the country (Skawatra, 2003). Life expectancy of rural women, which was 32 years in 1947, has gone up to 64 years today. The infant mortality has decreased considerably.

According to the Census of India 2001, the literacy percentage of women was only 54.16, though it has grown considerably since Independence. In 1951, the literacy rate of women was only 8.86 per cent. In 2001, it had raised manifold which went up to 54.16 per cent. The school enrollment has gone up to 99 per cent and every eligible girl child today, has all the freedom and opportunity to get education. They now have access to Higher Education.

Ever since India became free, there have been phenomenal changes in the condition of women. The constitution has given women the much needed status. They are now equal before law. There can be no discrimination by the state on grounds of gender. But, it is reported that in 1991, India had approximately 5157 dowry deaths, 20,611 molestation cases, 12,300 kidnappings and abductions, 10,283 cases of eve teasing, 15,949 instances involving cruelty by husband and relatives (Giri, 1998).

In matters related to economic development, women continued to be marginalized both in policy formulation and programme implementation. Low level of skills lead to lower wages and low earning (Agarwal, 2001). In terms of employment, she enjoys the same status as men and has to be given equal pay for equal work. Assurance has been given to promote harmony and to renounce practices derogatory to their dignity. Some of the recently enacted labour laws have facilitated the employment of rural women as unskilled labour in the organized and unorganized sectors.

Politically, the reforms in the Panchayat Raj Act have given greater share for women in rural governance. At present, the concept of Self-Help Groups for women, particularly in rural areas has given them an opportunity to organize themselves to engage in productive activities that could augment their earnings (Vanavarayar, 2003) which leads to their social and political empowerment.

Gender Disparity: According to Amartya Sen (2001), gender inequality is not one homogenous phenomenon but a collection of desperate and interlinked problems and the different kinds of gender inequality were displayed in mortality, natality, basic facility, special opportunity professions, ownership, and household matters. We shall look into the classification of gender disparity at birth, growth and survival.

Disparity at Birth: In being born as female children and in giving birth to children, women experience grave disparity, while the infant mortality reveals that the right to be born is denied, the maternal mortality speaks of the lack of medical care and attention to women.

Infant Mortality: Sex ratio (females per 1000 males) is a simple but very strong index of the long-term status of women's welfare. India is one of the few countries where males significantly outnumber females, and their imbalance has increased over time. According to Census of India 2001, the sex ratio is 933.

Table 1.1: Sex Ratio (1901—2001)

Year	*Tamil Nadu*	*India*
1901	1044	974
1951	1007	946
1961	992	941
1971	978	930
1981	977	934
1991	974	927
2001	986	933

In Tamil Nadu, the sex ratio has been raised to 986 (1991 sex ratio—974). The inter-district variations in TN have been striking. Thoothukudi has the highest sex ratio of 1049 and Salem has the lowest 929. In Dindigul district, the sex ratio is 986 on par with the ratio of the state.

For the 0-6 year population, Tamil Nadu (TN) figure of 939 is slightly above the Indian average of 924, but there is a general tendency of juvenile sex ratio in TN to decline. The districts of Salem (826), Dharmapuri (878) and Theni (893) have reported very low rates. Salem district has the dubious distinction of having the lowest juvenile sex ratio of 826 among all the districts in our country. Due to female infanticide in TN, thousands of infants are killed every year. In 1998, as per Primary Health Center (PHC) records, 3226 female infants were killed. It is concentrated in a core region of 7 districts namely Salem, Dharmapuri, Theni, Namakkal, Karur, Dindigul and Madurai. The general decline in juvenile sex ratio draws attention to safeguard the future of women.

Maternal Mortality: India's Maternal Mortality Rates (MMR) in rural areas are one of the highest in the world. From a global perspective, India accounts for 19 per cent of 911 lives births and 27 per cent of all maternal deaths. It is estimated that pregnancy related deaths account for one-third of them, considered preventable forever.

A factor contributes to India's high maternal mortality rate is the reluctance to seek medical care during pregnancy. It is viewed as a temporary condition that will disappear. The estimates nationwide are that only 40-50 per cent of women receive any antenatal care. In Tamil Nadu, it is available only for 81.9 per cent of pregnant mothers (Multi indicator survey, 1995) and maternal mortality rate has come down from 376 per 1,00,000 live births in 1992 (India: 453) to 150 in 1998. However, MMR was high in the Nilgiris, Perambalur and Sivagangai districts (TSDR, 2000).

Disparity at Growth: As female children grow, they are treated differently in getting food and health care; they do not even have educational opportunity as that of their male counterparts.

Food and Health Care: Surviving through a normal life cycle is a resource-poor woman's greatest challenge. Gender disparities in nutrition are evident from infancy to adulthood. In fact, gender has been the most statistically significant determinant of malnutrition among young children and malnutrition is a frequent direct or underlying cause of death among girls below age 5. Girls are breast-fed less frequently and for shorter durations in infancy in children and adulthood. Males are fed first and better. A primary way that parents discriminate against their girl children is through neglect during illness. Sometimes the sick, little girls are not taken to the doctor as frequently as are their brothers.

Education: Education can pave way for an overall development of individuals and for the society. Female literacy is not only an end itself, but also serves as a catalyst for overall performance in other segments too. General literacy levels of women in TN (64.55 per cent) have been always above the national average (India's female literacy: 54.16 per cent).

Table 1.2: Literacy in Tamil Nadu

Year	*Male (%)*	*Female (%)*	*Total (%)*
1951	31.73	10.06	20.85
1961	44.54	18.17	31.41
1971	51.78	26.36	39.46
1981	58.26	34.99	46.76
1991	74.88	51.30	63.72
2001	82.33	64.55	73.47

Source: Census of India (1951-2001)

Even though female literacy in Tamil Nadu has shown considerable increase, the gender gap between male and female literacy rates has continued. The need to narrow down the gap is urgent. The inter-district imbalance in literacy levels ranges from 49.10 per cent in Dharmapuri to 85.39 per cent in Kanyakumari.

Disparity at Survival: While working for their survival, women are not given equal wages, dignified treatment and their progress is suppressed through violence. However, women continue to show their determination by involving in governance. In rural areas, while the work participation of men had increased from 58.28 per cent in 1991-92 to 60.1 per cent in 1993-94, that of women increased considerably from 38.50 per cent to 47.8 per cent. While the increase of work participation of women has to be acknowledged, the types of work undertaken by them bring out clearly their subservient position in Tamil Nadu.

Table 1.3: Work Participation in Tamil Nadu

Type of Area	*1991-92 (%)*	*1993-94 (%)*
1. *Rural*		
• Male	58.28	61.1
• Female	38.50	47.8
2. *Urban*		
• Male	52.78	57.4
• Female	13.10	22.8

Source: Statistical Hand book of TN

Women's contribution to agriculture—whether it is subsistence farming or commercial agriculture, when measured in terms of the number of tasks performed and the time spent, is greater than men. The industries make *beedi* (hand rolled cigarette), manufacturing (60%), cotton mills (59%), cotton spinning (79%), cashew nut processing (84%) and manufacturing of matches that are surely not highly rewarding; some of them even create serious health hazards. Women's work participation mostly goes unrecorded and unrecognized. They work roughly twice as many hours as men. Nearly 27 per cent are accounted for by 'unpaid activities' performed by family labour (*The Hindu*, Sep. 5, 2000). Moreover, the situation and working condition of rural women in TN requires greater attention and provision.

Violence: Violence against women and girls is the most pervasive. Human rights violation is one of the most crucial social mechanisms by which they are forced into a subordinate position. Fear of violence is a cause of women's lack of participation in activities beyond their home as well as inside it. In recent years, there has been an alarming rise in atrocities against women in India.

Every 26 minutes, a woman is molested. Every 34 minutes, a rape takes place. Every 42 minutes, a sexual harassment occurs. Every 43 minutes, a woman is kidnapped. And every 93 minutes, a woman is burnt to death over dowry. One-quarter of the reported rapes involve girls under the age of 16 but the vast majorities are never reported although the penalty is severe, and convictions are rare.

Governance: Perhaps the most significant development for women in the last decade has been the introduction of 33 per cent reservation for women in local village level (panchayat raj) elections. More and more women have shown that once they have power, they are able to use it, to the benefit of society in general and women in particular. (http://www.twnside.org) However, there is ample delay. Currently, constitutional amendment bill being considered for approval by the Indian Parliament that will allow the Indian govt. to set aside 33 per cent of the seats in the Lok Sabha and other legislative bodies in the states exclusively for women.

Since the onset of Panchayat Raj Institutions (PRI), the percentages of women in various levels of political activity have risen from 4-5 per cent to 25-40 per cent. Through the experience of the Indian PRIs, one million women have actively entered political life in India. Since the creation of the quota system, local women—the vast majority of them illiterate and poor, have come to occupy as much as 43 per cent of the seats.

Life Cycle Approach: Women, as an independent target group, account for 495.74 million and represent 48.3 per cent of country's total population, as per the 2001 Census. Empowering women as a process demands a life-cycle approach. Therefore, every stage of their life counts as a priority in the planning process. Depending upon the developmental needs at every stage, female population has been categorized into 5 distinct sub-groups (population as projected for 2001). They include:

- Girl children in the age-group 0-14 years who account for 171.50 million (34.6 per cent), deserve special attention because of the gender bias and discrimination they suffer from at such a tender age;
- Adolescent girls in the age-group 15-19 years, who account for 52.14 million (10.5 per cent), are very sensitive from the viewpoint of planning because of the preparatory stage for their future productive and reproductive roles in the society and family, respectively;
- Women in the reproductive age-group 15-44 years numbering 233.72 million (47.1 per cent) need special care and attention because of their reproductive needs;
- Women in the economically active age group 15-59 years, who account for 289.40 million (58.4 per cent), have different demands like those of education, training, employment, income generation and participation in the developmental process, decision-making etc.; and
- The elderly women in the age-group 60+ years, numbering 34.87 million (7.0 per cent), have limited needs mainly relating to health, financial and emotional support.

We may conclude that women, who enjoyed a better status in historic times, slowly became secondary and subservient to men. However, the recent trend has been better and they are gradually equipping themselves on all fronts. To-day, the talk is about empowerment of women through organizing them into Self-Help Groups and making them dignified human beings.

1.4. Institutional Initiatives—Global Institutions

UNIFEM is the women's fund at the United Nations. It provides financial and technical assistance to innovative programmes and strategies to foster women's empowerment and gender equality. Placing the advancement of women's human rights at the centre of all of its efforts, UNIFEM focuses its activities on four strategic areas: (1) reducing feminized poverty, (2) ending violence against women, (3) reversing the spread of HIV/AIDS among women and girls, and

(4) achieving gender equality in democratic governance in times of peace as well as war.

UNIFEM works to enhance women's economic security by strengthening their rights to land and inheritance, increasing their access to decent work, and empowering women migrant workers in both sending and receiving countries. UNIFEM has worked with the Government to formulate a minimum standard contract for migrant women that is being used to monitor working conditions. In over 30 countries, UNIFEM supports national and local initiatives to include gender perspectives in budgeting processes, and to collect and use sex-disaggregated data in public policy formulation.

CEDAW

The call for a Women's Convention emerged from the First World Conference on Women in Mexico City in 1975. On December 18, 1979, the United Nations adopted the Convention on the Elimination of All Forms of Discrimination Against Women, also known as "The Treaty for the Rights of Women" or "CEDAW." Until the General Assembly adopted the Convention in 1979, no international document comprehensively addressed women's rights within the political, cultural, economic, social, and family life.

Often called an international "Bill of Rights" for women, CEDAW is the culmination of more than 30 years of work by the United Nations Commission on the Status of Women. The creation of this treaty was the first critical step in developing appropriate human rights language for women. This language addresses abuses (*for example*, physical, sexual, economic, and political) of women and promotes women's full enjoyment of their rights and well-being. CEDAW has been used to incorporate women's rights into national constitutions, update or eliminate discriminatory national laws, and influence court decisions in many countries.

Because of CEDAW, millions of girls who were previously denied access are now receiving basic education; measures have been taken against sex slavery, domestic violence and trafficking of women; women's health care services have improved, saving lives during pregnancy and childbirth; and millions of women have secured loans and obtained the right to own or inherit property. As of March 2004, 175 countries have ratified CEDAW. The United States is among a small minority of countries that have not ratified the treaty, including Iran, Sudan, and Somalia.

The goal articulated in Cairo is to 'bring about more equitable relationships between men and women, and empower women to participate more fully in development'. Therefore, a broad policy to be pursued by the 180 countries represented in Cairo is the empowerment of women.

1.5. National Initiatives for Women Empowerment

In order to empower the weaker and socially and economically deprived sections of the society, the Ministry of Welfare which was constituted on 25th September 1985, was renamed as the Ministry of Social Justice and Empowerment on 25th May 1998 during IX plan period. The responsibility for implementation of the schemes is shared between the Central and State Governments. The Department of Women and Child Development, since its inception, has been implementing special programmes for holistic development and empowerment of women with major focus on improving the socio-economic status of women. Some of the recent programmes and initiatives of women and development implemented by the Departments of Women and Development and Rural Development in the area of women's empowerment are as follows:

1.5.1. Women Development

In the Women and Child Development sector, the nodal Department of Women and Child Development also implements a few innovative schemes besides formulating policies and programmes; enacts/amends legislations affecting women and co-ordinates the efforts of both Governmental and Non-Governmental Organizations (NGOs) to raise the overall status of women on par with that of men. The programmes of the Department include: (i) empowering strategies; (ii) employment and income generation; (iii) welfare and support services; (iv) awareness generation and gender sensitization and (v) other enabling measures. These programmes play the role of being both supplementary and complementary to the other general development programmes in the sectors of health, education, labour and employment, rural and urban development, etc. Some of the important on-going interventions of the nodal Department during the Ninth Plan are detailed below:

- ***Empowering Strategies*:** The erstwhile programme of Indira Mahila Yojana launched in 1995, was recast as Swayamsidha in 2001 to empower women by generating awareness and helping them to achieve economic strength through micro-level income-generation activities and facilitate easy convergence of various services such as literacy, health, non-formal education, rural development, water supply, entrepreneurship, etc.

  Another empowering intervention refers to 'Swa-Shakti Project', sanctioned in 1998 for a five-year period till 2003 with assistance from the International Development Association and International Fund for Agricultural Development. Swa-Shakti has been in action in 57 districts of 9 states of Bihar, Chhattisgarh, Gujarat, Haryana, Jharkhand, Karnataka, Madhya Pradesh, Uttaranchal and Uttar Pradesh. Its major objective is to create an enabling environment for empowerment of women through setting up of self-reliant women's SHGs and developing linkages between SHGs and lending institutions in order to ensure women's continued access to credit facilities for income generation activities.
- ***Employment and Income Generation:*** The Support for Training and Employment Programme (STEP), launched in 1987, provides a comprehensive package of upgradation of skills through training, extension inputs and market linkages to poor and assetless women in the traditional sectors of agriculture, dairy farming, handicrafts, handlooms, animal husbandry, sericulture and fisheries. Since inception of this programme, about 6.1 lakh women have been covered under 133 projects launched in 19 states viz. Andhra Pradesh, Bihar, Chhattisgarh, Gujarat, Haryana, Himachal Pradesh, Karnataka, Kerala, Madhya Pradesh, Maharashtra, Manipur, Nagaland, Orissa, Sikkim, Tamil Nadu, Tripura, Uttaranchal, Uttar Pradesh and West Bengal. Nearly 60 per cent of the projects have been in the dairy sector. About 8,000 women's dairy co-operatives with more than 4 lakh members have been organised throughout the country mainly through the

initiative of State Cooperative Milk Federations. Another programme called Training-cum-Production Centres for Women (popularly known as NORAD) was launched in 1982-83 with the assistance from the Norwegian Agency for Development and Cooperation (NORAD). The scheme attempts to improve the lives of young women/girls especially school drop-outs and semi-literates, by extending training to non-traditional trades like electronics, watch assembling, computer programming, garment making, secretarial work, community health work, embroidery, weaving, etc.

Yet, another major programme of employment and training for poor and needy women, being implemented by CSWB, is the Socio-Economic Programme (SEP). Around 62 SEP Units were set up during the Ninth Plan to benefit about 3,100 women. The major reason for the failure to achieve the targets set for this programme was the decision to phase out the scheme and finally drop the same in the Tenth Plan.

The scheme of Condensed Courses of Education & Vocational Training for Adult Women (CCE & VT), being run by CSWB since 1958, aims to provide new avenues of employment through continuing education and vocational training for women and girls who are school drop-outs.

➢ ***Welfare and Support Services:*** Launched in 1972-73, the programme of Hostels for Working Women (HWW) aims to promote greater mobility for women in the employment market by providing safe and cheap accommodation to working women belonging to the lower income strata living away from home. Since inception of the scheme, 881 hostels were sanctioned with a capacity to accommodate 62,308 women till date, and their 8,226 dependent children in the attached 316 day-care centres. The programme of Short Stay Homes (SSH) for Women and Girls was launched in 1969 to protect and rehabilitate those women and girls who are in social and moral danger due to breakup of families, mental strain/stress, social ostracism, exploitation etc. At present, there exist 271 SSHs, benefiting more than 6,700 women.

The scheme of Assistance to Voluntary Organisations for

Education Work for Prevention of Atrocities against Women was started in 1982. Under this scheme, Women Study Centres and institutions of higher learning and voluntary organizations are given financial assistance for undertaking various activities relating to education. The General Grants-in-Aid to Voluntary Organisations through CSWB and for strengthening its field organisations is a multifaceted scheme providing financial assistance to voluntary organisations for rendering welfare services to women, children, aged and infirm, handicapped and other special groups through various programmes.

➢ ***Awareness Generation and Gender Sensitization:*** The Ninth Plan attached great importance to efforts that trigger changes in societal attitudes towards women and the girl child. An integrated media campaign-covering electronic, print and film media—which projects a positive image of both women and the girl child is the most important component of the Government's communication strategy. To sensitize the enforcement machinery, a countrywide gender sensitization programme was launched in 1991 in collaboration with United Nations Development Fund for Women, New Delhi. Special campaigns to combat atrocities against women were also launched throughout the country in collaboration with the State Home Departments and NGOs.

A set of 10 legal literacy manuals written in a simple and illustrated format was also published in 1992 with the aim of educating women about the laws concerning their basic rights. These manuals cover laws relating to working women, child labour, contract labour, adoption and maintenance, Hindu, Muslim and Christian Marriage Laws including right to property, dowry, rape, kidnapping and related police procedures. The Awareness Generation Project for Rural Poor Women (AGPRP) aims to identify the needs of these women and generate awareness amongst them about their rights and handling of social issues. Since 1986-87, the scheme has placed special emphasis on encouraging the participation of women in Panchayati Raj Institutions and learning about their role in national integration and communal harmony. The programme for Information and Mass Education creates public awareness through the multi-media strategy on issues relating to women.

Other Enabling Measures

The year 2001 was celebrated as 'Women's Empowerment Year'. During the year, various activities and programmes were taken up on different themes pertaining to women's social, political and economic empowerment. The Scheme for Women in Difficult Circumstances—'Swadhar' has been designed with a flexible and innovative approach to cater to the requirements of various categories of women in distress, in diverse situations under different conditions. The Scheme aims to provide basic needs of shelter, food, clothing and care to the marginalised women/girls living in difficult circumstances who are without any social and economic support. It also attempts to provide emotional support and counselling to such women and ensure their social and economic rehabilitation through education, awareness, skill upgradation and personality development through behavioural training etc.

1.5.2. Rural Development

In the field of Rural Development, anti-poverty programmes have been a dominant feature of Government initiatives in rural areas. The Swarnajayanti Gram Swarozgar Yojana (SGSY) was launched in 1999 with the objective of bringing the beneficiary families (swarozgaris) above the poverty line by providing them income-generating assets through a mix of bank credit and Government subsidy. It is envisaged that 50 per cent of SHGs in each block should be exclusively of women, who will account for at least 40 per cent of the swarozgaris. Since inception of the scheme, 7.4 lakh SHGs have been formed. Around 4.3 million swarozgaris, 24 per cent of whom were women, were assisted during the Ninth Plan.

The Jawahar Gram Samriddhi Yojana (JGSY) reserves 30 per cent of employment opportunities for women. During the Ninth Plan, around 3.9 million man-days constituting 28 per cent of the total employment generated under JGSY, were provided for women. The

Indira Awas Yojana (IAY) stipulates that houses under the scheme are to be allotted in the name of the female member of the beneficiary household or in the joint names of husband and wife. Priority is given to widows and unmarried women. Since its inception in 1985-86, 7.9 million houses have been built.

The National Maternity Benefit Scheme (now transferred to the Department of Family Welfare with effect from the year 2001-02) aims at assisting expectant mothers by providing them Rs. 500 each for the first two live births. Under the National Old Age Pension Scheme, central assistance is provided to women and men above the age of 65 years who have little or no regular means of subsistence. The Restructured Centrally Sponsored Rural Sanitation Programme, launched in 1999, ensures construction of village sanitary complexes exclusively for women, wherever the construction of individual household latrines are not feasible.

1.5.3. National Institutions

National Commission for Women: NCW, a statutory body set up in 1992, safeguards the rights and interests of women. It continues to pursue its mandated role and activities; viz. safeguarding women's rights through investigations into the individual complaints of atrocities; sexual harassment of women at work place; conducting Parivarik/Mahila Lok Adalats, legal awareness programmes/camps review of both women-specific and women-related legislations. investigates into individual complaints, atrocities, harassment, denial of rights etc. and takes suo moto remedial action to restore their legitimate rights. NCW, since its inception, investigated into a total number of 24,025 complaints, wherein dowry deaths and dowry harassments accounted for the maximum number. Open Adalats (public hearing) is the most innovative and informal style adopted by the Commission to hear the individual grievances. Out of the 41 legislations having direct bearing on women, the Commission reviewed and suggested remedial legislative measures in 32 Acts and forwarded the same to the government for necessary action, besides drafting a Bill on Sexual Harassment at the Work Places and a Bill on SAARC Regional Convention for Prevention and Combating Trafficking in Women and Children.

Amongst its success stories, the Commission requested the State Governments to reserve a certain percentage of resources for women even at the village level for programmes such as water supply, health services, nutrition, sanitation, etc. and reviewed the functioning of women's cells in governmental organizations and issued fresh guidelines to reactivate the cells. It has also organized many seminars/ workshops on important emerging problems of women, viz. impact of globalization on women, prevention of atrocities against women, economic empowerment of tribal women, girl child abuse, child marriages, empowerment of Dalit women, women in prostitution, images of women in the electronic media, rehabilitation of *devadasis*, besides conducting legal awareness camps in those states like Haryana, Punjab, Rajasthan, Bihar, Uttar Pradesh, etc. where the status of women is comparatively lower. The Commission has also been very successfully documenting information on many important social problems like that of rape, abortion, *devadasis*, sexual harassment, etc. besides sponsoring studies on various subjects related to women.

Central Social Welfare Board: The Central Social Welfare Board (CSWB) was set up in 1953 with the objective of promoting social welfare activities and implementing welfare programmes for women, children and handicapped through voluntary organisations. In 1954, the State Social Welfare Boards were set up in the States and UTs. The programmes implemented by the Board include socio-economic programme for needy/destitute women, condensed courses of education and vocational training courses for women and girls, awareness generation projects for rural and poor women, family counselling centers/voluntary action bureau, holiday camps for children, welfare extension projects in border areas and balwadis, Crèches and hostels for working women, etc.

Rashtriya Mahila Kosh: The National Credit Fund for Women (Rashtriya Mahila Kosh) was set up on 30 March 1993, with a corpus fund of Rs. 31 crore with the major objective of meeting the credit needs of poor women, particularly in the informal sector. The RMK is managed by a Governing Board comprising 16 members. The Minister of State for Women and Child Development is the Chairperson of the Kosh. The Kosh has sanctioned up to 30 April 2002, loans amounting to Rs. 11,093 lakh to benefit 4,23,125 women through 1,016 NGOs.

Panchayati Raj: The salient features of the Constitution (73rd Amendment) Act, 1992 related to women are:

(a) to provide reservation of seats for Scheduled Castes, Scheduled Tribes and women (not less than one-third of total seats).
(b) preparation of a plan for economic development and social justice;
(c) implementation of schemes for economic development and social justice in relation to 29 subjects given in the Eleventh Schedule of the Constitution (article 243-G) and
(d) the constitution of Gram Sabha, consisting of men and women registered in the electoral rolls relating to a village comprised within the area of Gram Panchayat.

Parliamentary Committee: The Parliamentary Committee for empowerment of women consists of 30 members, 20 members to be nominated by the Speaker among members of Lok Sabha and 10 members of Rajya Shaba. The functions of the committee include, inter-alia, considering the reports submitted by the National Commission for Women and to report on the measures taken by the Union Government for improving the status/condition of women.

1.6. Constitutional Safeguards for Women

The country's concern in safeguarding the rights and privileges of women found its best expression in the Constitution of India. While Article 14 confers equal rights and opportunities on men and women in the political, economic and social spheres, Article 15 prohibits discrimination against any citizen on the grounds of sex, religion, race, caste etc. and Article 15(3) empowers the State to make affirmative discrimination in favour of women. Similarly, Article 16 provides for equality of opportunities in the matter of public appointments for all citizens; Article 39 stipulates that the State shall direct its policy towards providing men and women equally the right to means of livelihood and equal pay for equal work; Article 42 directs the State to make provisions for ensuring just and humane conditions of work and maternity relief; and Article 51(A)(e) imposes a fundamental duty on every citizen to renounce practices derogatory to the dignity of women. To make this *de-jure* equality into *a de-facto* one, many policies and programmes were put into action from time to time, besides enacting/enforcing special legislations, in favour of women.

1.7. Women in Five Year Plans

Tenth Five Year Plan (2002-2007) intends to translate the National Policy for Empowerment of Women (2001) into action through:

- creating an environment to realize their full potential,
- allowing *de-jure* and *de-facto* enjoyment of all human rights and fundamental freedom by women,
- providing equal access to participation and decision-making,
- ensuring equal access to women to health care, education, employment and social security,
- elimination of all forms of discrimination against women,
- building partnerships with their society,
- mainstreaming a gender perspective into the development process.

As the time target set for achieving the goals in the Policy goes beyond the Tenth Plan, the following measurable/monitorable goals set in the Tenth Plan (Approach Paper) having a direct bearing on the empowerment of women and the girl child, will be adopted in the proposed Action Plans:

- Reduction of poverty ratio by 5 percentage points by 2007 and by 15 percentage points by 2012;
- Providing gainful (high-quality) employment to the addition to the labour force over the Tenth Plan period;
- All children in school by 2003; all children to complete 5 years of schooling by 2007;
- Reduction of gender gaps in literacy and wage rates by at least 50 per cent by 2007;
- Reduction in the decadal rate of population growth between 2001 and 2011 to 16.2 per cent;
- Increase in Literacy rate to 75 per cent within the Plan period;

- Reduction of IMR to 45 per 1000 live births by 2007 and to 28 by 2012;
- Reduction of MMR to 2 per 1000 live births by 2007 and to 1 by 2012; and
- All villages to have sustained access to potable drinking water by 2007.

To translate the above goals into action, the Tenth Plan reaffirms the major strategy of mainstreaming the gender perspectives in all sectoral policies and programmes and plans of action. This will help achieve the ultimate goal of eliminating gender discrimination and creating an enabling environment of gender justice, which would encourage women and girls to act as catalysts, participants and recipients in the country's development process. Further, women specific interventions will be undertaken to bridge the existing gaps.

Acknowledging the fact that women's equality in power sharing and active participation in decision-making, both in administrative and political spheres, is a very strong instrument to achieve the goals of empowerment, the Tenth Plan will initiate all necessary steps to guarantee equal access and full participation to women in decision-making bodies, including the legislative, executive, judicial, corporate, statutory bodies and their advisory Commissions/Committees, Boards etc. Affirmative action such as reservations/quotas, including in the higher political, administrative and legislative bodies, will also be considered, if necessary, on a time bound basis. Introduction of women-friendly personnel policies will be an additional feature during the Tenth Plan to encourage women to participate effectively in all the administrative decision-making processes.

The process of organising women into Self-Help Groups (SHGs), started during the Ninth Plan to provide them permanent fora for articulating their needs and contributing their perspectives to development, has made tremendous progress as it brought into action more than a million SHGs all over the country. Experience has already shown that these groups have been very effective institutions at grass-root level in facilitating access to women, be it for financial or material resources or services or for information. Therefore, the Tenth Plan will continue to encourage SHG model to act as the agents of social change, development and empowerment of women.

1.8. SHG and Women Empowerment

The Ministry of Rural Development is striving to bring about rapid and sustainable development through socio-economic transformation in rural India. It adopts an integrated approach towards improving the quality of life of rural poor and ensuring equity and effective people's participation. In this approach, non-government organizations, self-help groups and Panchayati Raj Institutions have been accorded important role in rural development (India, 2000). Of these, SHG is a 'people's scheme' and its organization is a significant step towards empowering women (Mittal, 1999). A Self-help Group is a voluntary group, formed to attain some common goals, most of its members have similar social identity, heritage, caste or traditional occupations and come together for a common cause and manage resources for the benefit of the group members (NABARD, 1998).

Women SHGs play a vital role in enhancing the knowledge, skill and good attitude of their members. As NABARD (1998) has described firstly, the members can transit from dependency to self reliance much faster through social mobilization and awareness creation than through economic interventions. Secondly, women form the basis of social mobilization. Therefore aiming for women's empowerment is the most cost effective strategy available, even for economic development and enhancing members to become self-dependent, self reliant, providing a forum for members for discussing their socio-economic problems, developing decision-making capacity and leadership qualities among members and equipping women with the basic skills required for understanding monetary transactions.

1.9. Literature Review

Having sketched the status and problems of women at the global and national level, and analyzed the interventions for women's development by the national and international agencies—both governmental and non-governmental, literatures pertaining to women empowerment have been reviewed in the ensuing chapter.

Chapter 2

Review of Literature

2.1. Meaning of Women's Empowerment

Empowerment means individuals acquiring the power to think and act freely, exercise choice and fulfil their potential as full and equal members of society. As per the United Nations Development Fund for Women (UNIFEM), the term women's empowerment means:

- Acquiring knowledge and understanding of gender relations and ways in which these relations may be changed.
- Developing a sense of self-worth, a belief in one's ability to secure desired changes and the right to control one's life.
- Gaining the ability to generate choices and exercise bargaining power.
- Developing the ability to organize and influence the direction of social change, to create more just social and economic order, nationally and internationally.

Thus, empowerment means a psychological sense of personal control or influence and a concern with actual social influence, political power and legal rights. It is a multi level construct referring to individuals, organizations and community. It is international, involving mutual respect, critical reflection, caring and group participation, through which people lacking an equal share of valued resources, gain greater access to and control over these resources. (Rappaport, 1987).

"Empowerment of women" is a topic that has been debated and deliberated world over. Deliberations and action plans have been prepared for the last 30 years in the four world conferences on women at Mexico city (1975), Copenhagen (1980), Nairobi (1985), and Beijing (1995). These conferences have helped to strengthen the socio-economic, political and legal dimensions of the role of women. In the Mexico conference, it was decided that the decade (1975-85) be celebrated as the decade for women. During the decade, in 1979, the UN adopted CEDAW (Convention on Elimination of Discrimination against Women) which, in 1993, was adopted by India.

In Copenhagen, the world community concentrated on poverty alleviation, imparting education, enhancing avenues for professional advancement and addressing the problems of women in developing countries. At the end of the decade, the women of developing nations advocated and ensured full participation at the Nairobi conference which discussed the issues of women in the third world countries. The Beijing Declaration and Platform for Action was comprehensive aiming for quality, development and peace, acknowledging the diversity of communities, religions, and indigenous rights and the uneven progress in empowerment and increasing poverty. The meet demanded equal participation of women in government and decision making processes (Mor, 2001).

Mohini Giri (1998), states that women all over the world are overwhelmingly concerned with the issue of gender equality through women's empowerment. The countries of the world, and the women's movement everywhere, during the past five decades that the United Nations has been in existence, organized in a systematic and sustained manner, the strategies and approaches that would effectively enable women to be equal partners in one's national progress and prosperity.

According to Sahay (1998), the actual definitions offered for "empower" are:

(1) to give power or authority to;
(2) give ability to; enable; permit, (*for example*, court of law is empowered to judge a person to be punished or not).

'Power' is the key word of the term 'Empowerment', which means having control over material assets like land and finance, intellectual resources like knowledge; information and ideas, and to generate, sustain and propagate an ideology (Apte, 1995). Empowerment emphasizes not only increasing the power of the individual but also the quality of life for the individual, the efficiency and autonomy of the individual (Lowe, 1996).

Empowerment has several other dimensions like social, economic, psychological and political. Social empowerment connotes formation of social capacities such as health, education, freedom and opportunities for realizing one's potentialities. Economic empowerment implies entitlement to employment, income, property, productive resources and benefits regardless of gender differences. Psychological empowerment signifies confidence building, acquisition of a sense of efficacy and ability to overcome feeling of helplessness. Political empowerment implies equal say in the decision-making process in the power structure at all levels from local to global. All these dimensions of empowerment are so intertwined with one another that over reliance on one to the neglect of the other are not likely to work (Sharma, 2000).

2.2. Concept of Empowerment

"Becoming powerful", the internal meaning of the term "empowerment" has gained significance to eliminate the gender disparity in India. Gender disparity manifests itself in various forms, the most obvious being the trend of declining female ratio in population. According to UNDP Human Development Report—2001, gender disparity can be seen through the lens of the Gender-related Development Index (GDI) and Gender Empowerment Measure (GEM), in which, India's GEM rank is 86 out of 94 countries (HDR, 1997) and GDI rank is 105 (HDR, 2001).

The antecedents of empowerment are a combination of traditions of mutual and self help and more recently, movements of liberation rights and social activism, strengthened by anti-racism, feminism critiques of inequalities and oppressions racing from social class, age, differences (Adams, 1996).

According to Suguna (2001), there is continued inequality and vulnerability of women in all sectors—economic, social, political, education, health care, nutrition and legal. As women are oppressed in all spheres of life, they need to be empowered in all walks of life. Active participation in social, economic and political spheres would help in enhancing process of decision-making empowerment and it will also give women the desired self respect and social dignity and these of course, are the pre-requisites of empowerment.

Asian and Pacific Centre for Women and Development (APCWD) defines empowerment as a process that aims at creating the conditions for the self-determination of a particular people or group. When this definition is applied to women, it may be considered as a process of creating conditions for their self determination. According to Pillai (1995), empowerment is a process of awareness and capacity-building leading to greater participation, to greater decision-making power and control and to transformative action and also further states, broadly, that women empowerment is an active, multi-dimensional process which enables women to realize their full identity and powers in all spheres of life.

Sharma (1993) defines women empowerment as a process aimed at changing the nature and direction of systemic forces which marginalize women. Batliwala (1995) has also defined women empowerment as the process of challenging existing power relations, and of gaining greater control over the sources of power. Chandra (1997) is of the opinion that in its simplest form, women empowerment means the manifestation of redistribution of power that challenges patriarchal ideology and male dominance. In tune with this, as Nayar (1998) views, women empowerment may be defined as the process by which the powerless gain greater control over the circumstances of their lives.

Empowerment of women is perceived as crucial to the development and growth of the family and community (Das, 1998). Kumar and Rani (2001) are of the opinion that empowerment of women is to create an enabling environment where women can freely exercise their rights both within and outside home, as equal partners along with men. In the views of Vanavarayar (2003), real empowerment does not come from outside, it has to come from within.

Women are to be empowered in more ways than one. Feminists talk of different kinds of empowerment—economic, social, political and integrated. Those who talk of economic empowerment think that women are economically weaker and if they are empowered economically, other kinds of empowerment are assured. Those who talk of integrated empowerment want women to be empowered economically, educationally and socially (Suriakanthi, 2000).

Clark and Stewart (1992) say that empowerment is a theme, which requires clarification. To some, empowerment is about increasing the power of the public over public activities, giving the public greater choice and/or greater and better-defined rights over those services. To others, it is about increasing the power of the public over both public and private sector activities. Advocates of the first position may argue that the public do not need empowerment in the private sector because the market gives power to the customer.

Empowerment, in its simplest form, means the manifestation of redistribution of power that challenges patriarchal ideology and the male domination. It is both a process and the result of the process. It is transformation of the structures or institutions that reinforces and perpetuates gender discrimination. It is a process that enables women to gain access to and control of material as well as information resources. The concept of women's empowerment, throughout the world, has it roots in women's movement. It is since the mid-1980s that this term became popular in the field of development, especially with reference to women (Chandra, 1997).

Empowerment is the means by which individuals, groups and communities take control of their circumstances and achieve their own goals, thereby being able to work towards helping themselves and others to maximize the quality of their lives (Adams, 1996).

Empowerment is also the process of challenging existing power relations and of gaining greater control over the sources of power. The goals of women's empowerment are to challenge patriarchal ideology to transform the structures and institutions that reinforce and perpetuate gender discrimination and social inequality and to enable poor women to gain access to, and control of, both material and informational resources. It can change existing power relations by addressing itself to the three dimensions of material, human and intellectual resources (Batliwal, 1994).

Empowerment is the process of enabling or authorizing an individual to think, behave take action and control work in an autonomous way. It is the state of feeling of empowerment to take control of one's own destiny. Empowerment is the process by which the powerless gain greater control over the circumstances of their lives. It includes both control over resources (physical, human, intellectual and financial) and over ideology (beliefs, values, and attitudes) (Dubashi, 2000).

Empowerment can be viewed as a means of creating a social environment in which one can take decisions and make choices either individually or collectively for social transformation. It strengthens innate ability by way of acquiring knowledge, power and experience. Some of the best examples of empowerment from many countries have used group process to break the isolation and seclusion of individuals. Group processes have also been used in credit programs to ensure individual accountability.

2.3. Theories of Women Empowerment

Various theories of empowerment have been enunciated by theorists like Zimmerman (2001) and Hall (1990), among others. These theories enable us to understand the basics and the process of empowerment. According to Zimmerman, as quoted by Fetterman (2001), empowerment processes are those in which attempts to gain control, obtain the needed resources, and critically understand one's social environment are fundamental. The process is empowering if it helps people develop their skills, so that they become independent problem solvers and decision-makers. Empowering processes vary across levels of analysis, according to Zimmerman. For example, empowering processes for individuals may include organizational or community involvement; empowering processes at the organizational level may include shared leadership and decision-making; and empowering processes at the community level may include accessibility to government, the media, and other community resources. This theory adds that the outcomes of the empowering processes also differ across levels of analysis. At the individual level outcomes might include situation-specific perceived control, skills and proactive behaviours; at the organizational level outcomes might include organizational networks, effective resource acquisition, and policy leverage; and at the community level outcomes might include evidence of pluralism, the existence of organizational coalitions, and accessible community resources.

Hall (1990) has presented an identity empowerment theory which is a clinical sociological one that has been built on documented patterns and predictabilities in interpersonal, family, and group behaviour. It is used as an integrated frame of reference regarding women and empowerment (Sahay, 1998). The theory assumes that empowered women make meaningful commitments and undertake effective, goal-oriented activities that they choose for themselves, can understand the strengths and weaknesses of their personal and collective past and present and can cope with conflict in their relationships. The theory of Oakley and Marsden (1984) has delineated the levels of participation leading to empowerment. The first level is the 'manipulatory' or 'therapeutic' level which places importance on mass mobilization campaigns like the literacy campaign. At the second level is the 'token' form of participation with the extension of information, consultation and collaboration of some sort like the beneficiary-oriented income-generating rural development programmes. At the upper levels are 'partnerships', 'delegated power' and 'citizen control'. This form of participation is encouraged by Non-governmental Organizations (NGOs) like Self Employed Women's Association (SEWA) (Prasad, 2002).

The Harvard framework for women's empowerment based on Sara Longwe's formulation talks of five levels of gender equality (Sharma, 2000). These five levels include welfare, access, conscientization, participation and control. At the welfare level, it is pointed out that women should not only be the recipients of material benefits but should also be partners in development. At the access level, women should have access to resources like educational opportunities, land, credit, wage employment and services. The conscientization level involves promotion of critical awareness about the structure of discrimination, exploitation and oppression of women. The participation level indicates women's participation along with men in decision-making within the family and public organizations including the Legislative Assembly, Parliament, etc. The control level is the ultimate level of equality and empowerment when women have control over their lives and their children and have a proactive role in development.

Stromquist (1993) has included four components of empowerment, namely, cognitive, psychological, economic and political. The cognitive component refers to women's understanding of their conditions of subordination and the causes of such conditions. The psychological component includes the development of feelings that will help women at the personal and societal levels to improve their condition as well as the formation of the belief that they can succeed in their change efforts. The economic component of empowerment requires that women be able to engage in productive activities that will allow them some degree of financial autonomy. The political component of empowerment entails the ability to analyse the surrounding environment in political and social terms.

These theories of empowerment enable us to understand the meaning of women empowerment and what aspects are to be kept in mind in empowering women.

2.4. Approaches to Women Empowerment

Women's empowerment, according to Bhasin (1985), involved the transformation of power relations at six different levels: Individual, family, group, organization, village community and society. In order to empower the rural poor especially the women, female development workers must first empower themselves.

The author identifies three approaches to women's empowerment: the integrated development approach, which focuses on women's survival and livelihood needs; the economic development approach, which aims to strengthen women's economic position; and the consciousness-raising approach, which organizes women into collectives that address the sources of oppression. To be effective, empowerment strategies must simultaneously address women's practical gender needs as well as strategic gender needs. Finally, an undemocratic environment and a fragmented understanding of the concept and process of empowerment will hinder experiments in empowerment.

2.5. Indicators of Women Empowerment

There are four major categories of indicators or parameters of change, viz. social, economic, political and environmental (Jonpal and Acharya, 1995).

Social Indicators are used to measure the change in the social relationship of people under the programme. In a poverty programme, this can be the change in relationship between the poor and the landlord, the poor and the money-lenders, the poor and the bank, or the relationship between men and women and the resultant increase in the status of women.

In an educational programme, it can be the change in the relationship between the people and the teacher, the change in the attitude towards education, etc. Economic indicators are used to measure the changes in the economic status of the target population, family or community. In a poverty programme, this can be the increase or decrease in the ownership of assets such as cattle, land holdings and jewellery, rate of unemployment, wage rate, level of migration, etc.

Political indicators are used in measuring political change or change in the power structure. In a poverty programme, this can be the nature of leadership which the target population is showing on poverty issues such as wages, employment, gaining access to social services, shifts in land cultivation, women's control over natural resources, etc.

Environmental Indicators are used to measure environmental changes. In a poverty programme, the indicators can be deforestation, women's time used to collect fuel and fodder, soil erosion, depth of underground water, nature of land use, drought, flood etc.

Therefore, one of the clearest indicators of women's empowerment is an increase in women's capacities and willingness to support other women and to work diligently towards strengthening women in their efforts to survive or to gain equality (Barvard, 1971). It is only through acknowledging women's and men's interdependency in constructive ways that women can enter into more powerful exchanges with men in society at large (Durkheim, 1966).

The Draft Country Paper of India for the 4th World Conference on Women, Beijing, 1995 proposed certain qualitative and quantitative indicators for evaluating women's empowerment (Sahay, 1998). The qualitative aspects included self-esteem and self-confidence, articulation, leisure time, work loads, roles and responsibilities, domestic violence, social customs, participation levels, bargaining power, access to information, women's collections, social attitudes, women's economic contribution and decision-making. Quantitative aspects included demographic trends, number of women in participation, access and control over resources, physical health status, literacy levels and political participation at the local level.

Rao and Rao (1999) classified indicators at three levels, namely, (i) Individual and her household, (ii) Community and Organizational and (iii) National levels. In the first level of individual and her household are included decision-making, work sharing, control over reproduction, pride and value, self-confidence and self-esteem, and ability to prevent violence. At the second level of community and organization, women's organization, funds mobilized, leadership, involvement and participation, trainings and legal rights were included. At the national level, awareness of social and political rights, integration of women in planning, women networks and publications, official visibility and recognition, and the degree of media attention were included.

Empowerment as a social process challenged the fundamental imbalances of power distribution and relations. It was a process of redistribution of power within and between families, societies and a process aiming at social equality which could be achieved through disempowering some structures, systems and institutions. Social empowerment promoted sustainable rural structure for dissemination of knowledge about health, nutrition, literacy, education, freedom and opportunities for realizing women's potentialities and adoption of new agricultural practices. The social empowerment scale employed indicators such as gender discrimination, female infanticide, dowry, marriage, poverty, caste and social justice to assess the level of empowerment of women.

Indicators of women's empowerment encompass various aspects of women's roles and status: Freedom of mobility, economic security, ability to make small, large independent purchases, participation in important family decisions, relative freedom from domination by the family, political and legal awareness and participation in political campaigns and public.

2.6. Impact of Self-Help Initiatives in India

In India, since Ninth Five Year Plan (1997-2002), SHG promotion has been given high importance. On the basis of observation of women SHGs from all over the nation, it is reported that a large number of women have become economically independent. They have been able to earn income through diverse activities of agriculture, horticulture, animal husbandry, and food processing such as preparing banana chips. They have organized themselves better. They have become better communicators in putting forth their views. They have been spontaneous in involving themselves in social work. They have been able to gain strength and are able to create confidence among women in general. Some women are even able to manage Public Distribution System (*The Hindu*, June 12, 2000).

Many SHGs have initiated literacy drive among their members. Through literacy programme, women have become independent learners who are conscious of the importance of their children's education. Some have even taken the role of change agents who have been able to stop distillation of arrack and the sale of *ganja* (*The Hindu*, April 22, 2000 and January 6, 2001).

2.7. SHGs and Women Empowerment

Improvement in economic status of women enables women to develop their leadership qualities. Rani (2000) in her study, 'Impact of socio-economic status on the emergence of rural women leadership', found out that socio-economic status was a significant factor in the emergence of rural women leadership. The study empirically established the fact that the socio-economic status had a significant impact on determining the emergence of rural women as leaders in Dindigul district of Tamil Nadu.

Empowering women is inevitable towards decreasing the incidence of domestic violence. Thakar (2001) did a study to gain an understanding of the phenomenon of violence of family members against married women. The findings showed that most of the battered women were not highly educated. Eight per cent of the battered women had been educated up to middle school only. The biggest group of battered women (30.33%) was educated up to primary level. In the case of torture, 53.8 per cent of the respondents were inflicted by their husbands themselves. The data showed that 414 women were being tortured mentally.

Reddy (2002) has brought out the advantages of Self-Help Groups. He narrated his experience in the book 'Empowering Women through Self-Help Groups and Micro-credit'. Various issues of importance to women like role of women in society, obstacles to their development, equality with men, girl's education, their participation in public affairs/community activities in villages etc., were explained to them in specially organized workshops. Since many of them were illiterate, pictorial charts and audio-visuals were extensively used to make them understand. Field tours were part of the training package, which were found to be very effective in motivating women to join self-help groups and take up several community activities that were of importance to them.

Rizwana's (2002) report on the experience in MRCP (Maharashtra Rural Credit Programme) and MAVML (Mahila Arthik Vikas Mahamandal Limited) reveals that both the programmes are mainly implemented for women SHGs. She found that as a result of these initiatives, women showed willingness to discuss the issues like status of women, health awareness and hygiene. They were fighting against social evils such as dowry system, early marriage of girls, alcoholism etc. They could operate bank accounts. Women were attending Village Development Assembly/Village Development Council meetings and were showing cooperation. They took initiative in social development activities. They were showing interest in functional literacy. Women were becoming active entrepreneurs and operating both at individual and group levels. Women were realizing the need for information and approaching the government offices, banks and other departments for procuring information. Women were now aware of the role of village officials. They were aware of their rights as citizens. They were also participatory in the implementation and evaluation of the programme. Women were also participating in programmes like *shramdan,* and the plantation programmes.

Vijayanthi (2003), in her study of SHGs, found that the awareness level of SHG members was maximum on the importance of environmental sanitation. Decision-making skill related to education of children was also maximum. The self-empowerment level was higher at family level. It included improvement in the social status of the family, commanding respect from neighbours, participating in community activities, motivating other women to join SHGs and making better decisions in the family.

When SHG members were given functional literacy training it enabled SHG members to develop their saving habit as well as to share their ideas confidently and maintain their record of activities (Raja, 2003). Subburaman (2003) found that majority of SHG members saved money out of their own earnings. The functional literacy organized for them helped them in increasing their competence level and there was a free flow in exchange of ideas, learning and practice. Majority of SHG leaders also had properly maintained the savings and loan ledgers and minutes book.

A study on the various factors which contributed to the success of groups listed the crucial role played by the NGOs, effective leadership, group cohesiveness, buoyant savings, contribution by the members, regular meetings, high percentage of attendance by members in the group meetings, peer group pressure leading to high repayment rate, changing attitude of men, healthy competition among the members, linkage with government programmes of rural development, formation of cluster committees, campaigning skills, participation of groups for common causes, linkage with other institutions and effective supervision by the NGOs. (Lalitha, 2002)

According to Ranjani K. Murthy (2001), there are different starting points that are possible for women's empowerment: economic strategies, political strategies, social strategies and integrated strategies. Ideally, the choice of the starting point should be defined by the women themselves (based on an analysis of their situation), rather than on a pre-defined assumption that one strategy is better than another throughout the country. The case studies in this collection strongly challenge the assumption of the Indian government, NGOs and aid agencies that micro-credit is the most suitable solution to women's poverty throughout India and in all contexts.

2.8. Strategies of Women Empowerment

Women empowerment programmes in vogue fall into three strategies:

- Empowerment through integrated rural development programmes (poverty alleviation programmes).
- Empowerment through awareness building and organizing women.

- Empowerment through economic interventions.

Empowerment strategies were likely to be effective if they support women to mobilize peer groups and community resources (Mahmud, 1994). Conscientization and psychological priming had been found effective strategies than economic intervention (Narasimhan, 1999). However, conscientization was not the only strategy of attitudinal change. Female education and planned socialization too are potent strategies (Sharma, 2000).

Empowerment strategies are varied and refer to those strategies which enable women to realize their full potentials. They consist of greater access to knowledge and resources, greater autonomy in decision-making, greater ability to plan their lives, greater control over the circumstances that influence their lives and finally factors which would free them from the shackles of customs, beliefs and practices. Unless they themselves become conscious of the oppression meted out to them and show initiative to push forward, it would not be possible to change their status much.

O'connell (1993) describes that Oxfam work to empower women and to end gender discrimination, suggests the strategies of education for consciousness and collective action. Other two-pronged strategy for empowering women focuses on alternative employment and alternative power structures at the local level, achieved through building and strengthening women's groups. Psychological empowerment signified confidence-building, acquisition of a sense of efficacy and ability to overcome feeling of helplessness (Sharma, 2000).

2.9. Measuring Women Empowerment

Empowerment is a planned process and its nature and quality of relationship over time, can be assessed. Changes in power relations were a definite part of the empowerment process. There was a tendency to progress from dependency through independence towards increased interdependence. It is not difficult to measure empowerment; but the difficulty lies in achieving it.

The GEM (Gender Empowerment Measure) used variables constructed explicitly to measure the relative empowerment of women and men in political and economic spheres of activities namely participation, decision-making and power over resources. Any meaningful attempt to measure empowerment would have to go beyond measuring the transfer of resources (physical, financial, human) to the least powerful. If empowerment was to be measured in changed relationships, change would need to be detected in both sides of the relationship. Those who were involved in the process of empowerment were the right persons to measure their empowerment (Taylor, 2000).

2.10. Spiral of Empowerment

According to Taylor (2000), the various dimensions of empowerment i.e. educational, economic, psychological, social and political were interlinked and could not be isolated. The most fundamental principle of system theory pointed to the fact that no single element of a system could change its relationships within the system, without change occurring in the systematic nature of society. Henceforth, increasing women's access to micro-finance and involvement in Self Help Groups (SHGs) was assumed to initiate a series of virtuous spirals of economic empowerment, increased well-being for women and their families and wider social and political empowerment (Mayoux, 1999).

Economic Empowerment

Economic empowerment endorses women's sense of work, the right to determine choices, the power to control their own lives within and outside home and their ability to influence the direction of social change and to create a just social and economic order nationally and internationally (Noyleen, UNIFEM). When the right to earning and savings, entrepreneurship skills, marketing ability, managerial capacity and ownership of assets were experienced by women, it could be approved that they are on the process of empowerment (Sharma, 2000).

Educational Empowerment

Education was the prime avenue for empowering women. The process of empowering entailed much more than awareness of alternatives women's rights and the nature of the requirements. It involved the breakdown of powerful sex stereotyping which prevented women from demanding their rights from men in position of authority for women, the process of empowerment entailed breaking away from the cycle of learned and taught submission to discrimination, earned from one generation of women to the rest (Katarina, 1993).

Psychological Empowerment

Psychological empowerment signified confidence building, acquisition of a sense of efficacy and ability to overcome feeling of helplessness (Sharma, 2000). The definitions of knowledge, self respect and other elements related to human beings may be culture specific. However, invariable of society the concepts of strong determination, assertive nature, motivation etc. revealed the psychological empowerment of the individual. Often, their self-confidence is expressed in their courage to meet the officials without any fear and to represent their problems and difficulties.

Political Empowerment

Political process was central to the empowerment process (Karl, Marilee). In this process, adequate information and resources had to be made available for women to make their own autonomous decision making. Empowerment was used to describe a process by which women become conscious of their own situation and organize collectively to gain greater access to public services.

The political empowerment indicators considered their basic political rights, role in decision-making bodies of the state and the central governments, representation in policy-making, participation in political campaigning, leadership quality and ability to politicize their problems. (Calman, 1992)

Technology and Empowerment

At the crucial juncture, the members of SHGs as well as organizers have realized the direct need to utilize the dynamism in personal, community, financial and technological resources. If not, these assets would be wasted like stagnated water or unused iron material.

Responding to their need, the experts have come out with the approach of technological transfer. Technology is considered as the key parameter for measuring development. In 'India 2020: A Vision for the New Millennium' (Kalam and Rajan, 1998), it is noted that without a pervasive use of technologies, we cannot achieve overall development of our people in the years to come. It was encouraging to comprehend that the SHGs were recognized as an opt mode to transfer technology to the rural India.

2.11. Development and Empowerment

The GEM (UNDP, 1997) measured gender equality in key areas of economic and political participation and decision-making. The third indices as power over economic resources was added together to derive the final GEM value. However, empowerment cannot just be considered as a question of rearrangement of power, both economic and political; it was also a matter of change of values (Sharma, 2000).

According to Hall (1992), the empowered women share the following characteristics: Empowered women define their attitudes, values and behaviour in relation to their own real interests. They have autonomy because they claim their freedom from existing male hierarchies, whether they live in traditional societies or modern, industrial societies. Empowered women maintain equal-mindedness, rather than act out roles that merely confront and challenge male dominance. Empowered women do not aim at being superior to men. They respond as equal and cooperate in order to work towards the common good.

Empowered women use their talents to live fulfilling lives. They have not only survived the harshness of their own subjugation. But they have also transcended their subjugation, thus moving themselves through survival to fulfilment. Empowered women maintain their strength in the presence of pressures of family, religion, and work and they contribute towards the empowerment of all women. Empowered women may continue to meet their family responsibilities and participate in religion. They choose to do so in ways that strengthen rather than debilitate them, however, which is also advantageous for others. Empowered women do not retreat from these traditional responsibilities but they forge their own ways of doing things.

2.12. Study on Women Empowerment

An attempt has been made to study the phenomenon of women in rural areas, especially understand the bottlenecks of women empowerment and to locate the determinants. Design of the study is presented in the ensuing chapter.

Chapter 3

Design of the Study

3.1. Statement of the Problem

Women are discriminated from cradle to grave and even before birth. Within the family, the members are governed by a set of norms and practices evolved by the head of the household who exercises power, authority and control over the members. Since men have access and control over resources, their role is clearly defined as bread winners and women are supposed to confine themselves to the role of 'home makers'.

Women indeed do not enjoy the rights and freedom they are entitled to because they are women. Although women are entering vocational fields, their household responsibilities and duties have not decreased. Women continue to struggle in playing a dual role. Their workload increases, especially when they enter the work force. There are numerous other constraints and obstacles in attaining women empowerment.

Women and their problems are being given much importance in our social milieu. Indian women have attained a great deal in the past few years but there are still areas of discrimination which exist. A multitude of factors are responsible for an increasing discrimination which eventually stalls their empowerment. Empowerment is a multi-dimensional concept. Women need empowerment in the economic, social, cultural, education, health and family welfare, political, organizational, and decision-making spheres. Women empowerment is not caused by a single or a small set but a galaxy of complex factors.

What are the constituents of women empowerment? What factors stimulate or stall women empowerment? What are the indicators of women empowerment? How do we measure women empowerment? How do the men respond to the process of empowerment of women? These are certain questions which prop up in the minds of any researcher on women empowerment.

Precisely to enlighten the researchers on the various issues raised above, the present study makes an effort to examine the present status of women, elicit their views on the concept of women empowerment, ascertain the views of men on women empowerment, examine the bottlenecks obstructing women empowerment and identify indicators which would help assess the level of women empowerment.

3.2. Objectives of the Study

The study had the following objectives:

(1) To assess the status of rural women and locate the deterrents hindering their empowerment.
(2) To evolve a set of determinants of women empowerment through consultations and study their relevance among a cross section of rural women.
(3) To elicit the views of men on the deterrents and determinants of women empowerment.
(4) To make an in-depth analysis of the life and work of select rural women.
(5) To analyze the policy implications of these deterrents and determinants to the Government and NGOs.

3.3. Scope of the Study

The study has been undertaken with the objective of examining the status of women and understand the process of empowerment taking place among the rural women. In particular, the study purports to highlight the deterrents which stall the process of women empowerment and locate the determinants which constitute women empowerment. In order to understand the process of empowerment, the study has taken a holistic view of the community, by studying the phenomenon at the individual, household, group and community levels. The study has harvested information regarding the process of empowerment at the household level, perception of local youth about empowerment of rural women, the opinion of experts, academicians and NGOs on the dimensions, deterrents and determinants of women empowerment and has elicited the views of Self Help Group women members on the indicators of women empowerment.

3.4. Operational Definitions

Six concepts used in the study have been operationally defined here.

- ***Empowerment:*** Empowerment is an active, multi-dimensional process which should enable women to realize their full identity and powers in all spheres of life. It would consist of greater autonomy in decision-making, greater ability to plan their lives, have greater control over the circumstances that influence their lives and free them from shackles imposed on them by custom, belief and practice (Laxmi Devi, 1998).

  Greater autonomy in decision-making refers to a process by which the will of the women prevails over the will of others in the family. The spectrum of areas encompass those which govern the day-to-day life of their family—in social, economic, educational, health, organizational, political and allied spheres. A steady transition from the largely 'men dominated' decision-making to 'men and women dominated' decision-making, eventually paving way for more 'women dominated' decision-making denotes their 'greater' autonomy in this regard.

  The concept of empowerment, for the purpose of the present study refers to the process by which women enjoy autonomy, freedom of articulation, work, mobility, and voting, participation in community activities, political participation, commanding power and influence, freedom from gender discrimination and violence against women, fighting for gender issues, and addressing the issue of domination by fostering equal partnership in domestic governance.
- ***Deterrent:*** Deterrent refers to a thing that makes somebody less likely to do something that deters them.

- ***Determinant:*** Determinant refers to a thing that decides whether or how something happens.
- ***Status of Women:*** Status is considered as the ascribed position of an individual or section of the community at par with the necessities arising out of the ecological and traditional conditions. Women's status is the position women enjoy in a given society. Status of women can be assessed through specific indicators. Status is largely used as a synonym for the 'role'. Role is treated as more dynamic aspect of status and role cannot be dissociated (Lynton, 1936).

The term status in the present study is examined from the angle of both the position the women enjoy in the study villages as well as their role in the family, group and the community. Specifically, aspects relating to their social, economic, educational, health, political and organizational status, women's share in domestic responsibilities, role in decision-making, access and control over resources and their awareness about social legislations and women welfare programme have been assessed to examine their status.

3.5. Hypothesis

Propositions emerge from our critical observations of societal transactions. In respect of women, we may note that they command different status in different religions such as Hindu, Muslim, and Christianity, as also among different communities within each religion. Some religions and communities are liberal or moderate while others are rigid and restrictive. Religion and community therefore exercise their influence in the process of women empowerment. Similarly, education of women, the organization of women in Community Based Organizations (CBOs), political participation of women and access and control over their income also impinge upon the process of women empowerment. Accordingly, the study has formulated certain hypotheses listed below:

- Greater the rigidity of religions/communities, slower the process of women empowerment.
- Greater the level of women's income, greater is their empowerment.

- Higher the literacy rate, greater the empowerment.
- Greater the organization of women (in Self-Help Groups), faster their empowerment.
- Greater the political participation of women, greater is their empowerment.

3.6. Type of Design

This study will fit more into diagnostic design, than the descriptive design, as it aims at locating the 'causes' of a problem and the possible solutions for it. Diagnostic design is similar to descriptive design but with a different focus. It is directed towards what is happening, why is it happening and what can be done about it. The present study aims at identifying the deterrents of women empowerment and also advocates some policy options the Government can consider in empowering the rural women.

3.7. Method of Study

Survey Method was used in conducting the study. Data were gathered from women heads of households, experts, rural youth and members of Self Help Groups in the study villages.

In addition to survey method, the study also used Case study and Observation methods. Surveys have the inherent limitations of being unable to go in-depth, into the nuances of individuals' life, work, struggle, and its success or failure. *Case Studies* bring about minute details from the cases studied, which the surveys can't. Hence, the study also used case study method among a dozen respondents, who were conspicuously distinct from their local counterparts.

The method of *observation* was used to analyze the various events, situations and programmes such as deliberations of Self-Help Group meetings, community infrastructure built up by women groups freedom of male-female interaction, education of girl children, freedom of mobility for women, inter-action process in households which casts its shadows on the element of domination, participation of women in community events/public forums (such as Gram Sabha), women from different religions in their places of worship and other women related issues.

3.8. Focus Group Discussion

Further, in order to know the perception of men as to what they feel about women empowerment, Focus Group Discussions were arranged. Besides discussions with men, this method was also used to elicit the views of women—who were members of Self-Help Groups as well as members of the community, on the deterrents and determinants of women empowerment. These discussions also enabled the rank ordering of various determinants of women empowerment.

3.9. Selection of Study Area

Dindigul, one of the 29 districts of Tamil Nadu, was selected for the study area. Rural areas of Dindigul district comprising 14 blocks, thus constituted the study area. The researcher identified the rural areas of this district for the study, because the study was intended to highlight the process of empowerment among rural women. Profile of Dindigul district is given at the end of this chapter.

Dindigul district was identified for the study because it is one of the backward districts, identified by the Union Planning Commission, Govt. of India, based on certain yardsticks (2004) for implementation of Rashtrya Sam Vikas Yojana (RSVY). Further, M.S. Swaminathan Research Foundation, Chennai had also selected Dindigul as one of the seven districts in Tamil Nadu, for implementation of its Hunger Free Area Programme based on the level of development assessed with reference to 25 important variables (1987). Moreover, Gandhigram Rural Institute, the institution of the researcher, is also located in this district. Hence, Dindigul district was selected for the study.

Out of 14 blocks comprising this district, six blocks were selected for the study in consultation with the Project Officer for District Rural Development Agency, and Tamil Nadu Women Development Corporation and District Social Welfare Officer. The criteria for selection of blocks were:

- Predominance of rural areas.
- Greater dependence on agriculture.
- Greater dependence of women in agriculture.

Thus, a total of six blocks were selected for the study as suggested by the officials. At the third level, we presented the list of all village panchayats to the respective Block Development officers in these six blocks. In consultation with the Extension Officer (Social Welfare) and Rural Welfare Officers, the officials suggested selection of one typical progressive village and one typical backward village based on the following criteria:

- The size of the village.
- Sex ratio
- The availability of public infrastructure in the village.

Figure 1: Map of Dindigul District

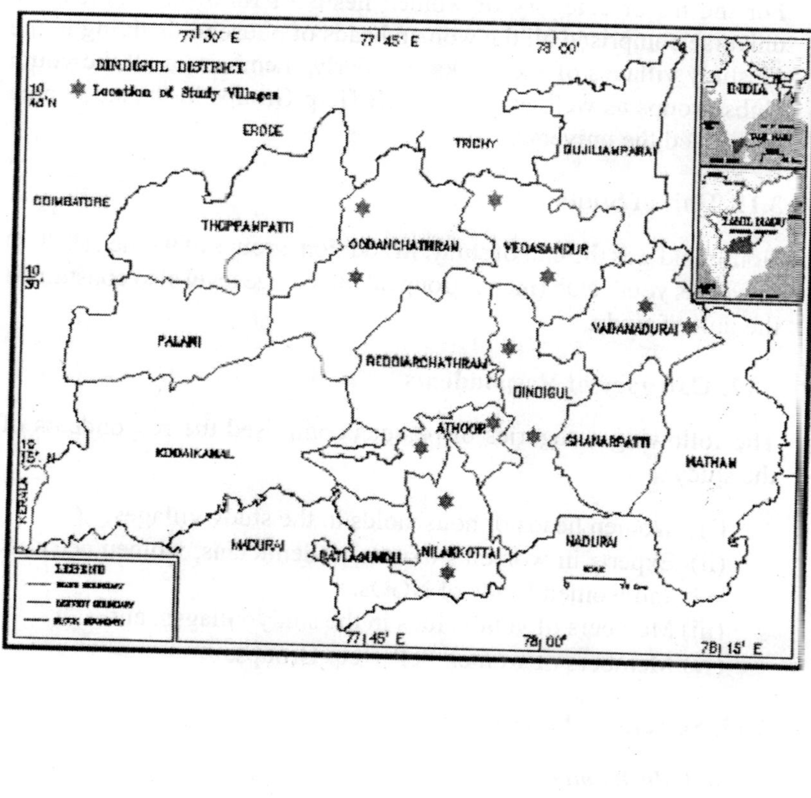

Table 3.1: List of Study Villages

Block	*Progressive Village*	*Backward Village*
Athoor	Pithalaipatti	Perumalkovilpatti
Dindigul	Periyapallapatti	Periyakottai
Nilakkottai	Mattaparai	Nakkaluthu
Oddanchathram	Markampatti	I. Vadipatti
Vadamadurai	Morepatti	Puthur
Vedasandur	Marambadi	Koovakkapatti

Accordingly, two villages were selected from each one of these blocks, making the total study villages to 12 in all.

3.10. Universe of the Study

For the major category of women heads of rural households, the universe comprised all the women heads of households living in the 12 study villages of six blocks. Similarly, members of all the youth clubs/groups as well as women Self-Help Groups in the study area comprised the universe.

3.11. Unit of Study

Household was the unit of study. In addition, groups of women (SHGs) as well as youth club (men's group) at the village level also constituted the unit of study.

3.12. Category of Respondents

The following categories of persons comprised the respondents of the study.

(i) Women heads of households in the study villages.
(ii) Experts in women's issues, academicians, women activists and women heads of NGOs.
(iii) Members of youth clubs in the study villages, and
(iv) Members of women Self-Help Groups.

3.13. Selection of Samples

Household Women

List of households available with the respective village panchayats were obtained initially. Details regarding the total population, male-female composition and sex ratio are given in the following table:

Table 3.2: Population Details of Study Villages

Blocks	*Villages*	*No. of Households*	*Total*	*Male*	*Female*	*Sex Ratio*
Athoor	Perumal Koilpatti	406	2064	1013	1051	1038
	Pithalaipatti	1026	5000	2300	2700	1174
Oddanchatram	Markampatti	283	1500	800	700	875
	I. Vadipatti	776	3957	2500	1457	583
Vadamadurai	Marambadi	721	3751	1989	1762	886
	Koovakkapatti	304	1700	960	740	771
Dindigul	Periakottai	167	900	500	400	800
	Periapallapatti	1626	8290	4080	4210	1032
Vadamadurai	Morepatti	335	1834	944	890	943
	Puthur	237	1352	897	455	507
Nilakkottai	Mattapparai	539	2750	1517	1233	813
	Nakkaluthu	352	1363	608	755	1241
	Total	6772	34461	18108	16353	10663

Simple random sampling method was followed in the selection of respondents from among the list of households provided by the respective village panchayats. Totally, a sample of 600 respondents-i.e. an arbitrarily fixed number of 50 per village in 12 villages, was selected from six blocks in Dindigul district, using equi-random sampling method.

From the pre-decided sample size of 50, every study village was stratified into religions and communities. Under the respective religions and communities, 50 respondents were selected proportionately, using stratified equi-random sampling method. Thus, a total of 600 samples were selected from 12 study villages.

Men's Group

Similarly, male members of the Youth Club/group in all the study villages, numbering around 20 in each club/group were invited for focus group discussions. The total number of participants in these meetings was 217.

Self-Help Groups

The study team held discussions with select Self-Help Groups, numbering six, selected from among the sample villages of Athoor,

Dindigul and Nilakkottai blocks. These blocks were purposively chosen for reasons of proximity. These Self-Help Groups supported the study in ranking the determinants identified by experts and activists.

Case Study Units

Respondents for the case study were identified among the women who were distinct from others in terms of their struggle in life and work—with resultant success or failure or both.

Case study was done on select women from each one of the study villages. Among the 12 such cases studied, 10 select case studies have been included in this report for brevity.

3.14. Sources and Type of Data

Sources of data include officials at the district level and block level, panchayat functionaries, activists, social workers, academicians, and scholars. Respondents who were the female heads of households, members of Self-Help Groups, and non-member public were the other sources. Members of youth club/groups as well as non-member youth who took part in group discussions served as yet another source.

From these sources, we collected both primary and secondary data. Literatures available in various research institutions and consultations had with experts on women empowerment, also supplemented the collection of primary and secondary data. Secondary data were collected from the records maintained at the village panchayat, BDO office, Mahalir Thittam project office, ICDS project office and NGO's official reports, census reports, articles and other published literatures.

3.15. Techniques of Study

Direct interview technique was followed in a face-to-face situation at the doorsteps of the women respondents. Interview schedule was used as the tool for data collection from the respondents.

Pre-designed and pre-tested interview schedules were used for collecting information from the women members of the study villages and women Self-Help Groups as well as men's group.

3.16. Pilot Study

A pilot study was conducted in two villages belonging to the village panchayats in Athoor block namely Velankannipuram in Chettiapatti panchayat and Kottaipatti in Kalikkampatti panchayat. The respondents were contacted to enlist their views on the broad areas of women empowerment and their responses served as the basis for constructing the tools of data collection.

3.17. Pre-Test

An interview schedule, initially prepared for a trial run, was administered to household women respondents as well as for Self Help Groups in these villages. The experiences gained from the pre-test helped to finalize the schedule with certain modifications in structuring and arranging the order of questions and also finalizing the appropriate questions/statements.

3.18. Tools of Data Collection

The study employed the following tools in the process of collection of data:

(1) Household interview schedule for the individual respondents.
(2) Group interview schedule for perception of men about women empowerment
(3) Interview schedule for eliciting the opinion of experts and activists on women empowerment.
(4) Indicators sheet for Self-Help Groups for rank ordering the determinants.
(5) An unstructured interview guide was also used in conducting the case study among select rural women.

Data were collected by trained Investigators using three types of interview schedules (viz., for household women, women groups and activists and experts) and an interview guide for Case studies.

These Investigators, who were graduates of Gandhigram, hailing from rural areas, were adequately oriented both in English and Tamil at the time of pilot study and pre-test. A translated Tamil version of the interview schedule was used by the Investigators. Respondents were clearly explained about both simple and complex concepts (including the status of women) during data collection process.

3.19. Data Collection and Analysis

The data were scrutinized and edited before they were subjected to coding and verification. Later, these data were computerized for tabulation and statistical processing. Data were analyzed using different statistical and tabulation procedures. Simple one way and two way tables were prepared using all the independent variables against empowerment variables. In addition to different types of tabular analysis, X^2 test of significance was used to identify the relationships of dependent variable with various independent variables.

3.20. Study Variables

Following were the independent and dependent variables studied:

- Religion
- Community
- Family Type
- Family Headship
- Age/Birth Order
- Pace of Birth (Rural/Urban)
- Marital Status
- Age at Marriage
- Type of Marriage
- Education
- Skill Training
- Occupation
- Household Income
- Respondent's Income
- Standard of living
- Membership in SHGs

Dependent Variables used in the study were:

- Reduction in Workload/Responsibility sharing.

- Decision-making.
- Access and control over resources.
- Domestic responsibilities sharing.
- Autonomy.
- Awareness about social legislations/women welfare programmes.
- Freedom of articulation, mobility, work, dress and voting.
- Participation in community activities.
- Political participation.
- Gender discrimination.
- Male domination.
- Violence against women.
- Power and influence.

3.21. Duration of the Study

The study was conducted during the period 2004-2005, and was updated by collecting additional data during 2006.

3.22. Probable Outcome

The study could be expected to aid the planners and policy-makers in gaining insight into the process of empowering rural women, based on which they would be able to fine-tune the existing and formulate new policies and draw up fresh plans for empowering the rural women.

Data collected for the present study, have been presented and analysed in the ensuing chapters.

Chapter 4

Response of the Rural Women

The status of rural women, sought to be studied through a sample of 600 respondents in the rural belts of Dindigul district, along with the indicators of empowerment and the factors facilitating as well as those stalling the empowerment of rural women, are analyzed in this chapter.

This chapter is divided into two sections—A and B. Section A deals with certain basic characteristics of all the respondents and the constituents of their overall socio-economic status. Details regarding deterrents and determinants of women empowerment are provided in Section B.

SECTION A

This section deals with data on the socio-economic status of sample respondents in the study area. Broadly they include:

- Religion and Community,
- Family type and Family headship pattern.
- Age, Birth order and Place of birth,
- Marital status of the respondents, and Age at marriage.
- Educational status of respondents and their spouse,
- Maternity details, number of deliveries and Antenatal and Post natal care.
- Availability of basic amenities.
- Occupation of respondents and their spouses.
- Vocational and leadership skills of respondents.
- Household income and Respondents' income.
- Domestic expenditure.

- Household Savings and Liabilities.
- Shouldering of domestic responsibilities.
- Household decision-making process.
- Access and control over productive assets.
- Membership in SHGs.
- Awareness about social legislations.
- Changes in social customs and social restrictions.
- Perception of women on men's rating of women's status.
- Problems faced by women and girl children.
- Sources of women's problems and methods of overcoming.

Data on the above aspects of the study are presented through tables with analysis and inferences.

Religion and Community

Religion and community play a pivotal role in the lives of both men and women, more so in the case of rural women. The social and cultural lives of women are woven around their religion and community, which would heavily impinge upon their empowerment. Table 4.1 throws light on the social composition of the respondents.

Table 4.1: Religion and Community Particulars of the Respondents

No.	Particulars	Number (n=600)	Percentage
1.	*Religion*		
	• Hindu	508	84.7
	• Christian	68	11.3
	• Muslim	24	4.0
2.	*Community*		
	• SC/ST	202	33.7
	• Most Backward Class	110	18.3
	• Backward Class	254	42.3
	• Forward Classes	34	5.7

Table 4.1 reveals that nearly 85.0 per cent belonged to the Hindus, 11.3 per cent to Christianity and 4.0 per cent of them were from Islam.

In respect of the community, 33.7 per cent of the respondents belonged to SC/ST and 60.6 per cent was from backward and most backward communities.

Respondents therefore, largely comprised Hindus (85.0%), and belonged to backward (42.3%) and scheduled communities (33.7%). Preponderance of respondents from a particular religion viz., Hindu and a sliding pattern of respondents from the other two religions viz., Christianity and Muslim show that the sample population is drawn from all the religions of the society, with a greater share from the predominant Hindu group.

Similarly, the picture on the community composition with two-thirds from Backward and Most Backward segments and one-third from SC/ST portrays the representation from all segments of the community, particularly a greater number among the Scheduled Castes and Tribes.

We may therefore infer that the views and opinions expressed by the respondents will represent a cross-section of the community and thus be comprehensive and holistic of the study area. In addition, the views of SC/ST sections are represented better in the study population.

Figure 2: Religion and Community of the Respondents

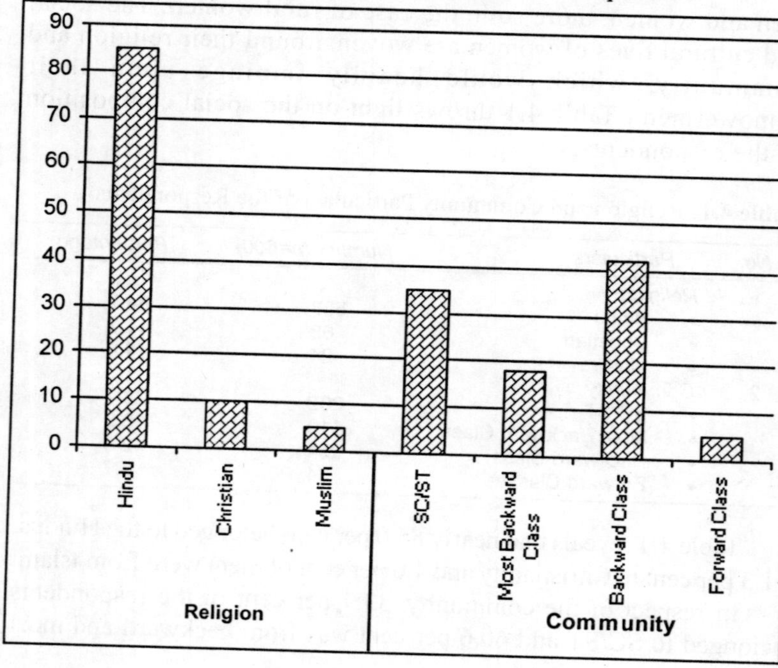

Table 4.2: Family Type and Pattern of Family of the Respondents

No.	Particulars	Number (n=600)	Percentage
1.	Family Type		
	• Joint family	157	26.7
	• Nuclear family	443	73.3
2.	Pattern of family		
	• Single member	24	4.0
	• Male headed	489	81.5
	• Female headed	87	14.5

Family Type and Headship

Table 4.2 brings out that 73.3 per cent of the respondents hailed from nuclear families, while the remaining 26.7 per cent represented joint families.

Further, 81.5 per cent respondents lived in male-headed families. Families headed by females comprised 14.5 per cent.

Table 4.3: Age, Birth Order and Place of Birth of the Respondents

No.	Particulars	Number of Respondents (n=600)	Percentage
1.	Age		
	• Below 35 years	291	48.5
	• Above 35 years	309	51.5
2.	Birth Order of Respondents		
	• First child	221	36.8
	• Second to Fifth child	165	27.5
	• Fifth to Eighth child	214	35.7
3.	Place of Birth		
	• Rural	538	89.7
	• Urban	62	10.3
	Total	*600*	*100.0*

Nuclear families (73 per cent) and male headed families (82 per cent) were predominant among the respondent households. Mason (1986) says that residence in a non-nuclear family, which in the Indian context, implies residence with in-laws for ever-married women, is likely to be a less 'empowering' setting than residence in a nuclear family, and with multiple generations co-residing, the probability of participation in, let alone control over household decisions, is less likely for women who have entered the family as brides.

From the above conclusion, we may infer that while the prevalence of more nuclear families represents the gradually changing scenario of nuclearization, in favour of empowering women, the preponderance of male headed families manifests the patriarchal hold of the respondent households.

Age, Birth Order and Nativity

Table 4.3 shows the details about the age, birth order and place of birth of the respondents. The age profile of respondents shows that 48.5 per cent were aged below 35 years while the remaining 51.5 per cent were aged above 35 years.

Thirty seven per cent of respondents were born as the first child to their parents. The birth order of about 28.0 per cent respondents ranged from second to fifth. Another 36.0 per cent were born as fifth to eighth child.

Figure 3: Age, Birth Order and Place of Birth of Respondents

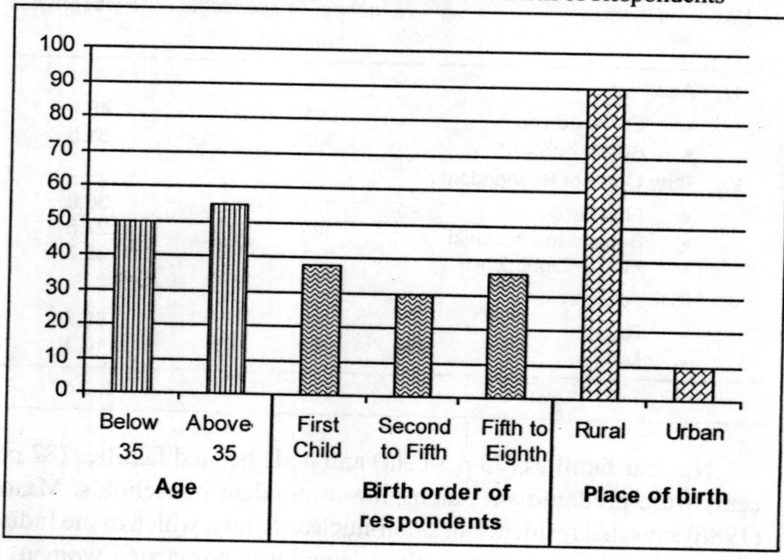

Nearly 90 per cent of the respondents were born in rural areas, while the rest (10 per cent) were born in towns or cities.

We may conclude that a near equal percentage of respondents belonged to the category of below 35 years (51.5 per cent) and above 35 years (48.5 per cent). Further, about 37 per cent of the respondents were born as the first child to their parents, and a large majority (90 per cent) were born in rural areas.

From the above conclusion, we may infer that a near equal divide between those aged below and above 35 years may contribute to a balance of views while the predominance of village born respondents may bring about a less progressive view towards empowerment.

Table 4.4: Marital Status, Age at Marriage and Type of Marriage of the Respondents

No.	Particulars	Number (n=600)	Percentage
1.	Marital Status		
	• Married	444	74.0
	• Unmarried	88	14.7
	• Widows, separated, divorces, deserted	68	11.3
2.	Age at Marriage		
	• 14—18	134	22.3
	• 18—21	384	64.0
	• 21 and above	82	13.7
3.	Type of Marriage		
	• Love marriage	115	19.2
	• Arranged marriage	485	80.8
4.	Relation to Spouse		
	• Close relatives	254	42.4
	• Relatives	178	29.6
	• Not known earlier	168	28.0
	Total	600	100.0

*Multiple responses

Marital Details

Marriage has a role to play in deciding the social status and living conditions of women in India. As the society is by and large patriarchal, the husband's social status defined the social status of woman, (Sahay, 1998).

Table 4.4 shows that married women were in large majority (74.0 per cent). Eighty six per cent of respondents were married at the young age of 14-18 and 18-21 years.

Eighty per cent of respondents had arranged marriage, while 19.2 per cent had love marriage.

Forty two per cent of respondents married within their close relatives while another 30 per cent married among their relatives.

We may infer from the above analysis that predominance of married women, their marriage at an early date and practice of arranged marriage reveal the prevalence of existing social norm among the sample population.

Table 4.5: Educational Status of the Respondents and their Spouses

No.	*Particulars*	*Number (n=600)*	*Percentage*
1.	Education of Respondents		
	• Illiterates	400	66.7
	• Primary and middle	163	27.2
	• Secondary and above	37	6.1
2.	Education of Spouses		
	• Illiterate	41	6.8
	• Primary	58	9.7
	• Middle level	459	76.5
	• Secondary level	33	5.5
	• Higher secondary	8	1.3
	• College/Professional	1	0.2

Education of Respondents and their Spouses

Table 4.5 gives an account of the educational status of the respondents, and their spouses.

Two thirds of the respondents were illiterate (66.7%). Only primary and middle level of education was received by a large majority of the respondents (27.2%). On the contrary, about 93 per cent of the spouses of the respondents were educated and 77 per cent of them had secondary level of education.

It may be concluded that only a third of the respondents were literate as against 93 per cent of their spouses. Women's illiteracy in the respondent households was found to be 10 times greater than that of their spouses. It is probable that they are less empowered. We may infer that illiteracy among majority of the respondents and a lower level of education among those literate may hinder women's empowerment.

Figure 4: Education of the Respondents and Spouses

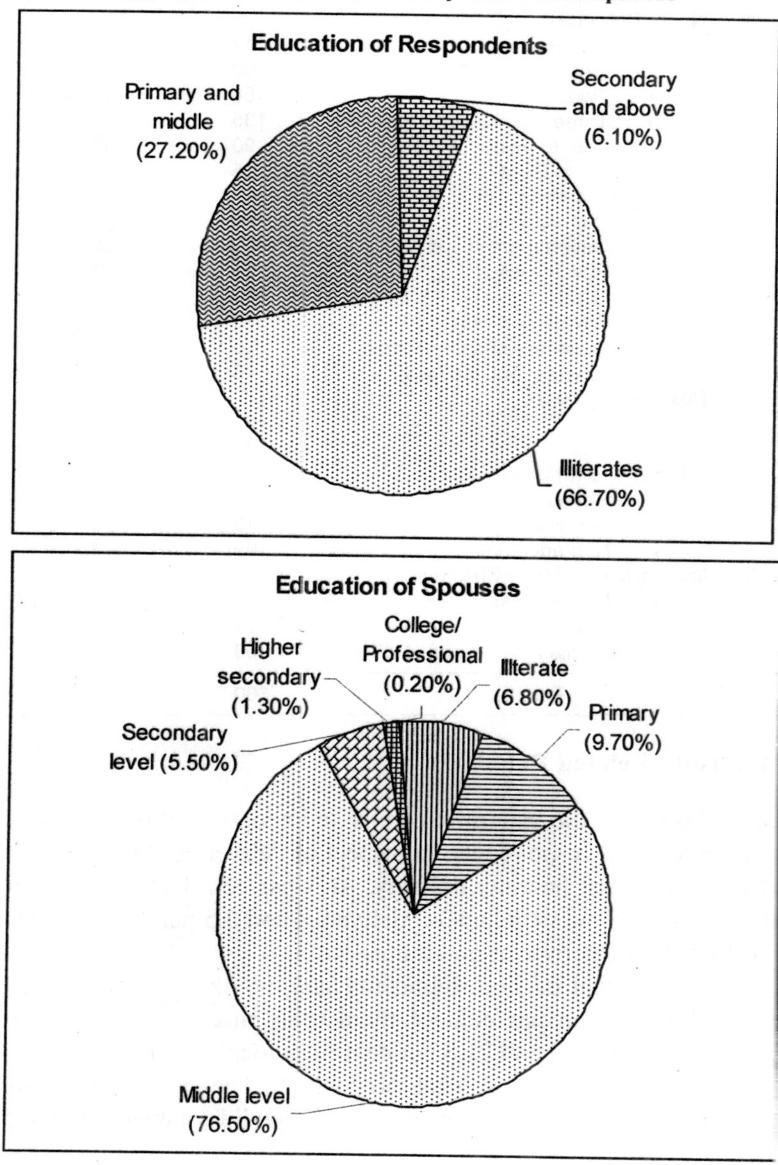

Table 4.6: Maternity Details and Adoption of Birth Control Measures by the Respondents

No.	*Particulars*	*Number (n=600)*	*Percentage*
1.	No. of Deliveries		
	• No response	112	18.6
	• One	90	15.0
	• Two	158	26.3
	• Three	135	22.5
	• Four to Five	90	15.0
	• Six to Eight	15	2.5
2.	Ante-natal Care		
	• No response	49	8.2
	• Government hospital	220	36.6
	• Private Hospital	131	21.8
	• Local	169	28.2
	• Private and local	10	1.7
	• Government and private	15	2.5
	• Government and local	6	1.0
3.	Post-natal Care		
	• No	469	77.3
	• Yes	131	22.7
4.	Adopter of Birth Control Measure		
	• Respondent	416	69.0
	• Spouse	15	2.5
	• Non-adopters	169	28.2
5.	Immunization of their Children		
	• No response	91	15.2
	• Fully	453	75.5
	• Partially	56	9.3
	Total	600	100.0

Maternity Related Details

Table 4.6 shows the maternity details and adoption of birth control measures by the respondents. In respect of deliveries, 18.6 per cent of them have not had any delivery, 41.3 per cent had one or two deliveries. 37.5 per cent had 3-5 deliveries and 2.5 per cent of them had from 5 to 8 deliveries and more.

Eight per cent of the respondents had not taken any ante-natal care. Thirty seven per cent of them took ante-natal care from government hospital and 21.8 per cent from local hospital.

With regard to the post-natal care, only 22.7 per cent of them had it while the remaining majority of 77.3 per cent did not take such care.

Figure 5: Ante-natal and Post-natal Care by the Respondents

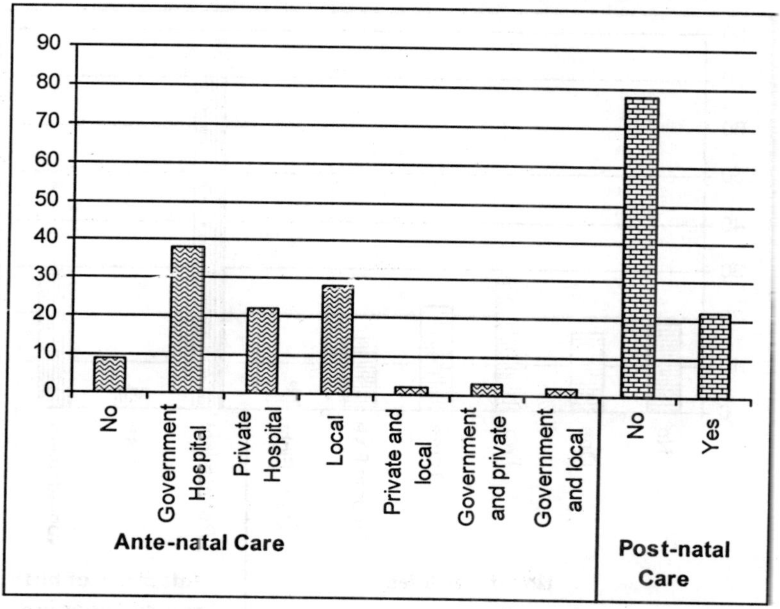

Birth Control Measures

Totally, 69 per cent respondents had adopted the birth control measures whereas only 2.5 per cent of their spouses had adopted such measures. Non-adopters constituted 28.2 per cent of the total respondents.

Seventy five per cent of the respondents had fully immunized their children while 15 per cent had not immunized at all.

The analysis shows that 64 per cent of the respondents had 2 to 5 deliveries. Ninety two per cent had taken ante-natal care from government and private hospitals but 77.3 per cent had not taken post-natal care. While 69 per cent of the respondents had adopted birth control measures, only 2.5 per cent spouses had done so. Seventy five per cent of the respondents had immunized their children fully.

We may infer from the above conclusion that facts such as deliveries ranging from 2 to 5, more ante-natal care but less post-natal care and preponderance of lesser women in family planning unfold that changes in terms of demographic trend and gender discrimination are slow.

Figure 6: Adoption of Birth Control Measure by the Respondents

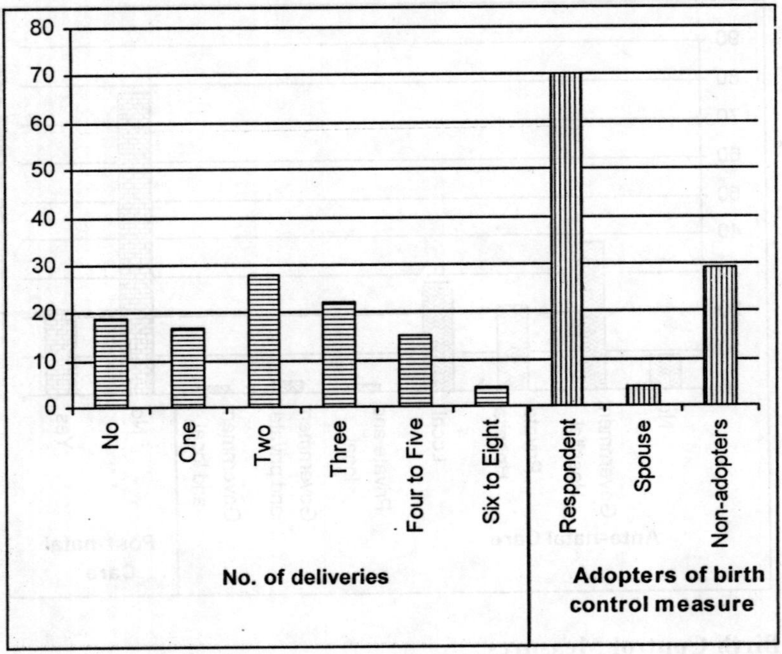

Table 4.7: Basic Amenities available in the Respondent Households

No.	*Particulars*	*Number (n=600)*	*Percentage*
1.	Drinking Water		
	• Private sources	329	54.8
	• Community sources	141	23.5
	• Own sources	130	21.7
2.	Toilet		
	• Not available	587	97.7
	• Available	13	2.3
3.	Type of Fuel		
	• Gas	345	57.5
	• Fuel wood	211	35.2
	• Kerosene	44	7.3
4.	Domestic Lighting		
	• Electrified	438	73.0
	• Not electrified	162	27.0

(*Contd.*)

(*Contd.*)

No.	Particulars	Number (n=600)	Percentage
5.	Basic Amenities		
	• Not available	295	49.2
	• Fan	97	16.2
	• Radio	72	12.0
	• Two wheeler	71	11.8
	• Tape Recorder	41	6.8
	• Television	24	4.0
6.	Home Gadgets		
	• No	434	73.3
	• Mixie	78	13.0
	• Grinder	28	4.7
	• Telephone	46	7.7
	• All	14	2.3
	Total	600	100.0

Basic Amenities

Table 4.7 presents the basic amenities and home gadgets available in the respondent households. Regarding the availability of drinking water for the respondent households, 21.7 per cent of them availed through own sources, 23.5 per cent through community sources and 54.8 per cent through private sources.

Except two per cent who had toilet facilities, 98 per cent of the respondent households did not have toilet facility.

Thirty five per cent of the respondent households used fuel wood, 57.5 per cent had gas and 7.3 per cent used kerosene for their domestic fuel.

Forty nine per cent of the respondent households did not have domestic necessities. Among others, 16.2 per cent had fan, 12.5 per cent transistor/radio, 6.8 per cent tape recorder and four per cent had television. About 12 per cent had two wheelers.

Out of the total respondent households, majority of them (73.3%) did not have any home gadgets. Thirteen per cent had a *mixie* and 4.6 per cent owned a grinder. About eight per cent had telephone connection.

We may conclude that private sources served as the major source of drinking water (53%), toilets were not available in 98 per cent households, electricity not available in 27 per cent households, no basic domestic necessities available in 49 per cent households and no home gadgets were available in 73 per cent of the households.

From the above conclusion, we may infer that non-availability of toilets in most cases, lack of electricity and other basic necessities and non-availability of basic necessities and home gadgets retain them under the backward rural fold.

Table 4.8: Occupation of Respondents and their Spouses—Before and After Marriage

Particulars	*Number*	*Percentage*
1. Present Occupation		
• Agricultural labour	225	37.3
• Domestic activities	199	32.9
• Self employment	89	14.5
• Non-Farm labour	77	12.7
• Salaried employment	10	1.7
2. Occupation Before Marriage		
• Domestic work	363	60.5
• Employed	122	20.3
• Studying	115	19.2
3. Occupation of Spouse		
• Farm labour	276	46.0
• Self employed	122	20.3
• No employment	76	12.7
• Salaried	65	10.8
• Non-farm labour	61	10.2
Total	600	100

Occupation—Present and Prior

Table 4.8 presents the occupation of respondents and their spouses—both at present and prior to their marriage. At present, 32.9 per cent of the respondents are engaged in their domestic activities, while 14.7 per cent were in self employment and 12.7 per cent of them as non-farm labourers. 37.3 per cent of them are engaged as agricultural labourers.

Prior to the marriage of the respondents, 20.3 per cent of them were employed, 19.2 per cent were studying and the remaining 60.5 per cent of them were engaged in domestic work.

Similarly, about 13 per cent of the respondents' spouses were not employed. Forty six per cent of them were in farm labour, 10.2 per cent employed as non-farm labour, 20.3 per cent in self-employment and 10.8 per cent were occupied in salaried employment.

We may conclude from the above analysis that 50 per cent of the respondents are in farm and non-farm labour activities at present. Prior to their marriage, 60 per cent were engaged in domestic work while the remaining were employed (20 per cent) or studying (19.2 per cent). Fifty six per cent of the spouses of the respondents were engaged in farm and non-farm labour.

The findings reveal the predominance of the sample respondents in farm and non-farm activities typical of rural settings and their views on women empowerment may be typical of a peasant society.

Studies have shown that unlike traditional farm/non-farm based labour activities, self employment programmes reduce the barriers to entrepreneurship by increasing women's access to credit and capital, technical expertise, management training and information and support networks. Since majority of the respondents are confined to the traditional activities, their opportunity to advance then, through self employment ventures, are largely restricted. Hence, their empowerment avenues remain closed because female entrepreneurship has the potential for women's empowerment.

Table 4.9: Vocational and Leadership Skills of the Respondents and their Benefits

No.	Particulars	Number	Percentage
1.	Vocational Skills (n = 48)		
	• Tailoring	23	47.9
	• Handicraft	17	35.4
	• Cooking	5	10.4
	• Basket making	3	6.3
2.	Pattern of Utilization (n = 48)		
	• Not utilized	21	43.75
	• Utilized	27	56.25
3.	Leadership and EDP Skills (n = 33)		
	• Accounting training	15	45.5
	• EDP training	13	39.3
	• Leadership training	5	15.2
4.	Training Institutions (n = 33)		
	• NGOs	21	63.7
	• Universities	4	12.1
	• Local organizations	4	12.1
	• Government	4	12.1

Vocational and Leadership Skills

Table 4.9 presents the vocational and leadership skills of the respondents and their benefits.

Eight per cent of the respondents possessed certain vocational skills, the major ones being tailoring (47.9%), and handicrafts (35.4%)

Little more than half of the respondents had utilized their vocational skills (50.3%) while others have not.

About six per cent of the respondents had undergone training in leadership and EDP (Entrepreneurship Development Programme) besides accountancy.

Thirteen per cent of the respondents acquired these skills and training from specialized training institutions, which include: Non Government Organizations (63.7%), Universities, local organizations and Government (12.1 per cent each).

Nearly one-tenth of the respondents have undergone skill training and about six per cent of the respondents in leadership and entrepreneurial development training. Fifty six per cent of the respondents have utilized their training. NGOs are the major training institutions who imparted training (63.7%).

Aspiration for skill acquisition among rural women is perhaps quite low, but has been growing steadily. However, utilization of skills in more cases augurs well for the prospects of empowering women.

Table 4.10: Occupation, Household Income and Annual Income of the Respondents

Particulars	*No. of Respondents*	*Percentage*
1. Household Annual Income		
• < Rs. 15,000	143	23.8
• Rs. 15,000-20,000	64	10.7
• Rs. 20,000-25,000	149	24.8
• Rs. 25,000-50,000	244	40.7
2. Annual Income of Respondents		
• No	66	11.0
• Below Rs. 3000	241	40.2
• Rs. 3000-5000	254	42.3
• Rs. 5000-10,000	29	4.8
• Above Rs. 10,000	10	1.7

Household Annual Income

Data on the annual income of the respondent households in Table 4.10 shows that one-third of the respondents had an income of less than Rs. 20,000 per annum, about one-fourth earned between Rs. 20,000 and Rs. 25,000, while the remaining two-fifths had Rs. 25,000 to Rs. 50,000 as their annual income.

Two-thirds of the respondents, therefore, had a higher income of above Rs. 20,000 per annum, whereas the remaining one-third had a lower income of below Rs. 20,000. We may infer from the analysis that about 60 per cent of the respondent households were nearly equivalent to families living below poverty line.

Figure 7: Annual Income of the Households and Respondents

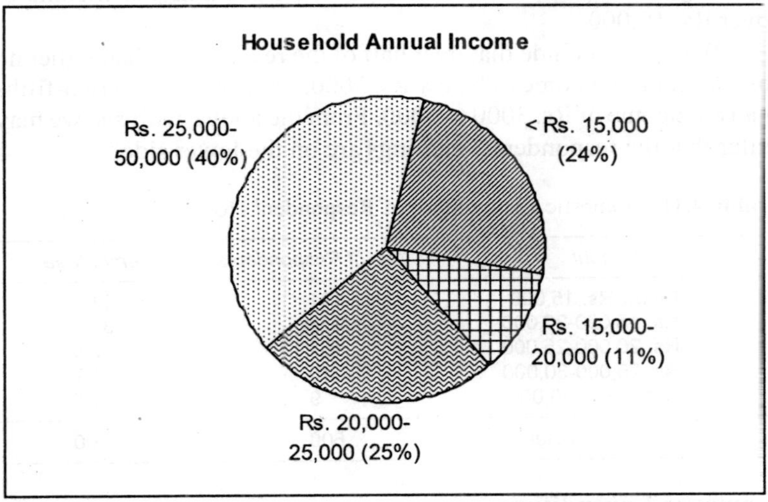

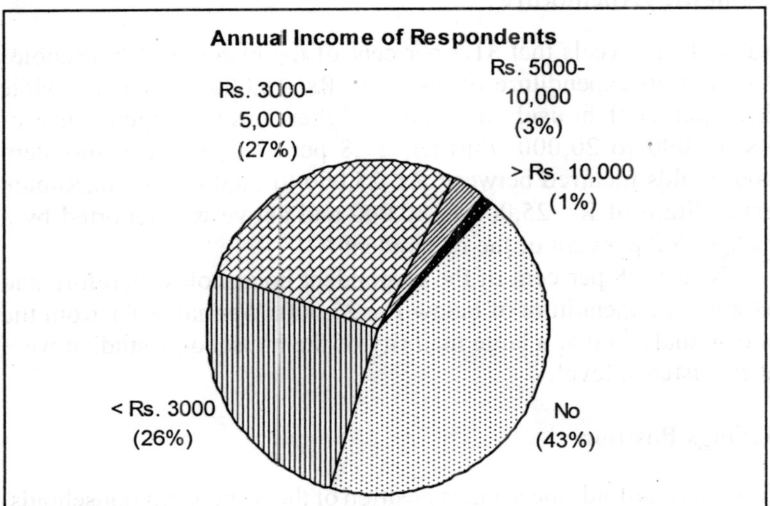

Annual Income of the Respondents

Table 4.10 shows that 11 per cent of the respondents did not earn while about 40.2 per cent had an income of below Rs. 3,000. Whereas 42.3 per cent of the respondents had an income of Rs. 3,000 to 5,000, 4.8 per cent of the respondents had an income of Rs. 5,000 to 10,000. A meagre two per cent of the respondents got a higher income of over Rs. 10,000.

We may conclude that over half of the respondents had either no or a minimum income of below Rs. 3000, while more than two-fifths had an income of Rs. 3000 to 5000. From the above analysis, we may infer that the respondents' earnings are on the lower side.

Table 4.11: Domestic Expenditure of Respondent Households

Sl. No.	*Amount*	*No. of Respondents*	*Percentage*
1.	Below Rs. 15,000	191	31.8
2.	Rs. 15,000-20,000	223	37.2
3.	Rs. 20,000-25,000	167	27.8
4.	Rs. 25,000-30,000	10	1.7
5.	Above Rs. 30,000	9	1.5
	Total	600	100

Domestic Expenditure

Table 4.11 reveals that 31.2 per cent of the respondent households incurred an expenditure of less than Rs. 15,000 per annum while 37.2 per cent households had a higher annual expenditure of Rs. 15,000 to 20,000. Further, 27.8 per cent of the respondent households incurred between Rs. 25,000 to 30,000. The maximum expenditure of Rs. 25,000 to 30,000 and above was reported by a meager 3.2 per cent of the respondents.

Nearly 98 per cent of the respondent households therefore had an annual expenditure of below Rs. 25,000. We may infer from the above analysis that a large majority of the households studied were at subsistence level.

Savings Position

Table 4.12 unfolds the savings position of the respondent households. More than three-fourths of the respondent households (76.2 per cent)

were reported to be saving. Among them, one-fourth had less than Rs. 1,000 as their savings. Forty four per cent of the respondents had a saving of Rs. 1,000 to 3,000, while others had a maximum savings of Rs. 5,000 and above.

Table 4.12: Savings Position of Respondent Households

Sl. No.	Amount	No. of Respondents	Percentage
1.	Below Rs. 1,000	115	25.2
2.	Rs. 1,000-2,000	108	23.6
3.	Rs. 2,000-3,000	93	20.4
4.	Rs. 3,000-5,000	75	16.4
5.	Above Rs. 5,000	66	14.4
	Total	457	100

We may conclude that nearly 86 per cent of the respondent households had a saving of less than Rs. 5,000 per annum. It may be inferred that functioning of Self-Help Groups in villages should have been instrumental in instilling the habit of savings among women in poor households.

Table 4.13: Liabilities of Respondents according to their Sources

Particulars	Bank (N = 600)	Cooperatives (N = 600)	Insurance (N = 600)	Private (N = 600)	SHG (N = 600)
Yes	67 (9.8)	63 (11.1)	48 (8.6)	92 (85.9)	80 (84.9)
No	533 (88.2)	567 (88.9)	552 (91.4)	508 (84.1)	520 (86.1)

* Multiple responses

Liabilities

Lack of liabilities gives peace and dignity and freedom from economic burdens and botherations, which forms the basis of empowerment. Liabilities of respondents show that a minimum of 8.6 per cent to a maximum of 86 per cent had borrowed from different sources. Borrowers from insurance companies, banks and cooperatives were at the minimum (8.6, 9.8 and 11.1 per cent respectively). As against this, 85 to 86 per cent respondents had borrowed from private sources and self help groups.

Figure 8: Liabilities of Respondents According to their Sources

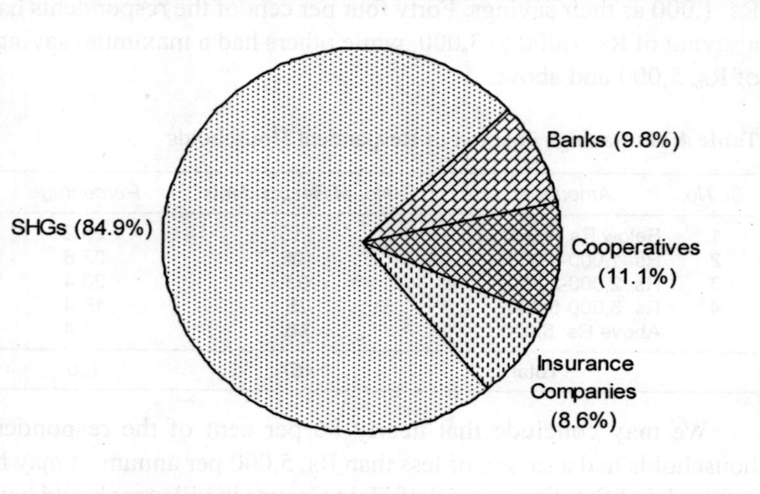

Table 4.14: Sharing of Domestic Responsibilities in the Respondent Households

Sl. No.	*Type of Responsibility*	*Respondents*		*Respondents and other Females*		*Men*	
		Member	*Percentage*	*Member*	*Percentage*	*Member*	*Percentage*
1.	Cooking	518	86.3	82	13.7	—	—
2.	Fetching drinking water	488	81.4	110	18.3	2	0.3
3.	Fetching drinking water in summer	480	80.0	103	17.2	17	2.8
4.	Washing of clothes	502	83.7	95	15.8	3	0.5
5.	Cleaning of vessels	504	84.0	92	15.3	4	0.7
6.	Collection of fuel wood	494	82.4	95	15.8	11	1.8
7.	Maintenance of house	496	82.6	88	14.7	16	2.7
8.	Care of the sick/disabled	507	84.5	89	14.8	4	0.7

The analysis in Table 4.13 reveals that respondents depended more on private sources (85.9%) and self-help groups (84.9%). Their dependence in banks, insurance and cooperatives has decreased. It also shows the predominance of private sources, slightly higher than the self-help groups. We may infer from the above conclusions that private sources still continues to be predominant and that the self-help groups have not been able to wean away the women from private sources. While greater dependence from private sources may curtail the process of empowerment, exclusive dependence on Self-Help Groups may contribute to greater empowerment.

Domestic Responsibility Sharing

Table 4.14 consists of details regarding the discharge of domestic responsibilities by the respondents in the categories viz., independently, with other family members and by the men in their households, in respect of certain basic domestic chores. These include cooking, fetching water, washing clothes, cleaning of vessels, collection of fuel wood, maintenance of the house and care of the sick and elderly.

Respondents took care of cooking responsibility at home independently in 86.3 per cent cases, and with other female members in the remaining (13.7%) households. No male member shared this responsibility.

Eighty to eighty seven per cent of the respondents shouldered the following responsibilities independently:

- Fetching of drinking water during summer
- Collection of fuel wood
- Maintenance of house
- Washing of clothes
- Cleaning of vessels
- Care of the sick/disabled

The other family members joined the respondents in the above tasks ranging from 14.7 to 18.3 per cent.

Men's share in the above tasks related to fetching of water during summer (2.8%), maintenance of house (2.7%) and collection of fuel wood (1.8%).

■ Care of the sick/disabled	84.5
■ Cleaning of vessels	84.0
■ Washing of clothes	83.7
■ Maintenance of house	82.6
■ Collection of fuel wood	82.4
■ Fetching of drinking water during summer	81.4

Men's share was limited to about two to three per cent in respect of fetching drinking water during summer, maintenance of house and collection of fuel wood. Family members assisted in all the activities ranging from 14 to 18 per cent.

We may infer from the above facts that cooking continues to be the prime preserve of women and the men keep away from all major domestic responsibilities. This reinforces the constancy in gender roles and the caution exercised by men from purveying into the women's domain.

Table 4.15: Members making Domestic-Related Decisions in the Respondent Households

No.	*Particulars*	*Respondents*	*Spouses*	*Both*
1.	Marriage of sons/ daughters	44 (7.3)	31 (5.2)	525 (87.5)
2.	Purchase of assets/ properties	42 (7.0)	35 (5.8)	523 (85.5)
3.	Number of children	52 (8.7)	31 (5.2)	517 (86.1)
4.	Education of children	47 (7.9)	36 (6.0)	517 (86.1)
5.	Adoption of birth control	56 (9.3)	29 (4.9)	515 (85.8)
6.	Borrowing/lending	51 (8.5)	36 (6.0)	513 (85.5)
7.	Employment of women/children	54 (9.0)	37 (6.2)	509 (84.8)
8.	Participation in SHGs	124 (20.6)	37 (6.2)	439 (73.2)
9.	Voting in elections	141 (23.5)	36 (6.0)	423 (70.5)
10.	Spending their income	65 (10.8)	501 (83.5)	34 (5.7)

Decision-Making

Lakshmi Devi (1998) states that in determining the status of women in India, factors such as the role women in decision-making with family and with community should be taken into consideration.

Table 4.15 deals with decision-making in the respondent households by the respondents, their spouse or both on matters of vital importance to the family.

Twenty four per cent respondents decided voting in elections, while another 20.6 per cent decided about their participation in self-help-groups. However, both the respondents and the spouses decided the above in 70.5 and 73.2 per cent cases respectively.

Between 84 and 86 per cent of the respondents and their spouses made decisions regarding:

■ Marriage of sons and daughters	87.5
■ Number of children they wish to have	86.1
■ Education of children	86.1
■ Adoption of birth control measures	85.8
■ Purchase of assets/properties	85.5
■ Employment of women/children/daughter	84.8
■ Borrowing and lending	84.3

On the other hand, decision on spending the earnings of the respondents was taken by the spouses in 83.5 per cent of the cases. Eleven per cent of the respondents decided about spending their income.

Figure 9: Decision-Making by Family Members

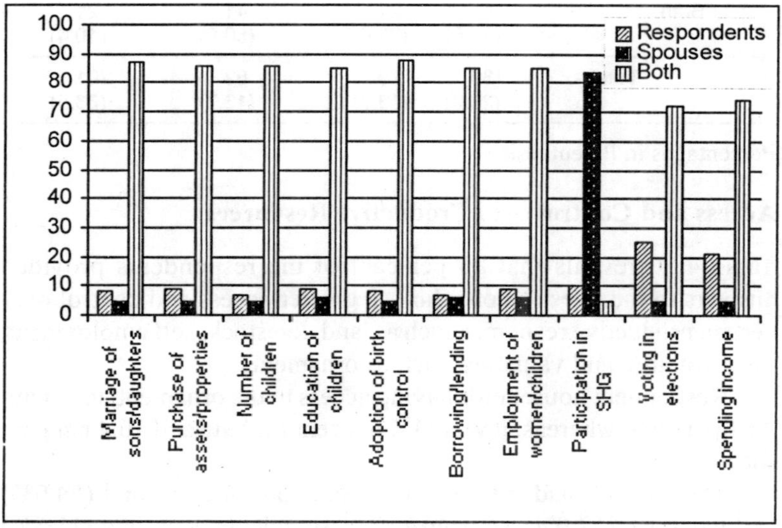

We may conclude that joint decisions (84 to 88 per cent cases) prevailed predominantly in respect of the number of children to be had, adoption of family planning, education of children, employment of women/children, marriage of sons/daughters and borrowing and lending. The spouses decided about spending the respondents' income (83.5%). The respondents decided about voting in elections (23.5%) and participation in Self-Help Groups (20.6%).

Decision-making process seems to be gradually emerging more partnership-based instead of the men's preserve. However, it still remains male-dominated. Women's freedom to vote in elections and participate in SHG activities and men's sway over spending their wife's income reveals the hold of men over women as well as their hold in select spheres.

Table 4.16: Access and Control of the Respondents over Productive Resources

No.	Particulars	Land	Livestock	Infrastructure	Ornaments
1.	Respondents	16 (11.5)	13 (16.4)	14 (17.1)	149 (74.1)
2.	Spouses	75 (12.5)	45 (57.0)	27 (32.8)	31 (15.15)
3.	Both	48 (34.5)	21 (26.6)	41 (50.0)	21 (10.4)
	Total	139 (23.2)	79 (13.7)	82 (13.7)	201 (33.5)

Percentages in Parenthesis

Access and Control over Productive Resources

Table 4.16 reveals that 80 per cent of the respondents provided answers to the question on who has greater access and control over certain productive resources such as land, livestock, self employment, infrastructure and valuables such as ornaments.

Respondent households having access to the ornament, tops with 74.1 per cent; whereas, it was 11.5 per cent for land and 16.4 per cent for livestock.

The spouses had greater access and control over land (54.0%) and livestock (57.0%) as against the respondents over land (11,5%) and livestock (16.4%).

Respondents therefore, have greater access and control over ornaments (74.1%), and their spouses have greater access and control over land and livestock (54.0 and 57.0%), both the respondent and their spouses have great access and control over the self employment infrastructure (50%) and land (34.5%).

Access of respondents over ornament and their spouses over land and livestock reveal that the men have a greater hold on productive assets.

Figure 10: Access and Control of Respondents over Productive Resources

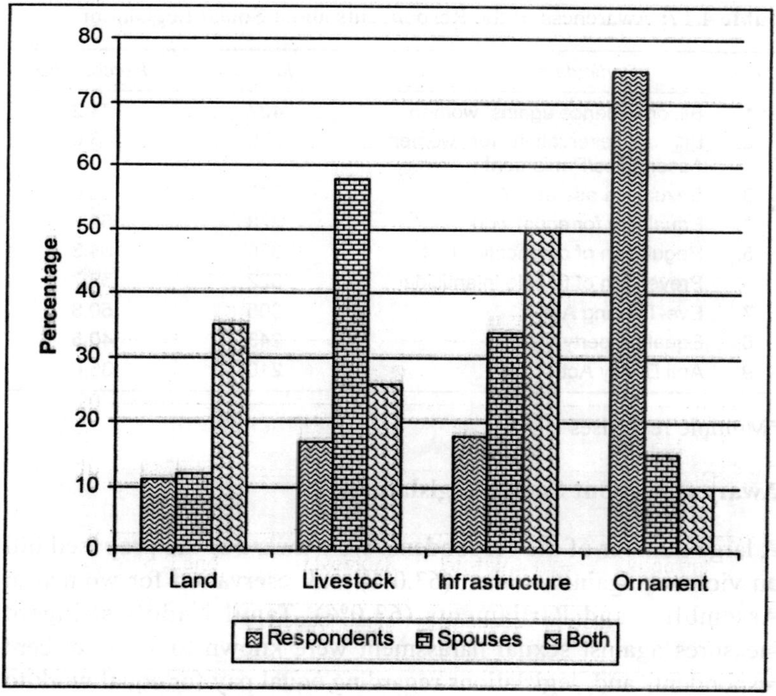

Membership in SHGs

Seventy three per cent of the respondents had enrolled as members in SHGs and the rest did not join SHGs. Almost three out of every four respondents were members of Self-Help Groups. Predominance of rural women in the ambit of community based people's organizations such as SHGs indicate the growing interest of women in group life and the grip of SHGs over the rural women.

Participation in Panchayat Elections

Regarding participation of women in panchayat elections, 14.3 per cent of the respondents participated in the election, of which more than half of them won while the rest lost. It is a good augury that, more than half of the contestants have won the panchayat elections. Growing number of women in civic bodies is a sure sign of women getting empowered.

Table 4.17: Awareness of the Respondents about Social Legislations

No.	*Particulars*	*Number*	*Percentage*
1.	Bill on violence against women	427	71.2
2.	Bill on reservation for women in Assemblies/Parliament	378	63.0
3.	Sexual Harassment Act	348	58.0
4.	Equal pay for equal work	328	54.7
5.	Regulation of diagnostics test	325	54.2
6.	Prevention of female infanticide	322	53.7
7.	Eve-Teasing Act	305	50.8
8.	Equal property rights	243	40.5
9.	Anti Dowry Act	210	35.0

*Multiple responses

Awareness about Social Legislations

A large number of the respondents were aware of the proposed bill on violence against women (63.0%) and reservation for women in Assemblies and Parliaments (63.0%). Tamil Nadu's stringent measures against sexual harassment were known to 58.0 per cent respondents and, legislations regarding equal pay for equal work to 54.7 per cent respondents. Prevention of female infanticide and regulation of diagnostic tests were familiar to about 54 per cent each of the respondents.

Majority of the respondents (51 to 71%) were aware of the Bill on violence against women, reservation for women in assemblies/ parliament, Sexual Harassment Act and legislations on prevention of female infanticide, regulation of diagnostic tests, and Eve Teasing Act.

It may be inferred from the above that greater awareness of women about various social legislations point out the growing concern among women for becoming part of the mainstream society.

Table 4.18: Opinion of Respondents on the Changes in Social Customs and Relaxation in Social Restrictions

No.	Particulars	Number (n = 600)	Percentage
1.	Marriage System		
	• Love marriage accepted	241	40.2
	• No change	144	24.0
	• Selection of partners	109	18.2
	• Inter caste marriage accepted	57	9.5
	• More empowerment	49	8.1
2.	Dowry Practice		
	• Dowry problem increased	306	51.0
	• Favour dowry	217	36.0
	• Dowry problem low	77	12.9
3.	Divorce		
	• Increased	334	55.7
	• No change	155	25.8
	• Decreased	111	18.5
4.	Role of Gender		
	• Equal importance for both sex	325	54.1
	• No change	162	27.0
	• Female baby accepted	113	18.9

Changes in Social Customs

Empowerment would consist of greater access to knowledge and resources, greater autonomy in decision-making, greater ability to plan their lives and free from shackles imposed on them by custom, belief and practice (Lakshmi Devi,1998).

Table 4.18 brings out the opinion of respondents on the changes in social customs and relaxation in social restrictions. Twenty four per cent of the respondents opined that no change has taken place in the marriage system. However, 49.7 per cent of them reported that they accept love marriage and inter-caste marriage.

Thirty six per cent of the respondents stated that there has been no change in the practice of dowry. While 51 per cent of the respondents felt that the practice has increased, 12.9 per cent said that it has decreased.

Twenty six per cent of the respondents felt that there is no change in the rate of divorce. While 18.5 per cent respondents opined that it has decreased, 55.7 per cent informed that it has increased.

There is no change in the role of gender according to 27 per cent of the respondents. However, 54.7 per cent of the respondents felt that equal importance is given to both the sex. About 19 per cent of the respondents informed that female baby is accepted nowadays.

We may conclude that 50 per cent of the respondents stated that inter-caste and love marriages are accepted by the society, 51 per cent have reported that dowry practice has increased and 55 per cent have opined that divorce rate has increased. Fifty six per cent of respondents have observed that there is equal importance given for both the sexes in society.

From the above conclusion, we may infer that growing acceptance of inter-caste and love marriages and the feeling of equal importance being given to both men and women provides assurances of an emerging trend towards gender-equality.

Table 4.19: Perception of Respondents on Men's Rating of Women's Status

No.	*Particulars*	*Number (n=600)*	*Percentage*
1.	Present Status of Women		
	• Secondary to men	308	51.3
	• Equal to men	263	43.8
	• Superior to men	29	4.9
2.	Men's Rating of Women Status		
	• Secondary to men	303	50.5
	• Equal to men	262	43.7
	• Superior to men	35	5.8
3.	Period Women Equal Men		
	• No.	257	42.8
	• Decision-making	216	36.0
	• Mobility	96	16.0
	• Earning skill and more skilful	31	5.2

Perception of Men's Rating

Table 4.19 presents the perception of men's rating of women's status by the respondents. Regarding the present status of women, 50.5 per cent of the respondents perceived their status as secondary to men and 43.7 of them reported it as equal to men. About five per cent have rated them as superior to men.

When asked how the men perceived their women's status, 51.3 per cent reported as secondary to men and 43.8 per cent of them as equal to men. About five per cent stated that they are assessed as superior to men.

When asked as to when the women would equal men, from the presently perceived status of secondary nature, 43 per cent answered in the negative. Thirty six per cent of the respondents stated that they will equal men when they are able to take all decisions governing them, independent of men; 16 per cent of the respondents said that when they have total freedom of mobility, they will equal men.

In their own perception, as well as in the perception of men, 51 per cent of the respondents have rated women as secondary to men, and 44 per cent considered them as equal to men. About six per cent rated them as superior to men.

While we can see that every other woman still feels that women are secondary to men in status, the view of their counterparts holding that they are equal to men or some perceiving to be superior to men is expected to consolidate and gradually tilt the scenario in favour of women.

Figure 11: Perception of Women on Men's Rating of Women

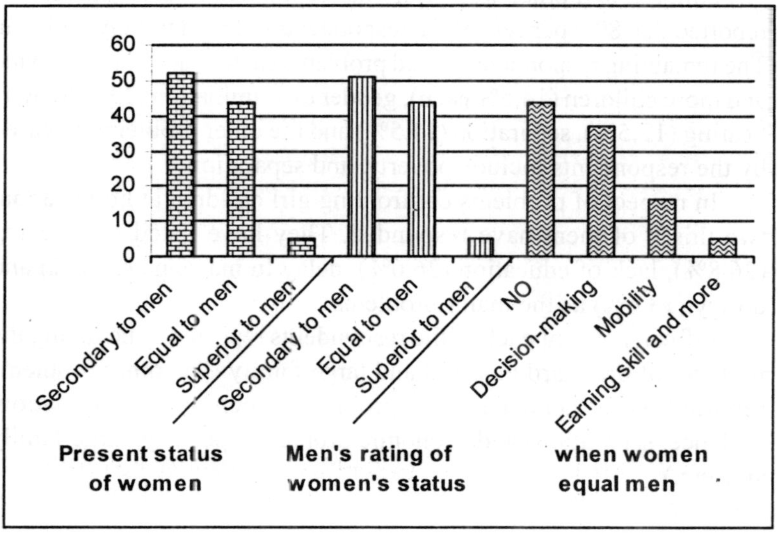

Table 4.20: Major Problems Faced by the Respondents, Girl Children and other Women

No.	Particulars	Number	Percentage
1.	Problems Faced by Respondents (n = 104)		
	• More children	15	14.5
	• Drunkard husband	15	14.5
	• Gender discrimination	14	13.5
	• Wife beating	13	12.5
	• Lack of regular income	12	11.5
	• Separated	12	11.5
	• Poverty	12	11.5
	• No issues	11	10.5
2.	Girl Children (n = 403)		
	• Not married yet	108	26.8
	• Eve-teasing	108	26.8
	• Lack of education	107	26.6
	• Dowry	55	13.6
	• Gender discrimination	25	6.2

Gender Based Problems

Table 4.20 presents the major problems faced by the respondents, girl children and other women in the respondent households. It was reported that 80.2 per cent of the respondents did not face any problem. The remaining respondents, faced problems such as drunkard husband and more children (14.5% each), gender discrimination (13.5%), wife beating (12.5%), separation (11.5%) and the other problems reported by the respondents include poverty, and separation.

In respect of problems confronting girl children at home, about two-thirds of them have responded. They have listed eve-teasing (26.8%), lack of education (26.6%), delay in marriage (26.8%) and dowry (13.6%) as the major problems.

Fifteen per cent each of the respondents reported to be facing the problem of drunkard husband and large family. The other problems reported were: gender related problems (such as discrimination, violence, separation) and economic problems (poverty, large family size etc.)

Eighty per cent of women saying that they do not have any problem seems to be rather unusual. Responses on the problems facing women belong to two categories viz., economic (more children, low income and poverty), and husband/men imposed (drunkard husband, wife beating, separation and gender discrimination). Perhaps they were inclined to think of only similar problems as a problem. Probably the respondents were guided by the

- Perception about what they considered as a problem and what is not
- Lack of serious problems confronting them in their perception
- Both actual and perceived role of self-help groups in solving their erstwhile problems

Table 4.21: Sources of Women's Problems and Proposed Methods of Overcoming

No.	Particulars	Number	Percentage
1.	Sources of Women's Problem (n = 600)		
	• Both	410	68.4
	• Men	149	24.8
	• Women	33	5.5
	• No response	8	1.3
2.	Methods of Solving (n = 592)		
	• Overcome the problems	268	45.3
	• Bear with the problems	324	54.7
	Total	600	100.0

Problems of Women

Table 4.21 gives the source of women's problems and methods of overcoming the problems, as reported by the respondents. Sixty eight per cent of the respondents have reported that both the men and women are the sources of problems, whereas 24.8 per cent have said that 'men' are the sources. It may be noted that 'women' as the source of all their problems was also cited by 5.5 per cent of the respondents.

When asked as to how they will solve their problems, they gave a crisp reply—either bear with the problems (54.7%) or overcome the problems (46.3%).

Figure 12: Sources of Women's Problems and Present Status of Rural Women

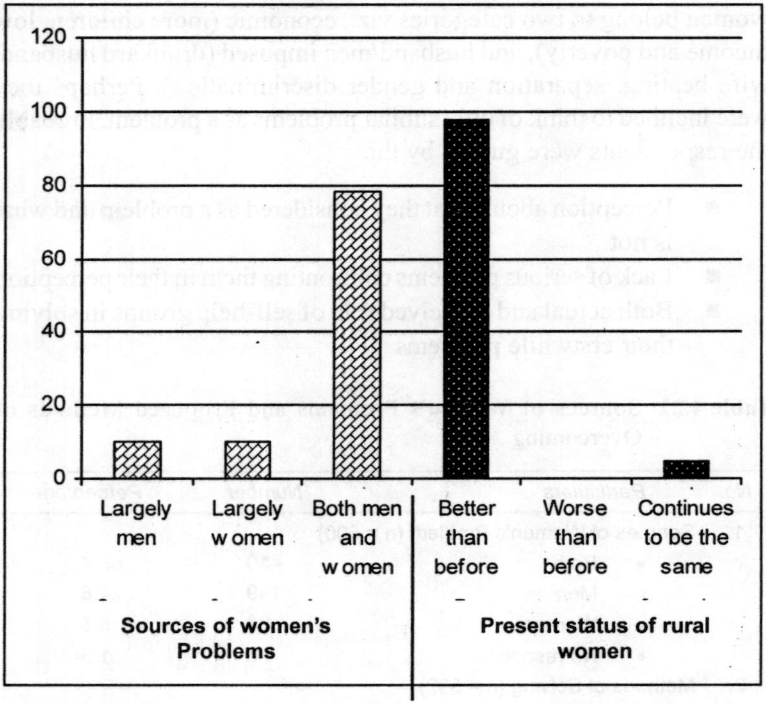

Nearly 70 per cent of the respondents realized that both the men and women are the sources of various problems confronting them while another one-fourth have attributed 'men' as the source. More than half of them have developed the tendency to bear with the problem (56.0%) or overcome it (44.0%).

We may infer from the above conclusion that acceptance by majority that the women's problems are caused by both the spouses, but one-fourth of them pointing out their fingers against men as singularly responsible, may highlight the decreasing role of men and increasing role of both the spouses in causing their problems.

SECTION B

In this section, data specifically related to women empowerment have been presented with analysis and interpretation. Tables dealing with the deterrents and determinants include the following aspects:

- Concept of women empowerment
- Ideal characteristics of empowered women
- Obstacles to women empowerment
- Yardsticks used in assessing women empowerment
- Indicators of women empowerment

  — Freedom of women
  — Community participation
  — Gender discrimination
  — Violence against women
  — Acquisition of power and influence
  — Overall empowerment

Towards the end, an attempt has been made to show the impact of certain independent variables on the five aspects of empowerment viz.,

- Level of freedom
- Level of participation
- Level of gender discrimination
- Level of violence against women
- Level of influence and power
- Overall empowerment

Concept of Women Empowerment

Table 4.22 depicts the views of respondents on the concept of women empowerment. Fifty two per cent of the respondents asserted that 'education' is basic for empowering women, while 17 per cent informed that 'employment' is necessary.

Table 4.22: Views of Respondents on the Concept of Empowerment

No.	*Particulars*	*Number*	*Percentage*
1.	Education	305	50.8
2.	Employment	102	17.0
3.	Decision-making	44	7.3
4.	Freedom of mobility	42	7.0
5.	Skills/capacity building	33	5.5
6.	Public participation	28	4.6
7.	Independence	22	3.6
8.	Managerial ability	9	1.5
9.	Equality of men and women	9	1.5
10.	Awareness	6	1.0
	Total	600	100

Figure 13: Views of Respondents on the Concept of Empowerment

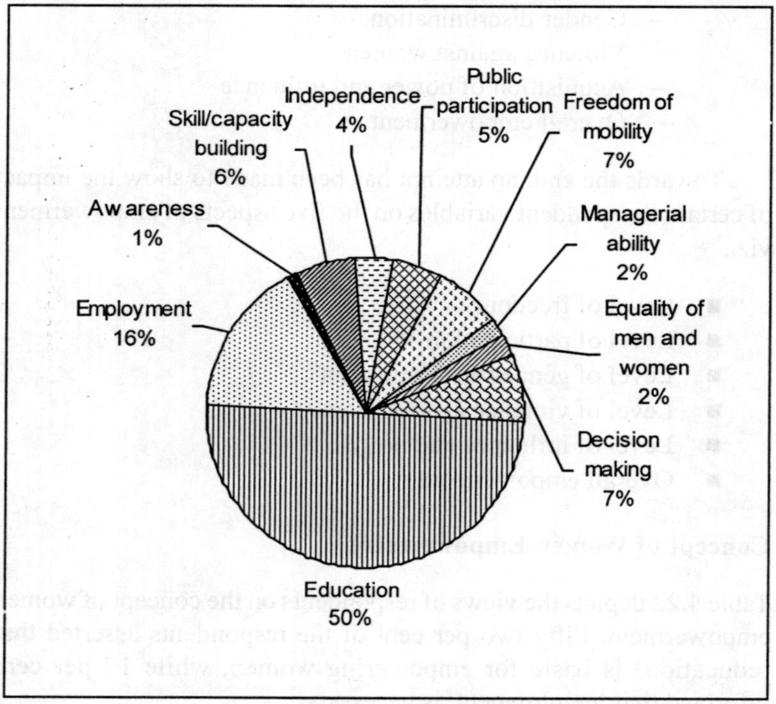

'Freedom' said another 7.0 per cent; skills and capacities and managerial ability reported 6.0 per cent, while 'participation' was suggested by about 5.0 per cent of the respondents. Independence, decision-making are the other ingredients needed for empowerment, as reported by the respondents.

It may be concluded that education (50.8%), employment (17.0%), greater freedom (7.0%), and public participation (5.0%) were considered the vital constituents of women empowerment.

The conclusion leads us to infer that respondents are of the opinion that education constitutes the fulcrum of women empowerment, supported by employment, freedom and public participation. This underlines the need for strengthening the foundation of girls' education.

Table 4.23: Ideal Characteristics of Empowered Women as stated by the Respondents

No.	*Particulars*	*Number*	*Percentage*
1.	Education	146	24.3
2.	Employment	125	20.8
3.	Freedom	117	19.5
4.	Self reliance	52	8.7
5.	Decision-making	51	8.6
6.	Courage	42	7.0
7.	Social acceptance	32	5.3
8.	Participation	27	4.5
9.	No response	8	1.3
	Total	600	100.0

According to Hall (1992), the encouraged women share certain characteristics. They have autonomy because they claim their freedom from existing male hierarchies. They maintain equal mindedness, they neither challenge male dominance nor aim at being superior to men, they maintain their strength in the presence of pressure of family, religion and work and contribute towards the empowerment of all women. Empowered women do not retreat from traditional responsibilities but they forge their own ways of doing things.

Figure 14: Ideal Characteristics of Empowered Women

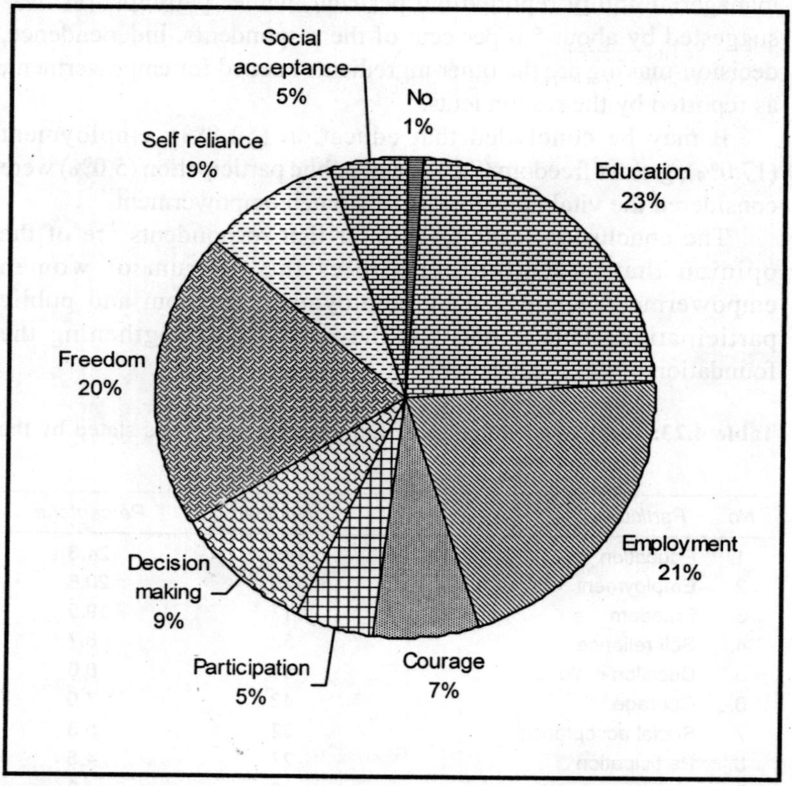

Ideal Characteristics

Table 4.23 presents the ideal characteristics of empowered women as expressed by the respondents. Listing out the ideal characteristics of empowered women, respondents have spelt out education (24.3%), employment (20.8%), and freedom (19.5%) as important. Power of decision-making, self reliance and courage were also reported by about 3 to 9 per cent each of the respondents as ideal characteristics.

Nearly two-thirds of the respondents have listed education, employment and freedom as the ideal characteristics which an empowered woman should possess.

Portraying the empowered woman as one, who is educated, employed and having freedom, the respondents reinvigorate the components of acquiring knowledge, providing livelihood and ensuring greater freedom as the foundations of women empowerment.

Table 4.24: Views of Respondents on the Obstacles to Women Empowerment and Methods of Overcoming

No.	*Particulars*	*Number (n = 600)*	*Percentage*
1.	Obstacles		
	• Poverty	197	32.8
	• Family members	115	19.2
	• Social outlook	90	15.0
	• Unemployment	60	10
	• Illiteracy	55	9.2
	• Superstition	44	7.3
	• Lack of awareness	39	6.5
2.	Measures to Overcome		
	• Awareness	257	42.8
	• Courage	102	17.0
	• Employment	71	11.8
	• Education	54	9.1
	• No response	49	8.2
	• Skill training	23	3.8
	• Freedom	44	7.3

Obstacles and Options

Table 4.24 depicts the views of respondents on the obstacles to women empowerment and methods of overcoming. Poverty was reported as an obstacle by 32.8 per cent of the respondents. Family members with restrictive nature (19.2%), societal outlook (15.0%), unemployment (10.0%), and illiteracy (9.2%) were expressed by the respondents as the other obstacles.

Commenting on the ways to remove these obstacles, 42. 8 per cent of the respondents suggested providing awareness, 17 per cent reported building up courage, and 11. 8 per cent suggested providing employment.

Social factors such as restrictive family members, negative societal outlook, superstition and illiteracy (50.7%) and economic factors such as poverty and unemployment (42.8%) served as the major obstacles in empowering the rural women.

Creating awareness and building up courage (59.8%), imparting education and skills (16.4%) and providing employment (11.8%) were suggested by the respondents for removing those obstacles.

Reporting poverty as the major obstacle, the respondents listed restrictive nature of family, unfavourable societal outlook, unemployment and illiteracy as the other obstacles, which indicate the need for a frontal attack on two fronts viz., economic and social—for freeing the women from the shackles of the problems.

Table 4.25: Freedom of Women as an Indicator of Empowerment

No.	*Particulars*	*Never*	*Sometimes*	*Always*
1.	Wearing dresses of your choice	163 (27.2)	293 (48.8)	144 (24.0)
2.	Travelling for long distance	488 (81.3)	96 (16.0)	16 (2.7)
3.	Choosing your employers	195 (32.5)	294 (49.0)	111 (18.5)
4.	Planning your family budget	191 (31.8)	279 (46.5)	130 (21.7)
5.	Voting in elections	207 (34.5)	280 (46.7)	113 (18.8)
6.	Refusing your spouse's sexual needs	299 (49.8)	223 (37.2)	78 (13.0)

(n = 600 each for every item from 1 to 6)

Freedom of Women

As shown in Table 4.25, in respect of wearing dresses of the respondents' choice, 48.8 per cent of the respondents replied that they had this freedom only 'sometimes', while 24 per cent had it 'always'.

For travelling 'long distance', 81.3 per cent of the respondents 'never' had freedom, while 16 per cent had it 'sometimes'.

Forty nine per cent of the respondents informed that they had the freedom to choose their employers 'sometimes', but 32.5 per cent 'never' had this freedom.

About 46 per cent the respondents had the freedom of planning their family budget and voting in elections 'sometimes'. When not in good health or during sickness, 37.2 per cent of the respondents had the freedom to refuse their spouse's sexual needs 'sometimes'; while another 13 per cent refused it 'always', whenever they wished to avoid.

Eighty one per cent of the respondents never had the freedom to travel long distances and about 32 to 35 per cent of the respondents never had the freedom to choose their employers, plan their budget or vote in elections. Half of the respondents never had the freedom to refuse their spouse's sexual needs when not in good health or while sick.

Participation by one out of every seven respondents, and half of them emerging victorious prove the emerging trend of women's gradual entry in politics and societal support.

While the women were restrained the freedom of long distance travel, reportedly for the safety of women, they were increasingly allowed the freedom of choosing their employers, planning their family budget and refusal of spouse's sexual needs. This shows the increasing role played by women on an equal footing with men.

Table 4.26: Participation in Community Activities as an Indicator of Empowerment

No.	Particulars	Never	Sometimes	Always
1.	Community participation	422 (70.3)	108 (18.0)	70 (11.7)
2.	Participation in strikes/agitations	453 (75.5)	92 (15.3)	55 (9.2)
3.	Visiting government offices	457 (76.2)	91 (15.2)	52 (8.6)
4.	Visiting police station	471 (78.5)	79 (13.2)	50 (8.3)
5.	Visiting panchayat office	470 (78.3)	84 (14.0)	46 (7.7)
6.	Articulation in public meetings	465 (77.5)	93 (15.5)	42 (7.0)
7.	Interaction with men/boys	469 (78.2)	80 (13.2)	51 (8.5)
8.	Membership in local institutions	494 (82.3	82 (13.7)	24 (4.0)

(n = 600 each for every item from 1 to 8)

Community Participation

Seventy per cent of the respondents never participated in community activities while the remaining (30%) could participate either 'sometimes' or 'always' as presented in Table 4.26. About 76 to 78 per cent of the respondents 'never' had an opportunity to participate in strikes/agitations, visit government offices, police stations and panchayat offices, articulate in public meetings and interact with males. Eighty two per cent of the respondents could 'never' be a member of local institutions.

The freedom for participation of women in community activities, strikes/agitations, local institutions, visit government offices, police stations and panchayat offices, articulate in public meetings and interact with men was available for 18 to 30 per cent of the respondents largely 'sometimes'. The remaining 70 to 82 per cent of the respondents 'never' got this freedom of participation.

It may be inferred that freedom of participation in social and community activities seems to be at low ebbs, with majority kept at bay, probably because men participated in such activities overwhelmingly.

Table 4.27: Gender Discrimination as an Indicator of Empowerment

No.	*Particulars*	*Never*	*Sometimes*	*Always*
1.	Food	512 (85.3)	75 (12.4)	13 (2.2)
2.	Dress	505 (84.7)	79 (13.1)	13 (2.2)
3.	Education of children	506 (84.3)	82 (13.6)	12 (2.0)
4.	Health care for children	500 (83.3)	90 (14.9)	10 (1.7)
5.	Health care for adults	490 (81.1)	99 (6.4)	11 (1.8)

(n = 600 each for item no 1 to 5)

Gender Discrimination

Table 4.27 shows that about 80 to 85 per cent of the respondents reported that they never faced gender discrimination in respect of food, dresses, education of children, health care for children and adults.

About 12 to 15 per cent of the respondents informed that they 'sometimes' experienced gender discrimination (only 6.4 per cent for adult health care), while about two per cent expressed that they always faced gender discrimination.

We may conclude that a majority of the respondents (80 to 85%) have stated that there was no gender discrimination in food, dress, education and health care for children and adults. However, 12 to 15 per cent reported discrimination 'sometimes' and two per cent 'always'.

It may be inferred from the above analysis that non-discrimination on the grounds of gender in the vital areas of basic needs fulfilment such as food, clothing, education and health care amply prove that women get their due share largely.

Table 4.28: Violence Against Women as an Indicator of Empowerment

No.	*Particulars*	*Never*	*Sometimes*	*Always*
1.	Incidence of eve-teasing	501 (83.5)	86 (14.3)	12 (2.0)
2.	Incidence of ill treatment	507 (84.5)	80 (13.3)	13 (2.2)
3.	Domestic violence	509 (84.8)	79 (13.2)	12 (2.0)
4.	Sexual harassment at work site	499 (83.2)	94 (15.6)	7 (1.2)
5.	Alcoholism of husband	488 (81.3)	96 (16.0)	16 (2.7)

(n = 600 each for item number 1 to 5)

Violence Against Women

As seen in Table 4.28, between 81 and 84 per cent of the respondents informed that they 'never' faced violence against women—such as eve-teasing, ill treatment, domestic violence, sexual harassment and alcoholism of husband. However, about 13 to 16 per cent of the respondents reported that they faced violence 'sometimes' and two to three per cent 'always'.

Nearly 13 to 16 per cent of the respondents, faced violence against women 'sometimes', while 2 to 3 per cent faced violence 'always' in the form of eve-teasing, ill treatment, domestic violence, sexual harassment at worksite and alcoholism of husband.

The fact that violence against women such as eve teasing, ill-treatment, domestic violence and sexual harassment and alcoholism of husband has affected (about one out of ever five women) points out the decreasing trend in violence against women.

Table 4.29: Acquisition of Power and Influence as an Indicator of Empowerment

No.	Particulars	Never	Sometimes	Always
1.	Acquisition of power/authority	461 (76.8)	106 (17.7)	33 (5.5)
2.	Bargaining/Negotiation	421 (70.2)	119 (19.8)	60 (10.0)
3.	Fighting for women's issues	442 (73.7)	112 (18.8)	46 (7.7)
4.	Influence by others	458 (76.2)	112 (18.8)	30 (5.0)
5.	Respect from others	461 (76.8)	110 (18.4)	29 (4.8)

*Multiple Responses (n=600 for every item from 1 to 5)

Power and Influence

Empowerment as a motivational construct (Bandura,1986), relies more on an understanding of empowerment through individual's internal needs for power and control and feelings of personal efficacy. Under this model, individuals perceive themselves as having power when they are able to control events or situation and deal effectively with the environment and situations they encounter. Conversely, individuals are likely to feel powerless in situations that they cannot influence or where they do not have time, resources or skills to be effective from a motivational perspective, intrinsically based on a need for self determination.

Table 4.29 brings out the distribution of power and influence enjoyed by the respondents as an indicator of empowerment. About 18 to 20 per cent of the respondents expressed that they gained power and influence 'sometimes' in such areas as acquiring bargaining/ negotiation skills, fighting for women's issues, influence by others and influencing others. Nearly 5 to 10 per cent of the respondents gained power and influence 'always', whereas the remaining 70 to 77 per cent of the respondents "never" gained such power and influence.

About 23 to 30 per cent of the respondents gained power and influence either 'sometimes' or 'always' in respect of acquiring, bargaining/negotiation skills, fighting for women's issues, influence by others and influencing others.

The fact that one out of every four respondents has been acquiring power and influence in the process of bargaining, negotiating and fighting for women's issues makes it a good augury for their increasing trend.

Table 4.30: Yardsticks used in Assessing Women Empowerment as Reported by the Respondents

No.	*Particulars*	*Number*	*Percentage*
1.	Education	316	52.7
2.	Employment	98	16.3
3.	Articulation	52	8.7
4.	Skills	31	5.2
5.	Participation	29	4.8
6.	Decision-making	24	4.0
7.	Courage	20	3.3
8.	Freedom	16	2.7
9.	Awareness	14	2.3
	Total	600	100.0

Yardsticks of Empowerment

Table 4.30 depicts the yardsticks to be considered in assessing women empowerment. More than half of the respondents have pointed out 'education' as a yardstick we may consider in assessing women empowerment. The other yardsticks suggested by the respondents were employment, (16.3%), articulation ability (8.7%), and acquisition of skills (5.2%), considered critical by the respondents as a yardstick to be used in assessing women empowerment.

Spelling out the specific yardsticks of measuring empowerment, the respondents pointing out their finger towards education, amply emphasize the need for strengthening women's education component, to be supplemented by employment opportunities and building up their articulation ability.

Figure 15: Yardsticks used in Assessing Women Empowerment

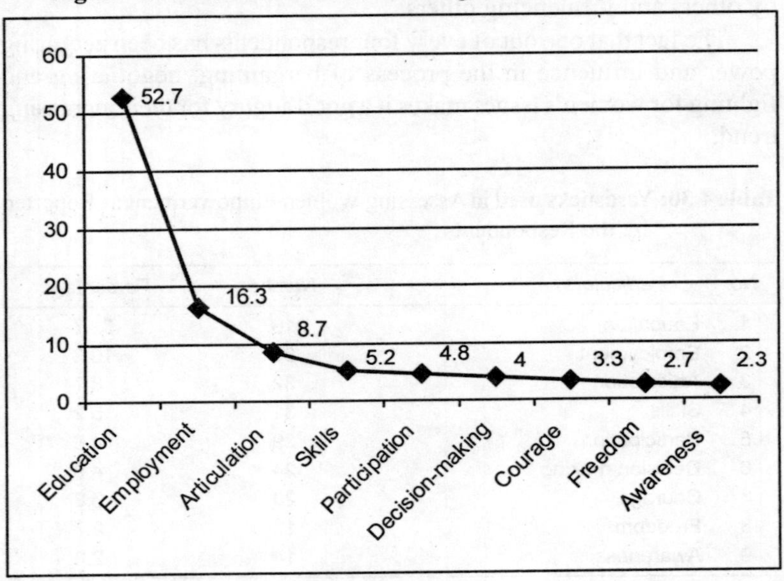

Independent Variables and Women Empowerment

An attempt has been made to study the relationship between certain independent variables and the dependent variable viz., the level of women empowerment, classified into 'high', 'medium' and 'low', based on score values.

The independent variables used in the study comprise the following:

1. Age
2. Birth order
3. Place of birth
4. Education
5. Vocational skills
6. Religion
7. Community
8. Family type
9. Marital status

10. Age at marriage
11. Occupation of Respondents'
12. Household annual income
13. Respondent's income
14. Membership in Self-Help Groups
15. Standard of living

Aspects of women empowerment analyzed in this section include the following:

1. Level of freedom
2. Level of participation
3. Level of gender discrimination
4. Level of violence against women
5. Level of influence and power
6. Overall empowerment.

Freedom and Empowerment

Table 4.31: Level of Freedom Among the Respondents

Sl. No.	*Variables*	*N=600*	*Level of Freedom (in percentage)*		
			Low	*Medium*	*High*
1.	Age				
	• 35 years or less	291	14.1	61.2	24.7
	• 36 years and above	309	11.3	61.2	27.5
	Chi-square		*1.341*	*df = 2*	*p = 0.511*
2.	Birth Order of Respondents				
	• First child	221	14.0	59.3	26.7
	• Second child	165	13.9	65.5	20.6
	• Third to fifth child	84	7.1	67.9	25.0
	• Sixth to eighth child	71	11.3	50.7	38.0
	• Above eighth	59	13.6	59.3	27.1
	Chi-square		*11.103*	*8*	*0.196*
3.	Place of Birth				
	• Rural area	538	13.6	61.3	25.1
	• Urban area	62	4.8	59.7	35.5
	Chi-square		*5.664*	*2*	*0.059*
4.	Education				
	• Illiterate	400	14.8	62.5	22.8
	• Primary education	113	5.3	69.0	25.7
	• Middle school and above	87	12.6	44.8	42.5
	Chi-square		*21.950*	*4*	*0.000*

(*Contd.*)

(*Contd.*)

Sl. No.	Variables	N=600	Level of Freedom (in percentage) Low	Medium	High
5.	Vocational Skills				
	• Skilled	100	10.0	55.0	35.0
	• Not skilled	500	13.2	62.4	24.4
	Chi-square		*4.998*	*2*	*0.082*
6.	Religion				
	• Hindu	508	13.6	63.6	22.8
	• Christian	68	5.9	44.1	50.0
	• Muslim	24	12.5	58.3	29.2
	Chi-square		*23.555*	*4*	*0.000*
7.	Community				
	• Forward class	34	5.9	52.9	41.2
	• Backward class	254	10.2	59.8	29.9
	• Most backward class	110	16.4	58.2	25.5
	• SC/ST	202	14.9	65.8	19.3
	Chi-square		*13.649*	*6*	*0.034*
8.	Family Type				
	• Joint family	157	10.8	51.6	37.6
	• Nuclear family	443	13.3	64.6	22.1
	Chi-square		*14.339*	*2*	*0.001*
9.	Marital status				
	• Married	444	13.1	61.7	25.2
	• Unmarried	88	10.2	64.8	25.0
	• Others	68	13.2	52.9	33.8
	Chi-square		*3.166*	*4*	*0.530*
10.	Age at marriage				
	• 14—18 years	134	14.9	60.4	24.6
	• 18—21 years	384	13.5	63.0	23.4
	• 21 and above	82	4.9	53.7	41.5
	Chi-square		*14.229*	*4*	*0.007*
11.	Occupation of Respondents				
	• House wives	209	11.0	62.7	26.3
	• Non farm labour	77	14.3	58.4	27.3
	• Agriculture labour	225	15.1	60.9	24.0
	• Self employment	89	9.0	60.7	30.3
	Chi-square		*3.838*	*6*	*0.699*
12.	Household Annual Income				
	• < Rs. 15,000	143	7.7	60.8	31.5
	• Rs. 15,001—20,000	64	4.7	73.4	21.9
	• Rs. 20,001-25,000	149	20.8	62.4	16.8
	• Rs. 25,001 and above	244	12.7	57.4	29.9
	Chi-square		*24.309*	*6*	*0.000*

(*Contd.*)

(Contd.)

Sl. No.	Variables	N=600	Level of Freedom (in percent age)		
			Low	Medium	High
13.	Annual Income of Respondents				
	• No	66	10.6	57.6	31.8
	• Below Rs. 2000	241	16.2	61.4	22.4
	• Rs. 2001-3500	254	11.0	62.6	26.4
	• Rs. 3501-5000	29	6.9	58.6	34.5
	• Rs. 5001-10000	10		43.3	56.7
	Chi-square		*17.202*	*12*	*0.142*
14.	Membership in SHG				
	• Member	164	16.5	54.3	29.3
	• Non member	436	11.2	63.8	25.0
	Chi-square		*5.154*	*2*	*0.076*
15.	Standard of Living Index				
	• Low (2-8)	367	17.2	63.8	19.1
	• Medium (9-16)	189	6.9	58.2	34.9
	• High (17-24)	44		52.3	47.7
	Chi-square		*38.091*	*4*	*0.000*

Level of Freedom Among the Respondents

Age group

Table 4.31 shows that the level of freedom in the mobility of women did not vary much between younger and older women. The proportion of women having high freedom of movement was 24.7 per cent among younger women, whereas it was 27.5 per cent for older women. The differences observed in the level of freedom of movement between younger and older women are not statistically significant.

Birth Order of Respondent

Relationship between birth order and freedom of movement showed that the early born respondents (as first to fifth child), had relatively lesser freedom than their counterparts born late to their parents (as sixth to eighth child and above). The differences observed in the proportion of women across the birth order of respondents, are not statistically significant.

Place of Birth

The level of freedom of movement of women varied between their places of birth. The proportion of women having greater freedom of movement was seen among women residing in urban areas (35.5%) than those in the rural areas (25.1%). The differences observed in the level of freedom of movement between women residing in rural and urban areas are statistically significant.

Education

Education plays a vital role in the freedom of movement of women. Degree of freedom of movement ascended along with the ascendance in the level of education of respondents. Lower level of freedom was noticed with illiterates and primary educated, whereas higher level of movement was found among those with middle school education and above. Education and freedom of movement were thus closely related. The differences observed in the level of freedom of movement between educated and non-educated women are statistically significant.

Vocational Skill

The level of freedom of movement of women varied according to their vocational skills. The proportion of women having high freedom of movement was 35.0 per cent among skilled persons, whereas it was 24.4 per cent for unskilled persons. Possession of skills thus positively influences the freedom of movement. The differences observed in the level of freedom of movement between skilled and unskilled respondents are statistically significant.

Religion

Religion exercises its influence in deciding the level of freedom among women. Larger proportions of the Christian women were having greater freedom of movement (50.0%) compared to the Hindu and Muslim respondents. Respondents from Hindu and Muslim religions had more medium level of freedom (i.e. 63.6 per cent and 58.3 per cent respectively). It is interesting to note that Muslim respondents had more 'high' level of freedom (29.2%), than their Hindu counterparts (22.8%). The differences observed in the level of freedom of movement among the women from different religions are statistically significant.

Community

Caste plays a pivotal role in deciding the level of freedom of movement for women. A greater proportion of forward caste women (41.2%) were having high level of freedom of movement, compared to those from backward class (29.9%), most backward class (25.5%), and SC/ST (19.3%) respondents. The freedom of movement and the backwardness of the community thus had inverse relationship. The differences observed in the level of freedom of movement among the women from various communities are statistically significant.

Family Type

The type of family has a role to play in the level of empowerment of women. A higher proportion of women from joint families (27.6%) were having greater freedom of movement. On the other hand, more nuclear families had 'medium' level of freedom (64.6%). The differences observed in the level of freedom of movement among the women with different family types are statistically significant.

Martial Status

Marital status of women is a factor which allows or restrains the freedom of movement. Data showed that higher proportion of those who were separated, divorced or widowed enjoyed greater level of freedom of movement (33.8%) compared to those who were married or unmarried (25.0% each). The role of men as husbands and parents in the family in restricting women's freedom was evident. Though differences are observed in the proportion of women having high level of freedom of movement between different marital statuses, the differences are not statistically significant.

Age at Marriage

Freedom of movement allowed to women seemed to be directly influenced by the age at marriage of the respondents. A higher proportion (41.5%) of married women, aged 21 years and above, were having high freedom of movement, compared to women aged 14-18 years and women aged 18-21 years. Age at marriage and freedom of movement had positive relationship in respect of medium and high level freedom. The differences observed in the level of freedom of movement among different age groups are statistically significant.

Present Occupation

The type of work one does also determines the level of freedom one enjoys. We may notice that the self employed and non-farm workers had a higher degree of freedom of movement (30.3 and 27.3 per cent respectively) than their counterparts engaged as housewives and farm labour (24.0 and 26.3 per cent respectively). Home and farm-bound workers had therefore restricted freedom of movement, than those in non-farm sector and the self employed. The differences observed in the proportion of women having high level of freedom of movement among different occupational groups are not statistically significant.

Household Annual Income

A higher proportion of women (31.5%), having a lower annual income of Rs. 15,000 and below, were having high level of freedom of movement, compared to those with an income level ranging from Rs. 15,000—20,000 and Rs. 20,000—25,000 (21.9 and 16.8 per cent respectively). Respondents from households having a higher income of Rs. 25,000 and above had a higher level of freedom (29.9%), though next only to those with a lower income of less than Rs. 15,000 per annum.

Freedom of movement was therefore noticed high at the extremes of income levels (the lowest income and highest income) and was seen in the inverse position between these two levels of income. The differences observed in the proportion of women having high level of freedom of movement between different income levels are statistically significant.

Income of Respondents

Relationship between the annual income of respondents and their level of freedom was found to be positive. Among respondents with lower income of Rs. 2,000 and below Rs. 2,001-3,000, a fewer percentage had higher levels of freedom (22.4 and 26.4 per cent respectively). On the contrary, among those with higher level of freedom, a higher percentage had high level of freedom (34.5 and

56.7 per cent respectively). The differences observed in the level of freedom of movement among different income groups of respondents are not statistically significant.

Membership in SHG

Membership of women in Self-Help Groups imposes its own demand for freedom of mobility. Data shows that the level of freedom of movement of respondents varied among membership in SHG. Among members of SHGs, the proportion of women having high level freedom of movement was 29.3 per cent, whereas it was 25.0 per cent among non-members. Membership in SHGs and freedom of movement had positive relationship. The differences observed in the level of freedom of movement between members of SHGs and non-members are statistically significant.

Standard of Living Index

Data shows that the level of freedom of movement of women constantly varied across their standard of living index. The proportion of women having high level freedom of movement was 47.7 per cent among those with high standard of living index, whereas it was 34.9 per cent for medium, and 19.1 per cent for low standard of living index. The differences observed in the level of freedom of movement among different standard of living categories are statistically significant. Freedom of movement therefore has positive and consistent relationship with the standard of living of the respondents. Higher standard of living and greater freedom of movement therefore seem to go together.

Gender Discrimination and Empowerment

Table 4.33: Level of Gender Discrimination Among the Respondents

Sl. No.	*Variables*	*Level of Gender Discrimination*			
		N	*Low*	*Medium*	*High*
1.	Age				
	• 35 years or less	291	8.6	25.8	65.6
	• 36 years and above	309	8.1	24.6	67.3
	Chi-square		*0.191*	2	*0.909*

(Contd.)

(*Contd.*)

Sl. No.	Variables	Level of Gender Discrimination			
		N	Low	Medium	High
2.	Birth Order of Respondents				
	• First child	221	7.7	28.5	63.8
	• Second child	165	8.5	23.0	68.5
	• Third to fifth child	84	4.8	29.8	65.5
	• Sixth to eighth child	71	9.9	25.4	64.8
	• Above eighth	59	13.6	11.9	74.6
	Chi-square		*10.627*	*8*	*0.224*
3.	Place of Birth				
	• Rural area	538	8.0	24.2	67.8
	• Urban area	62	11.3	33.9	54.8
	Chi-square		*4.221*	*2*	*0.121*
4.	Education				
	• Illiterate	400	7.8	19.5	72.8
	• Primary education	113	6.2	29.2	64.6
	• Middle school and above	87	13.8	46.0	40.2
	Chi-square		*36.142*	*4*	*0.000*
5.	Vocational skills				
	• Skilled	100	9.0	32.0	59.0
	• Not skilled	500	8.2	23.8	68.0
	Chi-square		*3.306*	*2*	*0.192*
6.	Religion				
	• Hindu	508	7.3	22.2	70.5
	• Christian	68	16.2	52.9	30.9
	• Muslim	24	8.3	8.3	83.3
	Chi-square		*46.162*	*4*	*0.000*
7.	Community				
	• Forward class	34	5.9	38.2	55.9
	• Backward class	254	9.8	30.7	59.4
	• Most backward class	110	5.5	22.7	71.8
	• SC/ST	202	8.4	17.3	74.3
	Chi-square		*17.407*	*6*	*0.008*
8.	Family Type				
	• Joint family	157	8.3	32.5	59.2
	• Nuclear family	443	8.4	22.6	69.1
	Chi-square		*6.212*	*2*	*0.045*
9.	Marital Status				
	• Married	444	7.9	25.7	66.4
	• Unmarried	88	11.4	22.7	65.9
	• Others	68	7.4	25.0	67.6
	Chi-square		*1.429*	*4*	*0.839*
10.	Age at Marriage				
	• 14—18 years	134	6.0	22.4	71.6
	• 18—21 years	384	8.1	24.5	67.4
	• 21 and above	82	13.4	32.9	53.7
	Chi-square		*8.533*	*4*	*0.074*

(*Contd.*)

(*Contd.*)

Sl. No.	Variables	Level of Gender Discrimination			
		N	Low	Medium	High
11.	Occupation of Respondents				
	• House wives	209	8.6	24.4	67.0
	• Non farm labour	77	10.4	29.9	59.7
	• Agriculture labour	225	7.6	21.8	70.7
	• Self employment	89	7.9	31.5	60.7
	Chi-square		*5.328*	*6*	*0.502*
12.	Household Annual Income				
	• < Rs. 15,000	143	4.2	25.2	70.6
	• Rs. 15,001—20,000	64	3.1	45.3	51.6
	• Rs. 20,001-25,000	149	10.1	18.8	71.1
	• Rs. 25,001 and above	244	11.1	23.8	65.2
	Chi-square		*23.722*	*6*	*0.001*
13.	Annual Income of Respondents				
	• No	66	10.6	39.4	50.0
	• Below Rs. 2000	241	5.4	21.6	73.0
	• Rs. 2001-3500	254	9.8	24.0	66.1
	• Rs. 3501-5000	29	3.4	27.6	69.0
	• Rs. 5001-10000	10	36.7	50	13.3
	Chi-square		*48.164*	*12*	*0.000*
14.	Membership in SHG				
	• Member	164	6.7	28.0	65.2
	• Non member	436	8.9	24.1	67.0
	Chi-square		*1.515*	*2*	*0.469*
15.	Standard of Living Index				
	• Low (2-8)	367	9.3	23.4	67.3
	• Medium (9-16)	189	7.4	28.0	64.6
	• High (17-24)	44	4.5	27.3	68.2
	Chi-square		*2.633*	*4*	*0.621*

Level of Gender Discrimination among Respondents

Age

The level of gender discrimination did not vary much between younger and older women as shown in Table 4.33. The proportion of women having high gender discrimination was 67.3 per cent among older women, whereas it was 65.6 per cent for younger women. The differences observed in the level of gender discrimination between younger and older women are not statistically significant.

Birth Order of Respondents

The level of gender discrimination did not show much variation across the birth order of the respondents. The results indicated in the table had an inconsistent pattern. Yet, when combined for medium and high level of gender discrimination, the early born (1st to 5th born) faced more gender discrimination (91.5 to 95.3 per cent) than those born later (6th to 8th born and above). The differences observed in the level of gender discrimination across birth order of respondents are not statistically significant.

Place of Birth

Data shows that a larger proportion (67.8%) of rural women faced higher gender discrimination compared to urban women (54.8%). Though differences are observed in the proportion of women having high gender discrimination between rural and urban areas, these differences are not statistically significant.

Education

The level of gender discrimination seemed to be high among the illiterate women (72.8%), as against the women educated up to primary level (64.6%) and middle level (40.2%). The differences observed in the level of gender discrimination among educated and illiterate women are statistically significant.

Vocational Skill

Higher proportion of unskilled women (68.0%) faced high gender discrimination when compared to skilled women (59.0%). Skilled women, therefore, had lesser risk of gender discrimination. Though differences are observed in gender discrimination between skilled and unskilled women, they are not statistically significant.

Religion

Larger proportion of Muslim women (83.3%) is having high gender discrimination when compared to Hindu (70.5%) and Christian women (30.9%). The differences observed in the gender discrimination across the three religions are statistically significant.

Community

A higher proportion (74.3%) SC/ST women were having high gender discrimination compared to most backward class (71.8%), backward class (59.4%) and forward class (55.9%) respondents. The differences observed in the level of gender discrimination among women from various communities are statistically significant.

Family Type

A greater proportion of nuclear family women (69.1%) were having high gender discrimination compared to those from joint families (59.2%). The differences observed in the gender discrimination between joint and nuclear families are statistically significant.

Marital Status

The level of gender discrimination did not vary much between marital statuses. The proportion of women having high gender discrimination was 67.6 per cent for 'others' (widowed, divorced & separated), whereas it was 66.4 per cent among married and 65.9 per cent among unmarried women. Married and widows/divorcees/separated, therefore, seemed to face greater discrimination than those who were not married. The differences observed in the level of gender discrimination between different marital statuses are not statistically significant.

Age at Marriage

A higher proportion of women married at the age group of 14-18 years (71.6%) are having high gender discrimination compared to women married in the age group 18-21 years (67.4%), and 21 years and above (53.7%). The early married women thus had a higher risk of gender discrimination. The differences observed in the level of gender discrimination among different age at marriage are statistically significant.

Present Occupation

Majority of agricultural labourers (70.7%) were facing high gender discrimination when compared to non-farm labourers (59.7%). A combined picture of high and medium level of gender discrimination showed the non-farm labourers were slightly less discriminated than the rest. Though the differences are observed in the proportion of women having high gender discrimination between different occupational groups, the differences are not statistically significant.

Household Annual Income

Data regarding household income level and gender discrimination shows that gender discrimination was higher (95.7 and 96.9%) at lower levels of income (<Rs. 15,000 and 15,000-20,000 respectively), for high and medium levels of participation combined.

At both these levels, it was found to be lower (89.9 and 89.0%) at higher levels of income (Rs. 20,000—25,000 and above Rs. 25,000 respectively). Level of gender discrimination across the income level was thus found to be inversely related. Though differences are observed in the proportion of women having high gender discrimination between different income levels, the differences are not statistically significant.

Income of Respondents

Relationship between the level of gender discrimination and the respondents' annual income were negatively correlated. Respondents with an annual income of below Rs. 2,000 and 2,001-3,500 had more respondents with higher level of gender discrimination (73.0 and 69.1 per cent respectively), whereas among those with higher income levels (Rs. 3,501-5,000 and 5001-10,000), only a lower percentage of them (66.0 and 13.3 per cent respectively) reported high level of gender discrimination. Level of gender discrimination therefore, decreased with the increase in the level of income. The differences observed in the level of gender discrimination among different income groups of respondents are statistically significant.

Membership in SHG

The level of gender of discrimination did not vary much between members and non-members of SHGs. The proportion of women having high gender discrimination was 67.0 per cent among non-members and 65.2 per cent for SHG members. Membership in SHGs had only slightly contributed for a lesser gender discrimination. The differences observed in the level of gender discrimination between members and non-members of SHG are not statistically significant.

Standard of living Index

Gender discrimination seems to be influenced by the standard of living of respondents. However, the trend appears to be in the reverse, as there was an increase in discrimination with higher standard of living. Women with a higher standard of living index were more highly discriminated (68.2%) than their counterparts with low (67.3%) and medium standard of living (64.6%). Though differences are observed in the proportion of women having high gender discrimination across different standards of living categories, the differences are not statistically significant.

Violence Against Women and Empowerment

Table 4.34: Level of Violence against Women among the Respondents

Sl. No.	*Variables*	*Level of Violence against Women*			
		N	*Low*	*Medium*	*High*
1.	Age				
	• 35 years or less	291	7.6	22.3	70.1
	• 36 years and above	309	10.7	18.1	71.2
	Chi-square		*2.936*	*2*	*0.230*
2.	Birth Order of Respondents				
	• First child	221	10.4	17.2	72.4
	• Second child	165	6.7	22.4	70.9
	• Third to fifth child	84	7.1	25.0	67.9
	• Sixth to eighth child	71	14.1	21.1	64.8
	• Above eighth	59	8.5	16.9	74.6
	Chi-square		*7.133*	*8*	*0.522*
3.	Place of Birth				
	• Rural area	538	8.9	19.9	71.2
	• Urban area	62	11.3	22.6	66.1
	Chi-square		*0.741*	*2*	*0.690*
4.	Education				
	• Illiterate	400	7.5	17.0	75.5
	• Primary education	113	7.1	25.7	67.3
	• Middle school and above	87	19.5	27.6	52.9
	Chi-square		*23.425*	*4*	*0.000*
5.	Vocational Skills				
	• Skilled	100	12.0	19.0	69.0
	• Not skilled	500	8.6	20.4	71.0
	Chi-square		*1.179*	*2*	*0.555*

(Contd.)

(*Contd.*)

Sl. No.	Variables	Level of Violence against Women			
		N	Low	Medium	High
6.	Religion				
	• Hindu	508	8.3	17.5	74.2
	• Christian	68	19.1	39.7	41.2
	• Muslim	24		20.8	79.2
	Chi-square		*34.155*	*4*	*0.000*
7.	Community				
	• Forward class	34	5.9	26.5	67.6
	• Backward class	254	7.1	29.1	63.8
	• Most backward class	110	11.8	13.6	74.5
	• SC/ST	202	10.9	11.4	77.7
	Chi-square		*27.350*	*6*	*0.000*
8.	Family Type				
	• Joint family	157	7.6	20.4	72.0
	• Nuclear family	443	9.7	20.1	70.2
	Chi-square		*0.595*	*2*	*0.743*
9.	Marital Status				
	• Married	444	10.1	19.6	70.3
	• Unmarried	88	6.8	23.9	69.3
	• Others	68	5.9	19.1	75.0
	Chi-square		*2.703*	*4*	*0.609*
10.	Age at Marriage				
	• 14—18 years	134	3.7	17.9	78.4
	• 18—21 years	384	10.4	19.3	70.3
	• 21 and above	82	12.2	28.0	59.8
	Chi-square		*11.321*	*4*	*0.023*
11.	Occupation of Respondents				
	• House wives	209	8.1	19.1	72.7
	• Non-farm labour	77	7.8	13.0	79.2
	• Agriculture labour	225	9.8	20.9	69.3
	• Self employment	89	11.2	27.0	61.8
	Chi-square		*7.056*	*6*	*0.316*
12.	Household Annual Income				
	• < Rs. 15,000	143	4.9	31.5	63.6
	• Rs. 15,001—20,000	64	12.5	20.3	67.2
	• Rs. 20,001-25,000	149	16.1	5.4	78.5
	• Rs. 25,001 and above	244	6.6	22.5	70.9
	Chi-square		*41.596*	*6*	*0.000*
13.	Annual Income of Respondents				
	• No	66	16.7	27.3	56.1
	• Below Rs. 2000	241	6.2	17.0	76.8
	• Rs. 2001-3500	254	10.2	20.9	68.9
	• Rs. 3501-5000	29	6.9	13.8	79.3
	• Rs. 5001-10000	10	16.7	56.7	26.6
	Chi-square		*32.303*	*12*	*0.001*

(*Contd.*)

(*Contd.*)

Sl. No.	Variables	Level of Violence against Women			
		N	Low	Medium	High
14.	Membership in SHG				
	• Member	164	9.8	23.2	67.1
	• Non member	436	8.9	19.0	72.0
	Chi-square		*1.508*	*2*	*0.471*
15.	Standard of Living Index				
	• Low (2-8)	367	8.2	19.6	72.2
	• Medium (9-16)	189	12.2	21.7	66.1
	• High (17-24)	44	4.5	18.2	77.3
	Chi-square		*4.581*	*4*	*0.333*

Level of Violence against Women among the Respondents

Age

The level of violence against women, as given in Table 4.34 did not vary much between younger and older women. The proportion of women facing high degree of violence was 71.2 per cent among the older women, and 70.1 per cent among younger women. The differences observed in the level of violence against women between younger and older women are not statistically significant.

Birth Order of Respondents

Respondents born after the eighth child in their family faced greater violence (74.6%) as against those born as first or second child (72.4 and 70.9%). The differences are not statistically significant.

Place of Birth

Rural women were facing high level of violence against women (71.2%) as compared to those from urban areas (66.1%). Though differences are observed in the proportion of women having high level of violence against women between rural and urban areas, they are not statistically significant.

Education

A large proportion of illiterate women (75.5%) were having high level of violence against women, compared to those with primary with (67.3%), middle and above levels (52.9%). The differences observed in the level of violence against women between various educational statuses are statistically significant.

Vocational Skill

The level of violence against women did not vary much between skilled and unskilled respondents. The proportion of women having high level of violence against women is 71.0 per cent among unskilled respondents, whereas it was 69.0 per cent among skilled women. The differences observed in the level of violence against women between skilled and unskilled women are not statistically significant.

Religion

Majority of Muslim women (79.2%) were facing high level of violence compared to Hindu (74.2%) and Christian (41.2%) women. The differences observed in the proportion of women having high degree of violence against women across different religious groups are statistically significant.

Community

A higher proportion of SC/ST women (77.7%) experience high level of violence followed by most backward class women (74.5%). forward class and backward class respondents faced violence in lesser number (67.6 and 63.8 per cent respectively). The differences observed in the proportion of women facing high degree violence across different communities, are statistically significant.

Family Type

The level of violence against women did not vary between joint and nuclear family respondents. The proportion of women facing high degree of violence was 72.0 per cent among nuclear family and 70.2 per cent in joint families. The differences observed in the level of violence against women between joint and nuclear family is not statistically significant.

Marital Status

Widows, separated and the divorced (75.0%) face high level of violence compared to those who are married (70.3%) and unmarried (69.3%). The differences are not statistically significant.

Age at Marriage

A larger proportion of women (78.4%) who got married in the age group of 14-18 years were having high degree of violence against women when compared to those married at 18-21 years (70.3%) and above 21 years (59.8%). The differences observed in the proportion of women having high level of violence across the different age groups of marriage are statistically significant.

Present Occupation

Women engaged in non-farm labour (79.2%) and domestic activities (72.7%) faced high level of violence compared to those in agriculture labour (69.3%) and self employment (61.8%). Though differences are observed in the proportion of women having high violence against women among different occupational groups, they are not statistically significant.

Household Annual Income

The influence of household income on the level of violence against women shows that a higher proportion (78.5 and 70.9%) of those having a total income between Rs. 20,000—25,000 and above Rs. 25,000 were facing high level of violence. As against this, among those having a lower income of less than Rs. 15,000 (63.6%) and Rs. 15,000—20,000 (67.2%), a lesser number of them faced high levels of violence. Level of income and violence against women therefore seems to be inversely related. The differences observed in the proportion of women having high level of violence across the different income levels are statistically significant.

Income of Respondents

Relationship between respondents' annual income and violence against women showed a fluctuating pattern. At the lower level of income (below Rs. 2,000), a higher percentage of respondents (76.8%) reported high level of violence, but it stood at 68.9 per cent for the next higher level of income (Rs. 2,001-3,500). The same pattern repeated for the next two levels of income.

However, when the two income levels were clubbed into below Rs. 2,000 to 3,500 and 3,501 to 10,000, the contrast was clear whereby, more respondents reported higher level of violence (i.e. 73%) at lower income (below Rs. 3,500) and fewer percentage of violence (i.e. 53%) at higher income levels (Rs. 3,500 to Rs. 10,000). Income level and violence against women therefore seemed to have an inverse relationship. The differences observed in the level of violence against women among different income groups of respondents are not statistically significant.

Membership in SHG

A majority of non-members (72.0%) are facing high level of violence compared to members of SHGs (67.1%). Participation in Self-Help Groups can be considered as necessary for a lesser violence. The differences are not statistically significant.

Standard of living Index

A large proportion of respondents having high standard of living (77.3%) faced high level violence compared to those with low (72.2%) and medium standard of living (66.1%). The differences are not statistically significant.

Power and Influence and Empowerment

Table 4.35: Level of Power and Influence among the Respondents

Sl. No.	*Variables*	*Level of Power and Influence*			
		N	*Low*	*Medium*	*High*
1.	Age				
	• 35 years or less	291	14.1	23.7	62.2
	• 36 years and above	309	17.2	30.4	52.4
	Chi-square		*5.884*	2	*0.053*
2.	Birth order of Respondents				
	• First child	221	15.4	29.4	55.2
	• Second child	165	13.9	27.3	58.8
	• Third to fifth child	84	20.2	21.4	58.3
	• Sixth to eighth child	71	15.5	32.4	52.1
	• Above eighth	59	15.3	20.3	64.4
	Chi-square		*5.712*	8	*0.679*

(Contd.)

(*Contd.*)

Sl. No.	*Variables*	*Level of Power and Influence*			
		N	*Low*	*Medium*	*High*
3.	Place of Birth				
	• Rural area	538	14.9	23.8	61.3
	• Urban area	62	22.6	56.5	21.0
	Chi-square		*39.787*	*2*	*0.000*
4.	Education				
	• Illiterate	400	14.8	23.3	62.0
	• Primary education	113	19.5	31.9	48.7
	• Middle school and above	87	14.9	39.1	46.0
	Chi-square		*13.973*	*4*	*0.007*
5.	Vocational Skills				
	• Skilled	100	23.0	37.0	40.0
	• Not skilled	500	14.2	25.2	60.6
	Chi-square		14.576	2	0.00-
6.	Religion				
	• Hindu	508	14.6	22.2	63.2
	• Christian	68	19.1	55.9	25.0
	• Muslim	24	29.2	50.0	20.8
	Chi-square		*54.551*	*4*	*0.000*
7.	Community				
	• Forward class	34	23.5	44.1	32.4
	• Backward class	254	15.4	40.2	44.5
	• Most backward class	110	17.3	21.8	60.9
	• SC/ST	202	13.9	10.9	75.2
	Chi-square		*64.814*	*6*	*0.000*
8.	Family Type				
	• Joint family	157	13.4	36.3	50.3
	• Nuclear family	443	16.5	23.9	59.6
	Chi-square		*8.994*	*2*	*0.011*
9.	Marital Status				
	• Married	444	14.9	23.4	61.7
	• Unmarried	88	17.0	40.9	42.0
	• Others	68	19.1	33.8	47.1
	Chi-square		*16.662*	*4*	*0.002*
10.	Age at Marriage				
	• 14—18 years	134	16.4	26.1	57.5
	• 18—21 years	384	15.9	24.2	59.9
	• 21 and above	82	13.4	42.7	43.9
	Chi-square		*11.901*	*4*	*0.018*
11.	Occupation of Respondents				
	• House wives	209	15.3	21.5	63.2
	• Non-farm labour	77	13.0	44.2	42.9
	• Agriculture labour	225	16.4	23.6	60.0
	• Self employment	89	16.9	34.8	48.3
	Chi-square		*19.772*	*6*	*0.003*

(*Contd.*)

(*Contd.*)

Sl. No.	Variables	Level of Power and Influence			
		N	Low	Medium	High
12.	Household Annual Income				
	• < Rs. 15,000	143	18.2	51.7	30.1
	• Rs. 15,001—20,000	64	7.8	46.9	45.3
	• Rs. 20,001-25,000	149	12.1	12.1	75.8
	• Rs. 25,001 and above	244	18.4	16.8	64.8
	Chi-square		*100.091*	*6*	*0.000*
13.	Annual Income of Respondents'				
	• No	66	12.1	40.9	47.0
	• Below Rs. 2000	241	10.4	24.1	65.6
	• Rs. 2001-3500	254	19.7	24.8	55.5
	• Rs. 3501-5000	29	24.1	34.5	41.4
	• Rs. 5001-10000	10	41.1	52.2	6.7
	Chi-square		*31.345*	*12*	*0.002*
14.	Membership in SHG	64	7.8	46.9	45.3
	• Member	149	12.1	12.1	75.8
	• Non-member	244	18.4	16.8	64.8
	Chi-square		*100.091*	*6*	*0.000*
15.	Standard of Living Index				
	• Low (2-8)	367	10.9	24.0	65.1
	• Medium (9-16)	189	23.8	29.1	47.1
	• High (17-24)	44	20.5	45.5	34.1
	Chi-square		*32.537*	*4*	*0.000*

Power and Influence

Age

Table 4.35 shows that more than three-fifths of the younger women, aged less than 35 years (62.2 per cent), had high level of power and influence, as compared to older women above 35 years (52.4%). The differences observed in the proportion of women having high power and influence between younger and older women, are statistically significant.

Birth Order of Respondents

More respondents born as ninth child (or above) to their parents, (64.4%) had high power and influence compared to those born as 2nd to 5th child (about 58.0%). Though differences are observed in the proportion of women having high power and influence between various birth orders, the differences is not statistically significant.

Place of Birth

More than 60.0 per cent of rural women were reported to have high power and influence, as against 21.0 per cent of urban women. The differences observed in the high power and influence possessed by rural and urban women are statistically significant.

Education

Sixty two per cent of illiterate women are having high power and influence compared to those with primary level education (48.7%) and middle level and above (46.0%). The differences observed in the proportion of women having high power and influence across their educational level, are statistically significant.

Vocational Skill

Three sixths of the unskilled women were having high power and influence as against 40 per cent of skilled women. The differences are statistically significant.

Religion

Sixty three per cent of Hindu women were having high power and influence compared to Christian (25.0%) and Muslim (20.8%) respondents. The differences are statistically significant.

Community

Seventy five per cent of SC/ST women were having high power and influence compared to 60.9 per cent from most backward class, 44.5 per cent from backward class and 32.4 per cent forward class respondents. The differences observed in the proportion of women having high power and influence among different communities are statistically significant.

Family Type

Almost 60 per cent of nuclear family women were having high power and influence compared to those from joint families (50.3%). The differences are statistically significant.

Marital Status

Nearly 62 per cent of married women were having high power and influence compared to 47.1 per cent of widows, separated and the divorced and 42 per cent of unmarried. The differences observed in the proportion of women having high power and influence across different marital status are statistically significant.

Age at Marriage

Sixty per cent of those who got married in the age group of 18-21 years were having high power (57.5%) followed by those married at 14-18 years, as against 43.9 per cent of those married above 21 years. The differences are statistically significant.

Present Occupation

Sixty three per cent of housewives were having high power and influence compared to 60.0 per cent of agricultural labourers, 48.3 per cent of self employed and 42.9 per cent of non-farm labour. The differences observed in the proportion of women having high power and influence across various occupational categories are statistically significant.

Household Income

Respondents having a higher household income of Rs. 20,000 to 25,000 and above Rs. 25,000 had a higher level of power and influence (75.8 and 64.8 per cent respectively). As against this, among those having a lower income of Rs. 15,000 and below and Rs. 15,000 to 20,000, only a less percentage of them (30.1 and 45.3 per cent respectively) had high level of power and influence. The results are statistically significant.

Income of Respondents

Power and influence and income level of the respondents were found to be negatively related. Among respondents with a lower income of below Rs. 2,000, more respondents (65.6%) had higher level of power and influence. This percentage constantly slided down the subsequent income levels and stood at 6.7 per cent for the income category of Rs. 5,001-10,000. The level of income of the respondents and the power and influence wielded by them were therefore inversely related. The differences observed in the level of power and influence among different income groups of respondents are not statistically significant.

Membership in SHG

Three-fifths of non-member women were having high power and influence, compared to 48.8 per cent of SHG members. The differences are statistically significant.

Standard of Living Index

Nearly two-thirds of women living in low standard of living category were having high power and influence compared to those in medium (47.1%) and high (34.1%) standard of living categories. The differences are statistically significant.

Factors influencing women Empowerment

Table 4.36: Level of overall Empowerment among the Respondents

Sl. No.	*Variables*	*Level of overall Empowerment*			
		N	*Low*	*Medium*	*High*
1.	Age				
	• 35 years or less	291	7.2	80.4	12.4
	• 36 years and above	309	7.8	76.4	15.9
	Chi-square		*1.658*	*2*	*0.436*
2.	Birth Order of Respondents				
	• First child	221	6.8	78.7	14.5
	• Second child	165	6.7	84.2	9.1
	• Third to fifth child	84	9.5	76.2	14.3
	• Sixth to eighth child	71	9.9	66.2	23.9
	• Above eighth	59	6.8	78.0	15.3
	Chi-square		*11.311*	*8*	*0.185*
3.	Place of Birth				
	• Rural area	538	7.1	78.4	14.5
	• Urban area	62	11.3	77.4	11.3
	Chi-square		*1.736*	*2*	*0.420*
4.	Education				
	• Illiterate	400	7.0	78.8	14.3
	• Primary education	113	7.1	80.5	12.4
	• Middle school and above	87	10.3	73.6	16.1
	Chi-square		*1.912*	*4*	*0.752*

(Contd.)

(*Contd.*)

Sl. No.	Variables	Level of overall Empowerment			
		N	Low	Medium	High
5.	Vocational Skills				
	• Skilled	100	7.0	80.0	13.0
	• Not skilled	500	7.6	78.0	14.4
	Chi-square		*0.198*	*2*	*0.906*
6.	Religion				
	• Hindu	508	7.5	76.6	15.9
	• Christian	68	8.8	85.3	5.9
	• Muslim	24	4.2	95.8	
	Chi-square		*9.902*	*4*	*0.042*
7.	Community				
	• Forward class	34	2.9	85.3	11.8
	• Backward class	254	7.5	79.1	13.4
	• Most backward class	110	9.1	80.9	10.0
	• SC/ST	202	7.4	74.8	17.8
	Chi-square		*5.471*	*6*	*0.485*
8.	Family Type				
	• Joint family	157	8.4	79.0	12.6
	• Nuclear family	443	5.1	76.4	18.5
	Chi-square		*4.519*	*2*	*0.104*
9.	Marital Status				
	• Married	444	7.4	77.3	15.3
	• Unmarried	88	9.1	81.8	9.1
	• Others	68	5.9	80.9	13.2
	Chi-square		*2.852*	*4*	*0.583*
10.	Age at Marriage				
	• 14—18 years	134	9.7	79.9	10.4
	• 18—21 years	384	6.5	77.3	16.1
	• 21 and above	82	8.5	80.5	11.0
	Chi-square		*4.580*	*4*	*0.333*
11.	Occupation of Respondents				
	• House wives	209	9.1	72.7	18.2
	• Non-farm labour	77	5.2	84.4	10.4
	• Agriculture labour	225	6.7	77.8	15.6
	• Self employment	89	7.9	87.6	4.5
	Chi-square		*13.008*	*6*	*0.043*
12.	Household Annual Income				
	• < Rs. 15,000	143	4.9	87.4	7.7
	• Rs. 15,001—20,000	64	3.1	92.2	4.7
	• Rs. 20,001-25,000	149	10.7	77.2	12.1
	• Rs. 25,001 and above	244	8.2	70.1	21.7
	Chi-square		*28.965*	*6*	*0.000*

(*Contd.*)

(*Contd.*)

Sl. No.	Variables	Level of overall Empowerment			
		N	Low	Medium	High
13.	Annual Income of Respondents				
	• No	66	9.1	81.8	9.1
	• Below Rs. 2000	241	5.8	78.8	15.4
	• Rs. 2001-3500	254	8.3	76.8	15.0
	• Rs. 3501-5000	29	3.4	86.2	10.3
	• Rs. 5001-10000	10	30.0	58.9	11.1
	Chi-square		*18.571*	*12*	*0.099*
14.	Membership in SHG	64	3.1	92.2	4.7
	• Member	149	8.2	70.1	21.7
	• Non member	244	10.7	77.2	12.1
	Chi-square		*28.965*	*6*	*0.000*
15.	Standard of Living Index				
	• Low (2-8)	367	8.2	80.4	11.4
	• Medium (9-16)	189	7.4	77.8	14.8
	• High (17-24)	44	2.3	63.6	34.1
	Chi-square		*17.551*	*4*	*0.002*

Level of Overall Empowerment among Respondents

Age

The level of total empowerment score did not vary much between the younger and older women (Table 4.36). The proportion of women having high empowerment score was 15.9 per cent among older women, whereas it was 12.4 per cent among younger women. The differences observed in the empowerment score between younger and older women are not statistically significant.

Birth Order of Respondents

Combined percentage of medium and high level of total empowerment score across the birth order of the respondents showed that those at the extremes—i.e. early born, as 1st and 2nd child and the late born, as eighth child or above had slightly higher score of about 93.0 per cent in each category, as against 90 per cent for those born as 3rd to 8th child. The differences observed in the proportion of women having high empowerment score among different birth orders are not statistically significant.

Place of Birth

The level of total empowerment score only slightly varied between rural and urban women. The proportion of women having empowerment score was 14.5 per cent among rural women, whereas it was 11.3 per cent among urban women. Also, the combined score of medium and high level of empowerment for rural women was 92.9 per cent, while it was 88.7 per cent for urban women. The differences observed in the level of empowerment score between rural and urban women are not statistically significant.

Education

Among the various categories of literacy levels, 16.1 per cent of middle level (and above) educated women were having high empowerment. This stands at 12.3 per cent for primary educated. The illiterates had an empowerment score of 14.3 per cent. In respect of the combined score for medium and high level of empowerment, the illiterates top with 93.1 per cent, followed by those primary educated (92.9%) and middle level educated (89.7%). The differences observed in the proportion of women having high empowerment score among different educational levels, are not statistically significant.

Vocational Skill

Fourteen per cent of unskilled women were having high empowerment score, compared to 13 per cent for skilled women. The differences are not statistically significant.

Religion

Sixteen per cent of the Hindu women were having high empowerment score (15.9%) compared to (5.9%) among the Christian women. Among Muslim women, 95.8 per cent had medium level of empowerment but none had a higher level of empowerment. The differences observed in the proportion of women having high empowerment score among different religious groups are statistically significant.

Community

Nearly 18 per cent of SC/ST women were having high empowerment score compared to backward class (13.4 per cent), forward class (11.8%) and most backward class women (10.0%). The differences observed in the proportion of women having high empowerment score across different communities are not statistically significant.

Family Type

Nineteen per cent of nuclear family women were having high empowerment score compared to 12.6 per cent among joint family The differences are not statistically significant.

Marital Status

Fifteen per cent of married women were having high empowerment score when compared to 13.2 per cent for the widows, divorcees and separated and 9.1 per cent for the unmarried women. The differences are not statistically significant.

Age at Marriage

Sixteen per cent of women who married in the age group of 18-21 years were having high empowerment score compared to 11.0 per cent of those who married above 21 years and 10.4 per cent for those who married early (15-18). The 'later married' have higher empowerment score than the 'early married'. The differences are not statistically significant.

Present Occupation

Eighteen per cent of housewives were having a high empowerment score compared to agriculture labourers (15.6 per cent), non-farm labourers (10.4%) and self employed women (4.5%). The differences are observed in the proportion of women having high empowerment score among different occupational groups. The differences are statistically significant.

Household Annual Income

The relationship between level of household annual income and the overall empowerment score showed positive relationship. The level of influence was low (7.7% and 14.0%) at lower levels of income (up to Rs. 20,000), whereas it recorded a slow rise in the higher slabs of household annual income Rs. 20,000-25,000 and above (14.2 and 21.7 per cent respectively). Household annual income has therefore influenced the overall empowerment score to some extent. The differences observed in the proportion of women having high empowerment score between different income statuses are statistically significant.

Income of Respondents

The influence of income of respondents on the total score of empowerment showed an inverse trend. At lower levels of income, more respondents had higher level of empowerment whereas at higher levels, the percentage was low.

In the income slabs of Rs. 2,000 and below and Rs. 2,001-3,500, about 15 per cent each of the respondents had higher level of empowerment. On the contrary, at the higher income brackets (Rs. 3,501-5,000 and 5,001-10,000), the percentage of those having higher level of overall empowerment was about 10 each. The annual income of respondents was therefore not positively related to the overall score of empowerment. The differences observed in the overall empowerment among different income groups of respondents are not statistically significant.

Membership in SHG

The empowerment score varied between SHG members and non-members. The proportion of women having high empowerment score was 21.7 per cent among members and 12.1 per cent for non-members. The differences observed in the empowerment score between members and non-members are not statistically significant.

Standard of Living Index

Thirty four per cent of women with high standard of living were having a high empowerment score compared to those with medium (14.8%) and low standard of living index (11.4%). The differences observed in the proportion of women having high empowerment score across different standard of living categories are statistically significant.

Chapter 5

Opinion of Experts on Women Empowerment

In order to elicit the views and opinions of the experts, activists, academicians and social workers on women empowerment, 50 respondents were contacted for the study. They were purposively selected, based on their association with women's issues and intervention programmes. All of them were females.

An interview schedule was pre-tested and administered on these respondents, who were largely from Gandhigram complex of institutions with academic, and activist background. Data were collected through direct interview method, at their doorsteps. The responses obtained from these respondents are presented below.

Table 5.1: Birth Order of Respondents

Sl. No.	*Particulars*	*No. of Respondents*	*Percentage*
1.	First child	12	24.0
2.	Second child	10	20.0
3.	Third child	02	04.0
4.	Fourth and above	26	52.0
	Total	50	100

Birth Order

Nearly a fourth of the respondents (24.0%) were born as the first child to their parents and 20.0 per cent were born as the second child. More than half of the respondents (52.0%) were born as the fifth child and above. Three-fourths of the respondents (76.0%) were born as second or subsequent child to their parents. The early born and late born enjoyed the status and commanded the respect due to their birth order from their parents and the sisters/brothers in rural communities, notwithstanding other factors like the sex and sex composition. Better status and greater respect enjoyed by the respondents may therefore influence the process of their empowerment

Table 5.2: Religion, Community, Education and Vocational and Life Skills of Respondents

Sl. No.	Particulars	No. of Respondents	Percentage
	Religion		
1.	Hindu	44	88.0
2.	Muslim	02	04.0
3.	Christian	04	08.0
	Total	50	100
	Community		
1.	Forward Castes	08	16.0
2.	Backward Castes	32	64.0
3.	Most Backward Castes	02	04.0
4.	Scheduled Castes	06	12.0
5.	Scheduled Tribes	02	04.0
	Total	50	100
	Education		
1.	Bachelor degree	02	04.0
2.	Master degree	22	44.0
3.	M.Phil	04	08.0
4.	Ph.D	20	40.0
5.	Technical training	02	04.0
	Total	50	100
	Skills and Talents		
1.	Typing	10	20.0
2.	Computer	16	32.0
3.	Oration	04	08.0
4.	No skills	20	40.0
	Total	50	100
	*Knowledge of Driving (n = 50) **		
1.	Cycle	22	44.0
2.	Moped	26	52.0
3.	Car	12	24.0
4.	Nothing	08	16.0

* Multiple responses.

Religion and Community

Eighty eight per cent of respondents belonged to Hindu religion, eight per cent were Christians and four per cent of the respondents were Muslims. Nearly nine-tenths of the respondents were Hindus.

Respondents belonging to backward caste constituted the majority (64.0%). The forward castes came next, sharing 16.0 per cent. Scheduled Castes and Scheduled Tribes together accounted for four per cent. On the whole, 68.0 per cent of the respondents were from backward castes and most backward castes.

Education and Skills

Forty four per cent of the respondents had PG degree while 40.0 per cent had Ph.D. degrees. Eight per cent had M.Phil., degree and four per cent of the respondents had UG degree. More than 90 per cent of the respondents thus had qualifications ranging from PG to Ph.D.

Forty per cent of the respondents did not possess any skill, 32.0 per cent possessed computer skills while another 20 per cent possessed typing skills. More than half of the respondents (52.0%) possessed typing and computer skills.

Fifty two per cent of the respondents knew to drive moped. Another 44 per cent knew cycling. Car driving was known to 24 per cent of the respondents.

More than three-fourths of the respondents (76.0%) had the knowledge of driving a moped or a car.

Among the 50 respondents, except one, all the others had a bank account in their names.

Respondents belonging to Hindu religion (80.0%), backward and most backward castes (68.0%), PG to Ph.D. qualified categories (90.0%), and bank account holders (98.0%) comprised the majority. More than half of the respondents possessed typing and computer skills and had the knowledge of driving automobiles.

Marital Details

Forty per cent of the respondents were unmarried, 44.0 per cent were married and eight per cent had got separated from their husbands.

Table 5.3: Marital Status, Type of Marriage, Education and Occupation of the Respondents and Spouses

Sl. No.	*Particulars*	*No. of Respondents*	*Percentage*
	Marital Status		
1.	Unmarried	20	40.0
2.	Married	22	44.0
3.	Divorced	02	04.0
4.	Widowed	02	04.0
5.	Separated	04	08.0
	Total	50	100.0
	Type of Marriage		
1.	Arranged marriage	22	73.3
2.	Love marriage	8	26.7
	Total	30	100.0
	Education of the Spouses		
1.	Illiterate	12	24.0
2.	School level	16	32.0
3.	UG level	16	32.0
4.	No response	06	12.0
	Total	50	100.0
	Occupation of Spouses		
1.	Govt. employees	18	36.0
2.	Private employees	18	36.0
3.	Business men	08	16.0
4.	Self-employment	04	08.0
5.	Wage labour	02	04.0
	Total	50	100.0

Widows and divorcees constituted four per cent each. Married respondents were thus in majority (44.0%), closely followed by the unmarried (40.0%).

Seventy three per cent of the respondents had arranged marriage while the remaining had love marriage.

Education and Occupation

Twenty per cent of the respondents' spouses had UG degree, while 16 per cent had completed their school education. Twelve per cent of them were illiterates. However, 52.0 per cent refused to divulge the educational status of their spouses.

Thirty six per cent each of the respondents' spouses were Government and private employees respectively. Sixteen per cent of them were business men. Eight per cent were engaged in self-employment.

We may conclude from the above analysis that 60 per cent of the respondents were married, 27 per cent had love marriage, 64 per cent of the respondents' spouses were literate, and 36 per cent of the spouses were in government employment.

Table 5.4: Dominating Member in the Present and their Parents' Families

Sl. No.	*Particulars*	*Nnmber of Respondents*			
		In their Present Family		*In their Parents' Family*	
1.	Male dominant	06	12.0	18	36.0
2.	Female dominant	00	00.0	02	04.0
3.	Both are equal	18	36.0	08	16.0
4.	Men are flexible	06	12.0	08	16.0
5.	Women are flexible	06	12.0	10	20.0
6.	Both are flexible	14	28.0	04	08.0
	Total	50	100	50	100

Dominant Family Member

The respondents were asked as to who is dominant in their present family—the men or women; similarly, in their parents' families, prior to their marriage.

Answering this, 36.0 per cent of the respondents informed that they were treated equally with men, in their in-laws' family, as against 16.0 per cent who were treated equally in their parents' family. In their parents' family, 36 per cent reported that they were dominated by men, as against 12 per cent in their present family. While four per cent of the respondents expressed that women dominated in their parents' family, one reported about women dominance in their present family.

More respondents (28.0%) reported that both the men and women were flexible in their present family as against their parents' families (8.0%).

On the whole, the dominance of men seems to be more in their parents' family (36%) than in their present family (8.0%). Both men and women were equally reported to be dominating in their present families (36%), more than their parents' families.

Table 5.5: Sources of Problems, Status of Women, and Men's Response to Women Empowerment

Sl. No.	*Particulars*	*No. of Respondents*	*Percentage*
	Sources of Women's Problems		
1.	Largely men	06	12.0
2.	Largely women	06	12.0
3.	Both men and women	38	76.0
	Total	50	100
	Present Status of Rural Women		
1.	Better than before	48	96.0
2.	Worse than before	0	00.0
3.	Continues to be the same	02	04.0
	Total	50	100
	Status Compared to Men		
1.	Secondary to men	32	64.0
2.	Equal to men	14	28.0
3.	Superior to men	04	08.0
	Total	50	100
	Men's Response to Women Empowerment		
1.	Half of the men support it	26	52.0
2.	Half of them oppose it	08	16.0
3.	Nobody supports	10	20.0
4.	Everybody supports	06	12.0
	Total	50	100

Sources of Women's Problems

While expressing their views on the major sources of problems women faced, 76.0 per cent of the respondents informed that they were caused by both men and women. On the other hand, 12 per cent informed that the problems were caused largely by men. As against this, another 12.0 per cent reported that it was largely due to women.

More than three-fourths of the respondents (76.0%) attributed the source of problems faced by women to both men and women.

Figure 16: Comparative Status of Women and Response of Men to Women Empowerment

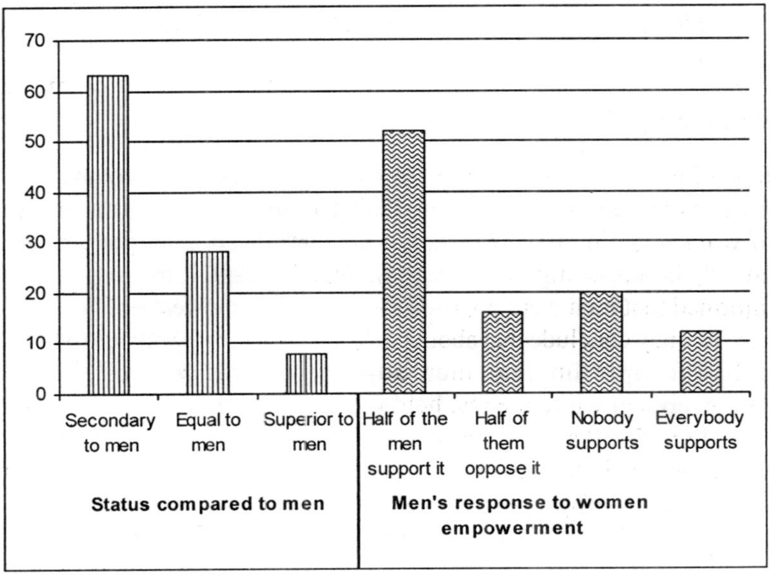

Present Status of Rural Women

The respondents were asked to give their opinion on the present status of women, in comparison with their previous status about 10 years before.

Ninety six per cent of the respondents said that status of rural women has become better than before, while the remaining four per cent felt that they still continue to remain the same as they were about 10 years ago. None of them had felt that it is worse than before.

There is an increasing recognition for the fact that women command better status than before, as reported by a vast majority (96.0%) of the respondents.

Comparative Status of Women

While comparing the present status of women with men, 64.0 informed that women are secondary to men. On the other hand, 28.0 per cent of them said women were equal to men. It may be noted that eight per cent of the respondents claimed that they are superior to men.

Nearly two-thirds of the respondents (64.0%) were of the opinion that women's status is secondary. The remaining 36 per cent respondents however held the view that women (28.0%) are either equal to men or even superior to men (8.0%).

Response of Men

Regarding the response of men to the empowerment of women, 52.0 per cent of the respondents said that half of the men supported the process of women getting empowered. On the other hand, 20.0 per cent felt nobody is supporting the process. Sixteen per cent of the respondents informed that men were opposed to women's empowerment.

We may conclude that about two thirds of the respondents (64.0%) hold the opinion that men support the process of women empowerment while the rest held the opposite view.

Three-fourths of the respondents opined that women's problems are caused by both men and women, 96.0 per cent informed that the present status of women is better than before, 64.0 per cent felt that women's comparative status is secondary to men, and over half of the respondents expressed that men support the process of women empowerment.

Table 5.6: Concept and Assessment of Women Empowerment at Various Levels

Sl. No.	*Particulars*	*No. of Respondents*	*Percentage*
	*Concept of Women Empowerment (n = 50)**		
1.	Freedom	38	76.0
2.	Self confidence	18	36.0
3.	Ability to control resources	18	36.0
4.	Decision-making	16	32.0
5.	Education and knowledge	14	28.0
6.	Regular income and family support	08	16.0
	*Measures of Women Empowerment (n=50)**		
1.	Psychological aspects	28	56.0
2.	Educational aspects	24	48.0
3.	Community participation and contribution	22	44.0
4.	Social aspects	20	40.0
5.	Economic aspects	18	36.0

(Contd.)

(*Contd.*)

Sl. No.	*Particulars*	*No. of Respondents*	*Percentage*
	At the Individual Level		
1.	Knowledge and skills	14	28.0
2.	Psychological development	14	28.0
3.	Economic activity	10	20.0
4.	Education and awareness	10	20.0
5.	Decision-making	02	04.0
	Total	50	100
	At the Family Level		
1.	Freedom to make decisions	16	32.0
2.	Prevention of violence and abuse	14	28.0
3.	Provide education and skills	12	24.0
4.	Counseling and awareness	06	12.0
5.	No discrimination	02	04.0
	Total	50	100
	At the Community Level		
1.	Providing opportunities of training	20	40.0
2.	Allow freedom and equality	14	28.0
3.	Support to helpless women	10	20.0
4.	Strengthen women's association	04	08.0
5.	Recognize women's activities	02	04.0
	Total	50	100

* Multiple responses.

Concept of Empowerment

Commenting on the concept of women empowerment, 76.0 per cent of respondents said that freedom of all kind—social, economic and political forms the basis of empowerment. Ability to control resources and exercise power (15.7%), decision making (14.0%), education and knowledge (12.5%) self confidence (10.0%) and regular income with economic support to family (7.0%) were also reported to constitute empowerment.

Respondents were asked to provide their suggestions regarding what needs to be done for empowerment of women at different levels—individual, family and community. Their suggestions are presented below.

Individual Level

At the individual level, rural women can be empowered through developing their knowledge and skills and psychological development—such as their boldness, self-confidence, determination and resolve—as reported by 28 per cent of the respondents each. Striving for economic activities and education and awareness were the other means expected, according to 20 per cent respondents each.

Family Level

In respect of what can be done at the family level, 32.0 per cent of the respondents felt that women should be encouraged to involve in decision-making process, 28.0 per cent suggested that family should prevent violence, and avoid gender discrimination and 24 per cent informed about helping girls to get education and acquire vocational skills.

Community Level

Regarding community level support, 40 per cent of the respondents suggested that women should be provided with opportunities of skill and leadership training, 28 per cent noted that they should be allowed freedom and equality of opportunities and 20 per cent felt that the community should support special categories of women such as widows, destitutes and the separated.

Assessment of Empowerment

When posed as how would they assess women empowerment, 56 per cent of the respondents pointed out psychological dimension should be assessed, while 48 per cent cited the educational dimension followed by community participation (44.0%) and social dimension (40.0%).

Freedom (76.0%), self confidence (36.0%) and ability to control resources and exercise power (36.0%) were listed by the respondents as the major attributes of empowerment of women.

Majority of the respondents have proposed instilling of courage and confidence and building up women's knowledge and skills at the individual level. Involvement in decision-making and prevention of violence was suggested at the family level. At the community level, it was stated that women should be provided with opportunities of training in vocational skills and allowed freedom.

In the process of assessing women empowerment, psychological make up of women commands priority in the minds of the respondents, followed by education and community participation.

Table 5.7: Dimensions of Women Empowerment and their Constituents

Sl. No.	*Particulars*	*No. of Respondents**	*Percentage*
	Dimensions of Women Empowerment (n = 50)		
1.	Social	18	36.0
2.	Cultural	12	24.0
3.	Health	10	20.0
4.	Economic	24	48.0
5.	Educational	18	36.0
6.	Psychological	10	20.0
7.	Training/Skill	10	20.0
8.	Political	10	20.0
9.	All the above	24	48.0
	Social Dimension (n=50)		
1.	Societal outlook and acceptance	22	44.0
2.	Eradication of social evils	14	28.0
3.	Freedom of mobility and involvement in organizations	12	24.0
4.	Equality in decision-making	10	20.0
	Economic Dimension (n=50)		
1.	Greater economic independence	18	36.0
2.	Involvement in income generation activities	16	32.0
3.	Own assets and access micro credit	12	24.0
4.	Equality in wages	10	20.0
5.	Solve problems	04	08.0
	Political Dimension (n=50)		
1.	Participation and performance	18	36.0
2.	Political knowledge and awareness	10	20.0
3.	Solve women's problems through political means	10	20.0
4.	Reservation and mobility	10	20.0
5.	Grassroot involvement and development	06	12.0
	Health Dimension (n=50)		
1.	Giving priority to health problems	18	36.0
2.	Good health	14	28.0
3.	Reproductive rights and family support	12	24.0
4.	Hygienic and healthy	10	20.0
5.	Knowledge and health care policies	06	12.0

(Contd.)

(*Contd.*)

Sl. No.	*Particulars*	*No. of Respondents**	*Percentage*
	Educational Dimension (n=50)		
1.	Compulsory education	18	36.0
2.	Quality education and reservation	12	24.0
3.	Knowledge and Self confidence	12	24.0
4.	Differential education for women	08	16.0
5.	Social barriers in girls' education	04	08.0

* Multiple responses.

Dimensions of Empowerment

When the respondents were asked to highlight the various dimensions of women empowerment, their responses were varied. Forty eight per cent said 'economic' empowerment is the major dimension while 36.0 per cent pointed out 'social' dimension and 'educational' dimension respectively. Twenty four per cent informed 'culture' as a dimension of empowerment. Health, psychological, political and skill dimensions were also cited by 20 per cent each of the respondents. Towards the end, 48.0 per cent of the respondents said that all the above dimensions are essential for women empowerment.

Figure 17: Dimensions of Women Empowerment

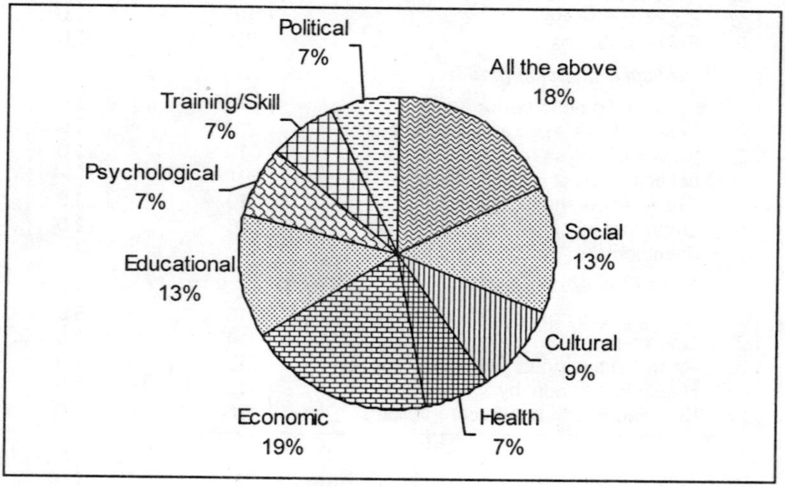

Social Dimension

Responding to the question as to what constitutes 'social' empowerment, 44.0 per cent of the respondents informed that the society should find greater space to accommodate the women in the following ways:

- accept and respect the women as dignified human beings,
- should make changes in patriarchal system,
- allow women's participation and decision-making in public areas,
- permit greater interaction with the male members of the society,
- allow women to take all the good things from society without gender barriers, and
- consciously change their hitherto held women suppressive social attitude.

Twenty eight per cent of respondents said that the following social evils should be eradicated:

- Dowry
- Violence against women
- Restrictions on widow remarriage
- Rape and sexual abuses
- Communal problems against women

Another 24 per cent expressed that freedom of mobility and involvement of women in community based organizations operating in their villages would pave way for social empowerment.

Economic Dimension

Elaborating on what constitutes economic empowerment, 36 per cent of the respondents listed out independence in employment, freedom to earn or spend, save or borrow, acquire or sell assets and take decisions as vital aspects. Thirty two per cent of the respondents expressed that involvement of women in income generation activities as the base for women empowerment. About one-fourth informed that women should own assets and command micro credit facilities, while one fifth of the respondents felt that giving women equal wages and not making under payment for her work are also important.

Political Dimension

Explaining what constitutes political empowerment, 36 per cent of them cited participation in elections and performing of political activities by the women. Moreover, 20.0 per cent each of the respondents said that political empowerment would comprise the following aspects:

- greater political knowledge and awareness,
- solving women's problems through political means,
- reservation of seats for women in elections, and
- greater mobility of women.

Health Dimension

By health empowerment, the respondents mean, giving priority to their health problems (36.0%) and protecting their health by keeping their mind and body sound (08.0%). Twenty four per cent of the respondents said that giving women reproductive rights and family support and maintaining sanitation, safe drinking water, healthy food and hygiene (20.0%) as the other dimensions of health empowerment. Acquisitions of knowledge on health care policies were also reported by the respondents (12.0%) as constituting health empowerment.

Educational Dimension

Educational empowerment includes providing compulsory education to girls from a minimum of Plus Two to a maximum of Graduate level, informed 36 per cent of the respondents. For another 24 per cent of the respondents, it means acquiring greater knowledge and developing self confidence. An equal number of the respondents said it is developing the quality of education, creating more opportunities and providing for reservations for women in admissions. Sixteen per cent of the respondents have suggested that women may be given differential education such as non-formal, continuing, functional, life-oriented etc.

Nearly half of the respondents informed that a multitude of dimensions—economic, social, political, cultural, education, health and psychological—comprised women empowerment. Among them, economic, educational and social dimensions were particularly emphasized by the respondents as constituting women empowerment.

Positive societal outlook and acceptance of women as equal partners in society (44.0%), eradication of social evils (28.0%) and allowing women the freedom of mobility and involvement of women in community organizations (24.0%) were reported by the respondents to constitute social empowerment.

Economic independence (36.0%), involvement in income generation activities (32.0%) and ownership of assets with access to micro credit facilities (24.0%) were highlighted as the vital shades of economic empowerment.

Participation of women in election and performance of political tasks (36.0%), and reservation of seats for women in elections (20.0% each) were expressed by the respondents as constituting political empowerment.

Giving greater attention to women's health problems (36.0%), striving for sound body and mind (28.0%) ensuring reproductive rights (24.0%) and safe drinking water, sanitation and hygiene (20.0%) were expressed as constituting the basis of health empowerment.

Providing compulsory education (36.0%) and reservation for women in admissions and acquiring more knowledge and self-confidence (24.0% each) were pointed out as the basis of educational empowerment.

Table 5.8: Strategies and Barriers to Women Empowerment

Sl. No.	*Particulars*	*No. of Respondents (n=50)**	*Percentage*
	Strategies		
1.	Education, knowledge and skill	46	92.0
2.	Economic support	32	64.0
3.	Social status	28	56.0
4.	Equal treatment	14	28.0
5.	Decision making	12	24.0
	Barriers		
1.	Social	46	92.0
2.	Educational	22	44.0
3.	Psychological	12	24.0
4.	Economic	08	16.0
5.	Tradition and language	08	16.0

* Multiple responses.

Strategies and Barriers

Table 5.8 throws light on various strategies of women empowerment and the barriers.

Strategies: Women can be empowered in the following ways as expressed by the respondents—through education, knowledge and skill (92.0%), developing them economically (64.0%), and by providing them with better social status (56.0%). Further, 28 per cent of the respondents suggested that by treating women equally with men and allowing them to take decisions, (24.0%) women can be empowered.

Barriers: Listing out the various types of barriers to women empowerment, 92 per cent of the respondents pointed out social barriers which include male supremacy, social stigma and secondary status. Education as a barrier was reported by 44.0 per cent of the respondents which refers to illiteracy, discrimination of girls' education and lack of awareness about the importance of girls' education among parents.

Table 5.9: Role of the Government, NGOs and Panchayats in Women Empowerment

Sl. No.	*Particulars*	*No. of Respondents**	*Percentage*
	Role of the Government		
1.	Policy formulation	20	40.0
2.	Economic support programmes	12	24.0
3.	Capacity-building	10	20.0
4.	Welfare and protection	06	12.0
5.	Government must take full responsibility	02	04.0
	Total	50	100
	Role of the NGOs		
1.	Training support	22	44.0
2.	Income generation activities	10	20.0
3.	Development programmes	08	16.0
4.	Support government policies	08	16.0
5.	Group formation	08	16.0
	Role of Panchayats		
1.	Encouraging women's participation	18	36.0
2.	Support government policies	12	24.0
3.	Development activities	08	16.0
4.	Reservation in politics	08	16.0
5.	Awareness generation	04	08.0
	Total	50	100

* Multiple responses.

Psychological barrier was expressed by 24 per cent of the respondents to denote the inhibitions and inferiority complex inherent in women. Sixteen per cent each of the respondents informed economic barriers (24.0%) and tradition and language respectively.

We may conclude that educating and imparting skills for women, providing them with economic support and giving them a better status in society would form the basic strategies of empowering women. Regarding barriers, social (92.0%), education (44.0%) and psychological barriers served as the prime impediments in women empowerment.

Role of Institutions

Table 5.11 presents the role of various institutions as suggested by the respondents.

- *Government*: In order to usher in the process of empowerment, the respondents have suggested the Government to promote empowerment-friendly social policies (40.0%). Areas of such policies include reservation in employment, education, health care protection, women development programmes, politics and legal protection. Economic support initiatives (24.0%) with capacity-building (20.0%) were proposed by the other respondents. Economic support refers to sponsoring of income generating activities, greater job opportunities, and strengthening of micro credit sector. Capacity-building relates to imparting of skill training, leadership training, awareness raising and women's participation in all such programmes.
- *Role of NGOs*: When asked how the NGOs can contribute to the women empowerment process, 44 per cent of the respondents pointed out training, while 20 per cent said through income generation activities. NGOs can contribute by sponsoring development programmes, said 16 per cent while another 16 per cent pointed out supporting of government policies as the means of encouraging women empowerment.

Table 5.10: Socio-Demographic Factors Influencing Women Empowerment

Sl. No	Particulars	Agree		Disagree		Neutral	
		Respons-es*	%	Respons-es*	%	Respons-es*	%
	Religion and Community						
1.	Religions promote empowerment	20	40.0	14	28.0	16	32.0
2.	Communities support empowerment	28	56.0	14	28.0	08	16.0
3.	Dalit communities more empowered	06	12.0	24	48.0	20	40.0
4.	Non-dalit communities more empowered	10	20.0	18	36.0	22	44.0
	Typology of Families						
5.	Nuclear families more empowered	28	56.0	10	20.0	12	24.0
6.	Joint families more empowered	10	20.0	20	40.0	20	40.0
7.	Female-headed families more empowered	34	68.0	08	16.0	08	16.0
8.	Male-headed families more empowered	0	—	36	72.0	14	28.0
9.	Rich families more empowered	28	56.0	10	20.0	12	24.0
10.	Poor families more empowered	08	16.0	28	56.0	14	28.0
11.	Farming families more empowered	10	20.0	30	60.0	10	20.0
12.	Non-farming families more empowered	04	08.0	26	52.0	20	40.0
13.	Educated families more empowered	34	68.0	08	16.0	08	16.0
14.	Female dominant families more empowered	20	40.0	14	28.0	16	32.0
	Age and Nativity						
15.	Young women more empowered (<35 years)	28	56.0	10	20.0	12	24.0
16.	Elderly women more empowered (>35 years)	12	24.0	18	36.0	20	40.0
17.	Rural women more empowered	10	20.0	32	64.0	08	16.0
18.	Urban women more empowered	24	48.0	10	20.0	16	32.0
19.	Women in NGO service area more empowered	28	56.0	14	28.0	08	16.0

(Contd.)

(*Contd.*)

Sl. No	Particulars	Agree		Disagree		Neutral	
		Responses*	%	Responses*	%	Responses*	%
	Education and Employment						
20.	Illiterate women more empowered	10	20.0	28	56.0	12	24.0
21.	Educated women more empowered	22	44.0	10	20.0	18	36.0
22.	Skilled/Trained women more empowered	28	56.0	04	08.0	18	36.0
23.	Employed women more empowered	28	56.0	10	20.0	12	24.0
24.	Unemployed women more empowered	0	0	38	76.0	12	24.0
	Awareness and Independence						
25.	Economically independent women more empowered	42	84.0	0	0	08	16.0
26.	Organized women in SHG more empowered	38	76.0	0	0	12	24.0
27.	Women with greater mobility more empowered	42	84.0	02	04.0	06	12.0
28.	Women with greater legal awareness more empowered	36	72.0	0	—	14	28.0
29.	Women with greater interaction with others more empowered	30	60.0	06	12.0	14	28.0
30.	Women with political involvement more empowered	30	60.0	10	20.0	10	20.0

* Multiple responses.

- *Role of Panchayats*: Responding to the question on the possible role of panchayats in promoting women empowerment, respondents suggested encouraging the participation of women in all panchayat activities (36.0%), supporting government policies (24.0%), sponsoring development activities and encouraging women's participation in civic elections through reservation (16.0% each).

Policy support in the spheres of employment, education, health care development and legal protection is the major contribution expected of the Government in the process of promoting women empowerment.

NGOs are expected by the respondents to support the process of women empowerment by organizing training programmes on imparting productive skills (44.0%) and by initiating income generating activities (20.0%)

Panchayats are expected by the respondents to encourage women's participation in panchayat sponsored development activities, and contest civic elections, in the process of empowering rural women.

Factors Influencing Women Empowerment

Table 5.10 gives an account of the opinion of the respondents to various statements presented before them.

Religion and Community

When asked about their opinion regarding the influence of social factors such as religion and community, 56.0 per cent of the respondents 'agreed' to the statement that community factor supported women empowerment, while 40.0 per cent agreed that religions promote women empowerment. Responding to the question on the empowerment status of women in *dalit* and non-*dalit* communities, majority (48.0%) disagreed that women in *dalit* communities are empowered. Similarly, 44 per cent of the respondents (neither agreed or nor disagreed) to the statement that women in non-*dalit* communities are empowered.

Typology of Families

The respondents were asked a set of questions regarding their opinion on the relationship between family and its typologies and its possible relationship to empowerment of women.

Responding to specific questions, the respondents agreed to the statements that women from educated families (68.0%), female headed families (58.0%), nuclear families (56.0%), rich families (56.0%), and female dominant families (40.0%) are more empowered.

Majority of the respondents have disagreed that women in farming families (60%) or non-farming families (52.0%) are more empowered.

Age and Nativity

In respect of the role of age, nativity and social service coverage of the respondents' areas by voluntary agencies, we may see from the table that 56.0 per cent of the respondents have agreed that young women (below 35 years) are more empowered than the elderly. Similarly, urban women are reported to be more empowered (48.0%) than their rural counterparts. Fifty six per cent of the respondents informed that women living in areas catered by voluntary agencies are more empowered (56.0%) due to their capacity-building and mobilization efforts among women.

Education and Employment

Regarding the possible influence of education, skill and employment on women empowerment, it is seen that educated (44.0%) employed (56.0%), and skilled trained women (56.0%) are reported to be more empowered. On the contrary, majority of them have disagreed that unemployed (76.0%) and illiterate women (56.0%) are more empowered.

Awareness and Independence

Majority of the respondents agreed to the statement that women with greater economic independence (84.0%), greater mobility (84.0%), better organization (76.0%) and more legal awareness (72.0%) were more empowered. Sixty per cent of the respondents agreed that women with political involvement and greater interaction with others are more empowered than others.

We may conclude that communities (56.0%), and religions (40.0%) are supportive factors in the process of women empowerment. More respondents agreed to the statement that non-*dalit* communities promoted empowerment (20.0%) than in *dalit* communities (12.0%).

Women hailing from families which are female-headed (68.0%), educated (68.0%), nuclear (56.0%), rich (56.0%) and female dominant (40.0%) are more empowered. Occupation was not reported to be exercising its influence on women empowerment.

Women belonging to younger age group (<35 years) (56.0%) hailing from urban families (48.0%) and those resident of NGO service areas (56.0%) are reported to be more empowered than their counterparts.

Women who have had education, training, skills and employment are reported to be more empowered.

We may conclude that economic independence, mobility, organization, legal awareness, political involvement and interactive nature enable women to be more empowered.

Chapter 6

Indicators of Women Empowerment

Response of Women Groups

Discussions were held extensively with women activists, social workers, academicians, research scholars and women staff working in non-government organizations. These respondents were purposively identified based on their association with women's issues, involvement in women related programmes and interest in women's problems.

They were specifically asked to offer their views on the indicators of women empowerment. Based on what they suggested as the main indicators, they were asked to spell out the probable constituents of each one of these indicators.

Accordingly, we could finalize ten major indicators and 50 items under these indicators. These indicators and the relevant items under each indicator were then taken to the study villages, numbering six. These villages are located in Athoor, Dindigul and Nilakottai blocks under different panchayats. These include:

Sl. No.	*Village*	*Panchayat*
1.	Kallupatti	Chettiapatti
2.	Kottaipatti	Kalikkampatti
3.	Ariyanallur	Munnilaikottai
4.	Jathigoundenpatti	Thoppampatti
5.	Melakottai	Ambathurai
6.	Alamarathupatti	Alamarathupatti

While in the first three villages, the schedule was administered among Self-Help Group members, in the later half, it was administered among groups of women, who are not part of Self-Help Groups at present.

Unanimity of the opinion among members with each group i.e. Self-Help Group women and non-Self-Help Group women prevailed on almost all the items of response. In the case of difference of opinions, the responses were rounded off to the majority opinion within the respective groups.

From among the various aspects reported to constitute a major indicator, the respondents were asked to rank order them from 1st to 5th so that we could include the five most important aspects of each indicator for a uniform and more focussed view of the components and their constituents comprising women empowerment.

Based on extensive consultations with the experts, NGOs as well as the SHG women, we had located ten areas which were identified as being relevant indicators of women empowerment. These areas were discussed among the women's group. The indicators are;

1. Basic needs fulfilment.
2. Availability of adequate resource base.
3. Health care.
4. Education.
5. Involvement in decision making.
6. Economic freedom.
7. Public participation.
8. Freedom of mobility.
9. Possession of certain qualities.
10. Government support.

Under each one of these headings, five related aspects were listed out. Three point rating scale was used to gather their assessment viz., 'agree. 'disagree', and 'don't know' with scores of three, two and one respectively.

Basic Needs

Under this heading, certain indicators such as fulfilment of essential needs such as food, shelter, work and money for essential expenses are included. The response of the two groups of women members are comparatively presented with its rating.

Table 6.1: Relevance of Basic Needs as an Indicator of Women Empowerment

Sl. No.	Indicators	SHG Women	NSHG Women
1.	Adequate and decent shelter for family members	Agree	Agree
2.	Decent work with a reasonable income and dignity in work place	Disagree	Agree
3.	Adequate money for essential expenses	Agree	Disagree
4.	Adequate food with necessary nutrients	Agree	Agree
5.	Fulfilment of essential needs such as clothing, drinking water, sanitation and energy requirements	Disagree	Disagree

Table 6.1 shows that both the groups of women had agreed that adequate shelter and food is an indicator of empowerment of women. But they disagreed with the statement on the fulfilment of essential needs such as water, clothing and sanitation and energy requirements. On the contrary, NSHG has disagreed with decent work and dignity in work place while SHG has disagreed with the need of money for essential expenses, because they do not consider it as an indicator of women empowerment.

Resources

Resources like good health for child bearing and work efficiency, productive assets, education, skill training and capital assistance for self employment were listed out among the group members as to whether these can be considered as an indicator. They have given their opinion on these indicators.

Table 6.2: Opinion of Respondents on the Relevance of Resources as an Indicator Women Empowerment

Sl. No.	Indicators	SHG Women	NSHG Women
1.	Good health for child bearing and work	Agree	Agree
2.	Productive assets for income generation	Disagree	Agree
3.	Minimum level of education necessary for life	Agree	Agree
4.	Training in vocational skills to augment income	Agree	Agree
5.	Capital assistance for self employment	Agree	Agree

As seen in Table 6.2, SHG and NSHG members have agreed with

all the statements, on good health, minimum education, vocational skills and capital assistance. Whereas the members of SHG have disagreed that productive asset for income generation will be an indicator for women empowerment. Because, they felt that providing assets may alone not be able to safeguard the women to earn their income.

Health Care

Health care is an essential component of women empowerment. Certain broad areas under health care are listed below along with their response:

Table 6.3: Opinion of Respondents on the Relevance of Health Care as an Indicator of Women Empowerment

Sl. No.	*Indicators*	*SHG Women*	*NSHG Women*
1.	Proper health care for common ailments	Agree	Agree
2.	Proper ante and post-natal care with institutional support for delivery	Agree	Agree
3.	Family planning should be done by men	Disagree	Disagree
4.	Small family size with adequate spacing of children	Agree	Agree
5.	Marriage should be conducted only after 21 years	Agree	Agree

Response of SHG and non-SHG group members in Table 6.3 has revealed that proper health care, ante and post-natal care with institutional support for delivery, small family size with adequate spacing of children and marriage after 21 years can be considered as the indicators of empowerment of women. Similarly, both the groups uniformly disagreed with the statement that family planning should be done by men. They expressed that men are doing hard work and hence it will affect their health. Instead, women can do it, felt both the group members.

Education

Education has been considered as one of the most critical inputs of development, especially in regard to the empowerment of people. In the lives of women, education plays a more important role in their empowerment. Table no. 6.4 gives the response of the SHG and non-SHG women on the various levels of education.

Table 6.4: Opinion on the Relevance of Education as an Indicator of Women Empowerment

Sl. No.	*Indicators*	*SHG Women*	*NSHG Women*
1.	Primary/Secondary education	Agree	Agree
2.	High School/Higher Secondary	Agree	Agree
3.	Polytechnic/Technical training	Agree	Agree
4.	Higher education	Agree	Disagree
5.	Vocational skills	Agree	Agree

Members of both the SHG and non-SHG have agreed that education up to school final, training in Polytechnics and Industrial Technical Institutions and imparting vocational skills will be necessary for women empowerment. In respect of higher education as an indicator, whereas the SHG women have agreed that it is necessary, the NSHG women have disagreed. This shows the awareness of Self-Help Group members about the need for higher education as an essential ingredient of women empowerment.

Decision-Making

Decision-making is an indicator which is related to the development status of women. Under this heading, the following statements were discussed:

Table 6.5: Opinion of Respondents on the Relevance of Decision-Making as an Indicator of Women Empowerment

Sl. No.	*Indicators*	*SHG Women*	*NSHG Women*
1.	Select the groom of her choice and marry	Agree	Agree
2.	Number of children/avoidance of sex preference/abortion/female infanticide/family planning	Agree	Agree
3.	Education of sons/daughters	Agree	Agree
4.	Farming/livestock/self employment related decisions	Agree	Agree
5.	Purchase/sale of property/valuable assets	Agree	Agree

The members of the two groups have accepted all the statements in Table 6.5, under the heading 'decision-making' like selection of groom of her choice, number of children to be had, abortion, female infanticide, family planning, education of children, decisions related to farming, livestock, self employment and purchase/sale of property.

Economic Freedom

Economic freedom is yet another important indicator of women's empowerment. The statements under this heading were presented to the group, listed below with their responses:

Table 6.6: Opinion of Respondents on the Relevance of Economic Freedom as an Indicator of Women Empowerment

Sl. No.	*Indicators*	*SHG Women*	*NSHG Women*
1.	Select/reject occupation as per her choice	Agree	Agree
2.	Receive/spend her earnings	Agree	Agree
3.	Borrow/repay loan for domestic purposes	Agree	Agree
4.	Save from their wages/income in Institutional/ private sources	Agree	Agree
5.	Buy materials/valuables for her/her family members	Agree	Agree

Economic freedom in the form of selection/rejection of occupation, spend their earnings, borrow/repay loans for domestic purposes, save their wages/income in institutional sources besides buying materials for her family requirements have been agreed by both the group members (Table 6.6).

Public Participation

Public participation is added as an indicator in assessing the development of women. The statements involved in this heading were discussed to enlist their opinion. They are:

Table 6.7: Opinion of Respondents on the Relevance of Public Participation as an Indicator of Women Empowerment

Sl. No.	*Indicators*	*SHG Women*	*NSHG Women*
1.	Participate in community level activities for public welfare	Agree	Agree
2.	Join women's group and initiate collective activities	Agree	Agree
3.	Vote for a candidate/party of her choice	Agree	Agree
4.	Contest election at panchayat level	Disagree	Disagree
5.	Actively participate in Gram Sabha meetings	Agree	Agree

Under the heading 'public participation', four statements, viz., participation in community level activities, women's group and Gram Sabha meetings and voting for a candidate/party of her choice were agreed by both the group members. They expressed that participation of women in public welfare activities will contribute to empowerment. But they disagreed that contesting in election is an indicator. Because women are compelled to contest in panchayat elections by the men in order to come to power through their women folk.

Freedom of Mobility

Freedom of mobility of women to any place and expression of their views is included as an indicator of women empowerment. The statements under this heading were discussed and their response recorded below:

Table 6.8: Opinion of Respondents on the Relevance of Freedom of Mobility as an Indicator of Women Empowerment

Sl. No.	*Indicators*	*SHG Women*	*NSHG Women*
1.	To articulate her views to family, group and community without fear or hesitation	Agree	Agree
2.	To visit various government/other offices or meet officials for personal, group and community issues	Disagree	Agree
3.	To travel without any support to long distances	Disagree	Disagree
4.	To send girls/women to distant places alone	Agree	Agree
5.	Availability of easy/quick means of mobility (vehicles for transportation)	Disagree	Disagree

Table 6.8 reveals that comparatively, both the self-help group and non self-help group members had agreed to the statements of articulating her views in family, group and community without fear or hesitation and send the girls/women to distant places. Whereas they disagreed with the availability of easy/quick means of mobility and traveling long distances without any support, the self-help group members have agreed that the visit to various government/other offices or meet officials for personal and community issues will empower women. However, the non-self-help group members have disagreed with this view.

Psychological Qualities

Women must have confidence in themselves and hope for progress which takes them to a higher level. They should have the courage to withstand and face any problem. The statements included under this heading and the opinions of the group are listed below:

Table 6.9: Opinion of Respondents on the Relevance of Psychological Qualities as an Indicator of Women Empowerment

Sl. No.	*Indicators*	*SHG Women*	*NSHG Women*
1.	Confidence in self/hope for progress	Agree	Agree
2.	Fearlessness and courage	Agree	Agree
3.	Uncomfortable with inequality/unease at discrimination	Agree	Agree
4.	Protest against atrocities/violence/harassment of women by men	Agree	Agree
5.	Desire for equality of women with men	Agree	Agree

All the statements under psychological qualities have been agreed by the women groups who participated in the discussion.

Government Support

Government support is another important indicator of women empowerment. The government formulates the policies and programmes for women's uplift from time to time.

Table 6.10: Opinion of Respondents on the Relevance of Government Support as an Indicator of Women Empowerment

Sl. No.	*Indicators*	*SHG Women*	*NSHG Women*
1.	Reservation in local panchayat elections	Agree	Agree
2.	Free education for girls in school	Agree	Agree
3.	Welfare schemes for widows/their daughters	Agree	Agree
4.	Legal protection in varied spheres	Agree	Agree
5.	Reservation for women in employment	Agree	Agree

Both the SHG and non-SHG group members have agreed with all the statements under the government support (in Table 6.10).

Based on the ten indicators, discussed among the members of the women group, the scores were found out for each statement. No rating was done to the response 'don't know'.

The scores obtained by the indicators were put to chi-square test. The formula for chi-square:

$$= \sum \frac{(fo - fe)^2}{fe} df_{(r-1)(c-1)}$$

fo = observed frequency
fe = expected frequency
df = degrees of freedom

The opinion scores are taken as observed frequency and expected opinion as expected frequency. The calculated chi-square values for the SHG group and non-SHG group are given below:

Table 6.11: Score Values of Factors Relevant to Women Empowerment

Sl. No.	*Indicators*	*Score Value*	
		SHG Women	*NSHG Women*
1.	Basic needs	4.4	4.4
2.	Resource base	30.0	16.6
3.	Health care	16.6	16.6
4.	Education	16.6	30.0
5.	Decision-making	30.0	30.0
6.	Economic freedom	30.0	30.0
7.	Public participation	16.6	16.6
8.	Freedom of mobility	4.4	5.4
9.	Psychological qualities	30.0	30.0
10.	Government support	30.0	30.0

Based on the scores, degrees of freedom are obtained as 5.99.

The chi-square values are used to frame null hypothesis to accept or reject the indicator framed for empowerment of women.

For example: $H_0 = H_1; H_0 \# H_1$

H_0 = Basic needs is not a women empowerment indicator
H_1 = Basic needs is a women empowerment indicator
(4.4) Calculated value < tables value (5.99)

H_0-accept. So women empowerment indicator doesn't include basic needs (opinion of women).

Based on this criterion, null hypothesis was framed to accept or reject the nine indicators.

Figure 18: Score Values of Factors Relevant to Women Empowerment

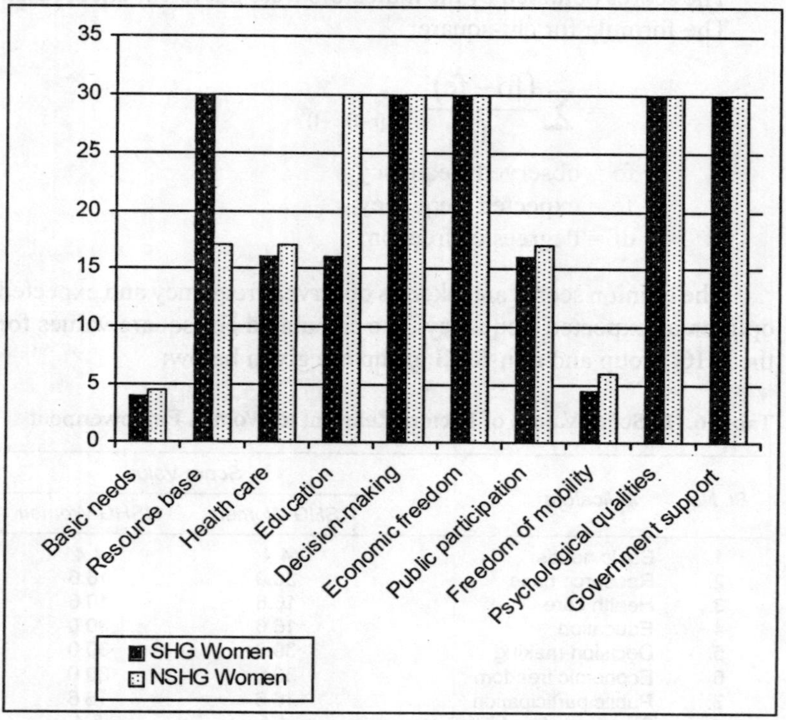

The conclusion given by the hypothesis is that basic needs and freedom of mobility and expression is not an indicator of women empowerment. On the other hand, resource base, health care, education, decision-making, economic freedom, public participation, psychological qualities and government support have been found to be the indicators of women empowerment.

Chapter 7

Perception of Men About Women Empowerment

Status of Women

Women are the world's largest excluded group and the first oppressed group in the history of mankind. Women's oppression is the widest form of oppression in the world, and they enjoy fewer privileges than men. According to United Nations 1991 statistics, women perform 67 per cent of the world's working hours, earn 10 per cent of the world's total income, constitute two-thirds of the world's illiterates and own less than one per cent of the world's property. Even though women make up half of the adult population and often contribute more than their shares to society both at home and outside, they are frequently excluded from position of power.

Though women's economic participation has been increasing, great inequalities remain between men and women in employment opportunities and rights, remuneration and recognition of women's economic participation. In any society, what women and men do varies enormously across the times. Women's work is usually less valued than men's work. If women are traders, trading will be viewed as menial and simple. If men are traders, it will be viewed as difficult and important. This lower valuation of perceived female characteristics and activities result in women being viewed as subordinate to men.

If we could turn to the very basic issue of health and survival, we would find compelling evidence of discrimination against females in many nations of the world. Women make up less than 5 per cent of the world's heads of State, heads of major Corporations and top positions in International Organizations. Women are not just behind men and political and managerial equity, but they are a long way behind. This is in spite of the fact that women are found in large numbers in lower level positions of public administration, political parties, trade unions and business.

Overall, women have fewer job opportunities than men and are disproportionately found in lower paid and less prestigious occupations. They earn far less even when performing the same work as men. Women hold only a small proportion of management positions and are seldom, in the leadership of trade unions, which may explain at least in part, women's weak position in regard to rights such as maternity leave, job security and the provision of social services as child care. Women who work outside the home are still responsible for the domestic work of the household and thus near a double work burden which is an obstacle both to better employment opportunities and to social and political participation.

The Government of India designated the year 2001 as the year of women's empowerment. Consequently, the policies and programmes incorporated the women empowerment component in all its dimensions. The Non-Government Organizations, donor agencies and development activists have also been embarking upon various activities aimed at empowering women. Educational institutions, industrial houses and financial institutions too have joined this mission. The Parliament and the political parties have been debating on giving one-third reservation for political empowerment of women in Assemblies and Parliament. The entire sub-continent is therefore, seized of empowering women in a multitude of spheres such as economic, political, educational, reproductive health and so on.

Concept of Empowerment

By the word 'empowerment' we mean power within. Young states "the term echoes the general emphasis within the mainstream on unleashing the capacity of individuals to be more entrepreneurial and more self-reliant". Empowerment is a process of awareness and capacity-building to greater participation and decision-making power.

Empowerment is an active, multi-dimensional process, which should enable women to realize their full identity and use their powers in all spheres of life. It would consist of greater autonomy in decision-making, greater ability to plan their lives, have greater control over the circumstances that influence their lives, free them from shackles imposed on them by custom, belief and practice (Lakshmi, 1998).

De Beavoir, in her book "The Second Sex", asserts that "one is not born but rather becomes a woman". Gender and sex are two distinct concepts, which explain the causes of subordination of women. Long before the women's decade, cross-cultural research showed that rather than being pre-determined or natural, almost all such perceived characteristics have been shaped and constructed by society. The word 'gender' therefore describes the socially determined characteristics, whereas 'sex' refers to those which are biologically determined. Gender plays a crucial role in developing woman's attitude and defining her roles. Several issues pertaining to women thus originate from 'gender' but not from sex.

Gender is thus defined as social construct, subject to variations across the time as distinguished from sex which is a constant biological factor. Our interventions in empowering women should concentrate more on the gender dimension. In this context, the role performed and status enjoyed by women in society, vis-à-vis the perception of men about women's role and status and their reactions to the empowerment of women assumes significance.

Micro-Study

One of the objectives of the study was to probe into the response of men towards gender discrimination and gender equality. The responses were elicited from men in all the 12 study villages, keeping in mind that there should be no bias with regard to the study, by interviewing women alone, as they may naturally favour gender equality.

The researcher therefore organized 'Focus Group Discussion' in the 12 study villages separately among men who were asked to be articulate and express their views on gender discrimination and gender equality. A small segment of those who gathered at the instance of the researcher, were averse and left the scene and while the larger group stayed back in order to express their views and arguments for and against women empowerment.

A minimum of 14 to a maximum of 19 youth participated in the discussions in each village. The discussions focused on eliminating gender discrimination and promoting gender equality. A series of related questions were put to them and the answers recorded. Each discussion took about of 1½ to 2 hours and their responses are presented here.

Interactive discussion, in focus group situation, with members of local youth groups, operating in the study villages unearthed their views and opinions on certain vital issues listed below:

- Family planning,
- Registration of assets,
- Education of girl children,
- Employment,
- Marriage,
- Freedom of interaction,
- Sex,
- Crimes against women,
- Gender roles,
- Media exposure,
- Equal property rights,
- Reservation for women,
- Legislation for women,
- Self-help groups, and
- Dowry.

Major view points of the respondents on each one of the above issues are highlighted.

Family Planning

The mindset of most of the respondents is tilted in favour of women undergoing family planning, as 90.0 per cent of the groups considered family planning as the women's domain. As a contrast, one group held a different view in this regard. The youth from Marambadi village opined that child birth is the grace of god and men should not tamper with the biology of women.

They were opposed to family planning regardless of men or women. Airing their views on family planning, they advanced the following reasons:

- Men are hard workers, earning their bread, often for the family too.
- By undergoing family planning, men cannot afford to be on rest for long, for post-operative care. But the women can, since they are the prime bearers and carers of children.

None of the groups have advocated family planning for men folk, which unfolds the mental predisposition of men on this vital issue.

Education of Girl Children

Except one group, all the youth groups (90.9%) interacted with felt that education of girls is a must. With higher education, women who have a restricted choice of occupation will largely benefit in diversifying their career options and unleashing their potentials, almost on a par with men. Education, they felt will be the most potent weapon in empowering the women. The group with a dissenting voice (at I. Vadipatti village) cited the wastage of girls' education when they are married or forced to discontinue their studies by their parents under cultural compulsions.

Lack of school nearby, travel to a distant place, poor economic background, and fear of possible love affair which might seal off the fate of their daughter's marital life daunted the parents from continuing their studies, the group felt. On the whole, the large scale preference of men for women's education reveals the changing mindset of men.

Inter-Caste Marriage

More than half of the group members (63.6%) welcomed the practice of inter-caste marriage. In the remaining, 27.3 per cent were opposed, while 9.1 per cent maintained neutrality.

Those who welcomed, added that inter-caste marriages with parents' permission are better. Polygamy, not inter-caste marriage, should be shunned, observed the group. Those who opposed cautioned that it will affect the lives of children in future. They apprehended that inter-caste marriages will widen the communal divide, further the existing communal rivalry and destroy the social harmony. The neutral group felt that it is left to the individual partners and their families to welcome it or condemn it, according to their socio-cultural milieu. All the groups, however, felt that widow remarriage especially among young widows, should be encouraged and that early marriage discouraged.

In sum, we may note that there is an increasing support for the emerging practice of inter-caste marriages and opposition for traditional practice of polygamy.

Sex Preference

More than half of the group members (54.5%) preferred a boy baby while (9.1%) welcomed any child. Respondents advocating male child felt that only the sons take a good care of their parents in their old age. Those opposing it were of the view that parents living in poor conditions, cannot afford to bring up and marry off a girl child even with a minimum dowry, which would again increase the debt burden of parents.

Gender Role

All the group members felt that women should not be given total freedom of work as there is less security for women at work places. The men exercised control over women where they apprehended insecurity or risk for women. Poor people, the men reported, prefer male child more than female child, primarily to avoid payment of dowry, and run into debt. With increasing literacy and growing awareness, there is a slide in the male child preference, the group informed. They observed that there is greater freedom of mobility, articulation, wearing of modern dresses, selection of life partners, participation in decision-making at home and initiating economic activities which were the male domains hitherto, freedom of interaction with boys and voting in elections, all of which would empower women.

Equal Property Rights

Ninety one per cent of the group members were against giving women the right to equal property for the obvious reason that women are given a huge share as dowry. Those who favoured equal rights felt that parents should share their wealth with their children equally, regardless of sex and be prudent in respect of dowry.

Dowry

All the group members acknowledged the practice of dowry but attributed the blame on the bride's side. While demanding action, they suggested that both the givers and takers of dowry should be punished. The members pointed out that almost all the poor and middle income parents give away all or their major wealth and earnings, which works out to more than the share of their sons.

Registration of Property

When asked to comment on the practice of men registering properties in women's name, 90.9 per cent of the groups welcomed this on the ground that it would be safer to have the properties in women rather than in men's name. It will also be a safeguard for women in the event of exigencies of men. In some cases, they practiced this system so that men's liability does not affect their property, especially in respect of alcoholic, gambling and unfaithful husbands.

In the case of one group (9.1%), they argued against this practice on the ground that only the men work hard and acquire properties and that they would not want to borrow from banks/cooperatives in women's name.

Employment

More than 90 per cent of the men did not concur with the proposition that women were working hard and put in longer hours of work. They argued that men can do women's work but not the reverse and hence preferred discrimination in wages in favour of men. One group (9.1%) however differed with the majority opinion and proposed abolition of the system of division of labour, as the women are involved in almost everything that men do.

Crimes against Women

The groups were divided in their opinion towards punishment for crimes against women—nearly half of them (45.5%) proposing stringent punishment for the erring persons, while 54.5 per cent advocating punishment for the erring women too. The proponents wanted the root cause of eve-teasing to be located and eliminated. Wherever the women themselves were found to be responsible as sources of provocation, the men wanted awarding stricter punishment.

Freedom

Nearly three-fourths of the groups interviewed (72.7%) felt that men allow freedom to their wives but they do not go anywhere alone. Similarly, the freedom of articulation is scantily used by women as they have an inherent fear in freely interacting with men. Regarding the freedom of dress, the group cautioned that the women should conform to local norms and should not attempt changes of radical nature.

Another 27.3 per cent of the groups felt that as teenage girls lack experience and maturity in choosing their life partner, it is advisable that the girls/women should not be given freedom. The groups did not encourage interaction of girls with boys. Such a freedom, they apprehended, would gradually zero down to one-to-one contact, which may result in unwanted risks such as teenage sex, unwanted pregnancies, early marriage, young motherhood, abandonment by men etc. Instead, the parents should play an upper hand, remarked the group.

Media Exposure

Eighty two per cent of the men's group interviewed expressed their unhappiness over vulgar exposure of women in the media in seductive postures for the shake of making more money, in total disregard to its impact on youth by the greedy women with attractive physique. The group advocated stringent punishment for such unethical practices. Telecast of these programmes on TV has greater negative impact on the school going children, added the group. They advised that parents should guard their children against watching such channels and programmes.

Reservation for Women

Reservation in civic bodies for women is essential, felt 63.6 per cent of the groups, while 27.3 per cent observed that they were only proxies for their powerful husbands. A lone group opined against reservation for women. Advocates of reservation advanced the argument that women leaders are more honest, not corrupt, sincere, easily approachable and concerned about the community than their male counterparts. Hence, they suggested hiking the percentage, from the existing 33.3 per cent to 50 per cent. They compared the better performance of the women panchayat leaders at present with their erstwhile male leaders. The opponents, on the other hand, revealed that the women are only proxies and their men-folk are the *de facto* leaders, making most of the vital decisions on women's behalf. In one group, the men argued that women, like men, had equal right to contest elections and hence, the question of reservation for women does not arise.

Legislation for Crimes Against Women

All but one group favoured the legislation for crimes committed against women. Women, by nature, bore the brunt of insults and injuries heaped on them by their husbands or in-laws and seldom revealed. Such legislations, the groups felt, would be an alarm to the offenders and a safeguard to women who would dare to expose the unbearable torture and harassment. These legislations would change the course of our cultural traditions of male dominance and female tolerance, and would pave the way for peace and dignity.

One group opposed any special legislation on the ground that the existing crime punishment would be suffice. Alcoholism is the prime cause of men's suppression and violence against women, the group added. Liberal policy on free flow of alcohol and stringent measures against violence against women are diametrically opposed to each other. The group therefore wanted the government to study the underlying causes of violence and strike at them.

Self-Help Groups

Almost all the men's groups interviewed, welcomed the idea of self-help groups for women. After the formation of SHGs, the group informed that there are concrete changes in women's lives. Women have become articulate, aware, active, informed, credit worthy, more caring, and are concerned about domestic activities, besides supporting their husbands. There is a spurt in their participation in the community activities, observed the group and added that they are able to see a visible change in their economic status at home and social status in the community.

Views on Women Empowerment

The various men's groups interviewed, advanced the following views on women empowerment:

- Men did not always treat women as subordinates and secondary, but it is the women who always think that they are vulnerable, and discriminated.
- Government has scores of welfare and development programmes for women but the women evince low interest and hence there are fewer takers for such programmes. Other measures of government for women will have the same fate and hence won't achieve the desired purpose.

The group also asserted that the women are getting empowered on their own and hence there is no need for government or other external agencies to assist in this process.

Obstacles

Pointing out the forces blocking women empowerment, the group listed the society, in-laws, men and the women themselves as responsible for blocking their progress.

The group welcomed empowerment of women in respect of education, employment, decision-making and articulation ability. The success of women in most cases, argued the group, derived from the strength of the men.

Attributes

Attributes such as education, empowerment, courage, self confidence, decision-making power and freedom enabled women empowerment. The barriers included poverty, culture, family situation and neighbours, the groups listed.

Conclusion

Men's group were in support of girls' education, inter-caste marriage with the permission of parents, registration of property in women's name, initially as a safety for the property but subsequently as a safeguard for women against the exigencies of men, expressed their concern against the vulgar exposure of women in the media, advocated reservation for women in panchayats, favoured legislations for crimes committed against women, and welcomed the idea of Self-Help Groups for women.

On the other hand, they were against men undergoing family planning, preferred boy baby over girl babies, opposed giving total freedom to women, blamed the bride's side for dowry and proposed punishment not only for the dowry takers but also for the dowry givers, disagreed with the commonly held view that women work hard and put in longer hours, advocated punishment not only for eve-teasers but also for provocative women, claimed that they give freedom of mobility to women but blamed the women that they do not avail it, expressed displeasure at the vulgar exposure of women and advocated stringent punishment not only for the film producers but also for the artists concerned, observed that women leaders are only a proxy to their powerful male spouses, refuted the claim that the men always subjugated the women and pointed out that not only the men but also the in-laws and the women as responsible for hindering women empowerment.

The above conclusion clearly reveals the stand taken by men with respect to the multitude of women-related issues, which is supportive in certain spheres but opposing in certain other spheres. Wherever they opposed, they justified it as 'in the interest of women, for the safety of women, for the future of women etc'. Secondly, men's fingers were pointed against girls, women, and their in-laws for problems or issues such as dowry, eve-teasing, and registration of property which are traditionally considered to be more male-induced.

We may therefore, infer from the above conclusion that men have always been dominating women and suppressing them wherever and whenever possible. Empowerment of women is not a matter relished but only resented by men. Men's desire to reign supreme over women will hardly vanish in a substantial manner at least in the near future.

Men's views on empowering women from its various dimensions often conflict than they concur; consensus was visible only in socially inevitable issues like education, self-help groups etc. At the same time, there seems to be a beginning of dilution of the hard-line attitude of men in giving women their due share in society. Orientation and sensitization of men therefore should be given an equal importance in our effort to empower the women.

Chapter 8

Summary of Findings and Conclusion

8.1. Purpose of the Study

As depicted under the chapter on Methodology, the study on "Empowering Rural Women—Locating the Deterrents and Determinants" was undertaken with the following objectives:

(1) To assess the status of rural women and locate the deterrents hindering their empowerment.
(2) To evolve a set of determinants of women empowerment through consultations and study their relevance among a cross section of rural women.
(3) To elicit the views of men on the deterrents and determinants of women empowerment.
(4) To make an in-depth analysis of the life and work of select rural women
(5) To analyze the policy implications of these deterrents and determinants to the Government and NGOs.

In order to accomplish the objectives stated, the study contacted five categories of respondents viz.,

- Household women, numbering 600 from 12 villages in six blocks of Dindigul district, selected through stratified equi-random sampling method,
- Experts, academicians and activists (numbering 50, purposely selected),
- Members of youth clubs/groups in all the 12 study villages,

- Self-Help Groups numbering six, selected purposely from Athoor block, and
- Household women purposely selected for case study from among the 12 study villages.

This chapter gives the summary of findings from the responses obtained from the above respondents.

8.2. Findings of the Study

A. Responses of Household Women

Socio-Economic Background

- Respondents largely comprised Hindus (85.0%). Sixty one per cent of the respondents belonged to Backward Classes and Scheduled Castes.
- Seventy three per cent of the respondents hailed from nuclear families, and the rest belonged to joint families.
- Male headed families constituted the majority (85.0%). Female headed families comprised 15 per cent of the respondent households.
- Fifty two per cent of the respondents were aged below 35 years, while the remaining 48 per cent were above 35 years.
- About 37 per cent of the respondents were born as the first child to their parents. Ninety per cent of the respondents were born in rural areas.
- Married women were in majority (74.0%). Among them, 86 per cent of respondents were married at the young age of 14-18 and 18-21 years. Seventy eight per cent of respondents had 'arranged' marriage while the remaining had 'love' marriage. Forty two per cent of respondents married within their close relatives while another 30 per cent had married among their relatives.
- Two-thirds of the respondents were illiterates. Majority of the literate respondents had studied only up to primary and middle levels. On the contrary, among their spouses, only

seven per cent were illiterates, and 82 per cent had middle and secondary level education.

- Sixty four per cent of the respondents had 2 to 5 deliveries. Ninety two per cent had taken ante-natal care from government and private hospitals, including local sources. On the contrary, 77 per cent had not taken post-natal care. Seventy six per cent of the respondents had immunized their children fully. Nearly 70 per cent of the respondents had adopted birth control measures, as against only about 3 per cent spouses.
- Sixty five per cent of the respondents were engaged in farm and non-farm labour activities at present. Prior to their marriage, 60 per cent were engaged in domestic work while the remaining were employed (20%) or studying (19.2%). Fifty six per cent of the spouses of the respondents were engaged in farm and non-farm labour.
- Eight per cent of the respondents had undergone skill training and five per cent of the respondents in leadership and entrepreneurial development training. Fifty six per cent of the respondents have utilized their training. Two thirds of all these trainees were imparted training by NGOs.
- About one fourth of the respondent households had an annual income of less than Rs. 15,000, 36 per cent got Rs. 15,000—Rs. 25,000 and 41 per cent had an income of Rs. 25,000—50,000. Regarding respondents' income, 40 per cent earned less than Rs. 3000, while another 40 per cent earned between Rs. 3000 and Rs. 5000.
- Ninety seven per cent of the respondent households had an annual domestic expenditure of less than Rs. 25,000.
- Three-fourths of the respondents borrowed from private sources while 65 per cent borrowed from Self-Help Groups. Banks and co-operatives catered to over half of the respondents.
- Eighty six per cent of the respondents had a saving of not more than Rs. 5,000.
- Private sources served as the major source of drinking water (55%), toilets were not available in 98 per cent of respondent

households, while electricity was not available in 27 per cent households.

- Basic household amenities were not available in 49 per cent households while no home gadgets were available in 73 per cent of the households.

Status of Women

The respondents played a major role in discharging various domestic responsibilities (80 to 87%) which include:

Care of the sick/disabled	(85.0%)
Collection of fuel wood	(82.0%)
Cleaning of vessels	(84.0%)
Fetching of drinking water	(81.0%)
Washing of clothes	(84.0%)
Fetching of water during summer	(80.0%)
Maintenance of house	(83.0%)

- Men's share was limited to about two or three per cent in respect of fetching drinking water during summer, maintenance of house and collection of fuel wood. Other family members too assisted in all the activities, ranging from 14 to 18 per cent.
- Joint decision by the spouses (84 to 88 per cent cases) prevailed predominantly in respect of number of children to be had, adoption of family planning, education of children, employment of women/children, marriage of sons/daughters and borrowing and lending.
- The spouses decided about spending the respondents' income in the case of 84 per cent households. The respondents themselves decided about voting in elections (23.5%) and participation in Self-Help Groups (20.6%).
- Respondents had greater access and control over ornaments (74.1%). Their spouses had greater access and control over land and livestock (54.0 and 57.0%). Both the respondents and their spouses had greater access and control over self employment infrastructure (50%) and land (34.5%).

- Fifty per cent of the respondents stated that inter-caste and love marriages are accepted by the society, 51 per cent reported that dowry practice has increased and 55 per cent opined that divorce rate has increased. Fifty six per cent of respondents observed that equal importance is given for both the sex in society.
- Majority of the respondents (about 51 to 71%) were aware of the following social legislations:
  - — Bill on violence against women (71%),
  - — Reservation for women in assemblies/parliament (63%),
  - — Regulation of diagnostic tests (54.2%),
  - — Prevention of sexual harassment (58%)
  - — Legislations on prevention of female infanticide (53.7%), and
  - — Eve teasing (50.8%).
- Regarding the present status of women, 51 per cent of the respondents perceived their status as 'secondary' to men, while 44 of them perceived it as 'equal' to men. About five per cent rated them as 'superior' to men.
- When asked as to how the men perceived women's status, 51 per cent of the respondents reported it as 'secondary' to men, while 44 per cent considered them as equal to men.
- Seventy three per cent of the respondents had enrolled as members in SHGs and the rest did not join SHGs.
- Fourteen per cent of the respondents participated in the panchayat elections, of which more than half of them had won.

Opinion on Gender Issues

- Eighty one per cent of the respondents reported that they never had the freedom to travel long distances. About 32 to 35 per cent of the respondents did not have the freedom to choose their employers, plan their budget or vote in elections. Half of the respondents did not have the freedom to refuse their spouse's sexual need when they were unwilling.

- The freedom for participation of women in community activities, strikes/agitations, visit local institutions, government offices, police stations and panchayat offices, articulate in public meetings and interact with men was not available for a large majority.
- Majority of the respondents (80 to 85%) stated that there was no gender discrimination in food, dress, education and health care for children and adults.
- About 13 to 16 per cent of the respondents faced violence against women 'sometimes', while 2 to 3 per cent faced violence 'always' in the form of eve teasing, ill treatment, domestic violence, sexual harassment at work site and alcoholism of husband.
- Between 23 and 30 per cent of the respondents informed that they gained power and influence either 'sometimes' or 'always' in respect of acquiring bargaining/negotiation skills, fighting for women's issues, influence by others and influencing others.

Gender Related Problems

- Twenty per cent of the respondents reported to be facing gender related problems (such as discrimination, violence, alcoholic husbands, separation) and economic hardships (poverty, large family size etc.)
- Eve-teasing (36.2%), lack of education (19.0%), delay in marriage (19.0%) and dowry (16.8%) were reported as the major problems confronting girl children at home.
- Nearly 70 per cent of the respondents realized that both the men and women were the sources of various problems confronting them while another one-fourth attributed 'men' as the source.
- More than half of them informed that they have developed the tendency to bear with the problem (56.0%). In contrast, 44 per cent informed that they will rather overcome their problems.

Empowerment—Constituents and Constraints

- Listing out the various constituents of women empowerment, respondents noted education (51.7%), employment (17.0%), greater freedom (7.7%), and public participation (5.0%) as vital.
- Social factors such as restrictive family members, negative societal outlook, superstition and illiteracy (50.7%) and economic factors such as poverty and unemployment (42.8%) were identified as the major obstacles in empowering the rural women.
- In order to remove those obstacles, the respondents suggested creating awareness and building up courage (59.8%), imparting education and skills (16.4%) and providing employment (11.8%) as instrumental.
- The respondents considered education, employment, articulation ability (8.7%), and acquisition of skills (5.2%) as critical yardsticks to be used in assessing women empowerment.
- Nearly two-thirds of the respondents listed education, employment and freedom as the ideal characteristics of an empowered woman.

Factors Influencing Empowerment

- The level of empowerment of women was studied across a set of independent variables—such as age, birth order, nativity, literacy skill, religion and community, family type, marital status, age at marriage, occupation and standard of living.
- The level of total empowerment score did not vary much between younger and older women. The proportion of women having high empowerment score was 15.9 per cent among older women, whereas it was 12.4 per cent among younger women.
- Combined percentage of medium and high level of total empowerment score across the birth order of the respondents showed that those at the extremes—i.e. early born, as 1st and

2nd child and the late born, as eighth child or above had a slightly higher score of about 93.0 per cent in each category, as against 90 per cent for those born as 3rd to 8th child.

- The level of total empowerment score only slightly varied between rural and urban women. The proportion of women having empowerment score was 14.5 per cent among rural women, as against 11.3 per cent among urban women. Also, the combined score of medium and high level of empowerment for rural women was 92.9 per cent, while it was 88.7 per cent for urban women.
- Among the various categories of literacy levels, 16.1 per cent of middle level (and above) educated women were having high empowerment. This stood at 12.3 per cent for primary educated. The illiterates had an empowerment score of 14.3 per cent.
- Fourteen per cent of unskilled women were having high empowerment score, compared to 13 per cent for skilled women.
- Sixteen per cent of the Hindu women were having high empowerment score compared to six per cent among Christian women. Among Muslim women, 95.8 per cent had medium level of empowerment but none had a higher level of empowerment.
- Nearly 18 per cent of SC/ST women were having high empowerment score compared to Backward Class (13.4%), Forward Class (11.8%) and Most Backward Class women (10.0%).
- Nineteen per cent of nuclear family women were having high empowerment score compared to 12.6 per cent among joint family women.
- Fifteen per cent of married women were having high empowerment score compared to 13.2 per cent for the widows, divorcees and separated and 9.1 per cent for the unmarried women.
- Sixteen per cent of women who married in the age group of 18-21 years were having high empowerment score compared to 11.0 per cent of those who married above 21 years and

10.4 per cent for those who married early (15-18). The 'later married' had higher empowerment score than the 'early married'.

- Eighteen per cent of housewives were having a high empowerment score compared to agriculture labourers (15.6%), non-farm labourers (10.4%) and self employed women (4.5%).
- Thirty four per cent of women with high standard of living were having high empowerment score, compared to those with medium (14.8%) and low standard of living index (11.4%).

B. Views of Experts on Empowerment

Experts comprising professionals, heads of NGOs, academicians, and activists were contacted in order to elicit their views on women empowerment.

Status of Women

Respondents belonging to Hindu religion, backward and most backward castes, PG to Ph.D. qualified categories, and bank account holders comprised the majority. More than half of the respondents possessed typing and computer skills and had the knowledge of driving.

Nearly a fourth of the respondents (24.0%) were born as the first child to their parents, while more than half of the respondents (52.0%) were born as the fifth child and above.

The dominance of men seemed to be more in their parents' family (36%) than in their present family (8%). Both men and women were equally reported to be dominating in their present families (36%), more than in their parents' families (16.0%).

Three-fourths of the respondents opined that women's problems are caused by both men and women. A vast majority (96%) informed that the present status of women is better than before. Nearly two-thirds of the respondents (64%) felt that women's status, compared to men is only secondary. Over half of the respondents expressed that men support the process of women empowerment.

Majority of the respondents proposed instilling of courage and confidence (28%) and building up women's knowledge and skills (28%) at the individual level. Involvement in decision-making (32%) and prevention of violence (28%) was suggested at the family level. At the community level, it was stated that women should be provided with opportunities of training in vocational skills (40%) and allowed freedom (28%).

Dimensions of Empowerment

Nearly half of the respondents informed that a multitude of dimensions—economic, social, political, cultural, education, health and psychological—comprised women empowerment. Among them, economic (40%), social (36%) and educational dimensions (36%) were particularly emphasized by the respondents as vital for women empowerment.

Respondents highlighted the major components of each one of the five dimensions of women empowerment. They are as follows:

- Positive societal outlook and acceptance of women as equal partners in society (44.0%), eradication of social evils (28.0%) and allowing women the freedom of mobility and involvement of women in community organizations (24.0%) were reported by the respondents as constituents of social empowerment.
- Economic independence (36.0%), involvement in income generation activities (32.0%) and ownership of assets with access to micro credit facilities (24.0%) were highlighted as the vital ingredients of economic empowerment.
- Participation of women in election and performance of political tasks (36.0%), and reservation of seats for women in elections (20.0% each) were expressed by the respondents as the major planks of political empowerment.
- Giving greater attention to women's health problems (36.0%), striving for sound body and mind (28.0%), ensuring reproductive rights (24.0%) and safe drinking water, sanitation and hygiene (20.0%) were expressed as constituting the components of health empowerment.

- Providing compulsory education (36.0%) and reservation for women in admissions and acquiring more knowledge and self-confidence (24.0% each) were pointed out as the foundations of educational empowerment.
- In order to accomplish the task of empowering women, education and imparting skills for women (92.0%), providing them with economic support (64.0%) and giving them a better social status in society (56.0%) were suggested by the respondents as the basic strategies of empowering women.
- Regarding the barriers, social (92.0%), educational (44.0%) and psychological barriers (24.0%) were stated as the chief impediments in women empowerment.

Role of Institutions

Responding to the probable role the government, NGOs and Panchayats can play in empowering women, the respondents gave the following views:

- Empowerment-friendly social policies in the spheres of employment, education, health care development (40.0%) economic support programmes (24.0%) and capacity-building programmes (20.0%) were suggested as the major contribution expected of the Government in the process of promoting women empowerment.
- NGOs were expected by the respondents to support the process of women empowerment by organizing training programmes in imparting productive skills (44.0%) and by initiating income generating activities (20.0%).
- Respondents expected the Panchayats to encourage women's participation in panchayat sponsored development activities, and contest civic elections (37.0%) and support government policies (24.0%) in the process of empowering rural women.

Factors Influencing Empowerment

Respondents were given 30 statements and asked to give their response on a three point scale viz., agree, disagree and neutral. The statements belonged to five major categories pertaining to religion and community, typology of family, age and nativity, education and employment and awareness and independence. Their responses are presented in the following paragraphs.

Religions (40.0%) and communities (56.0%) proved supportive in the process of women empowerment. More respondents agreed to the statement that non-dalit communities promoted empowerment (20.0%) than the dalit communities (12.0%).

Women hailing from families which are female headed (68.0%), educated (68.0%), nuclear (56.0%), rich (56.0%) and female dominant (40.0%) were reported to be more empowered. Occupation was not reported to be exercising a greater influence on women empowerment, although women in farming families were informed to be more empowered (20.0%) than their non-farm family counterparts.

Women belonging to younger age group of below 35 years (56.0%), hailing from urban families (48.0%) and those residents of NGO service areas (56.0%) were reported to be more empowered than their counterparts.

Further, women who have had education (44.0%), training (56.0%), skills and employment (56.0%) were reported to be more empowered.

Factors such as women with economic independence (84.0%), mobility (84.0%), organization (76.0%), legal awareness (72.0%), political involvement (60.0%) and interactive nature (60.0%) were pointed out to enable women empowerment.

C. Response of Women Groups on Indicators of Empowerment

Nine areas were identified by the experts as being relevant indicators of women empowerment. Those areas were discussed among two sets of women's group viz. self-help groups, and non-SHG women groups, numbering three each. The indicators include:

(1) Basic needs fulfilment
(2) Availability of adequate resource base
(3) Health care
(4) Education
(5) Involvement in decision-making
(6) Economic freedom

(7) Public participation
(8) Freedom of mobility
(9) Psychological qualities
(10) Government support

Under each one of these headings, five related aspects were listed out. Three point rating scale was used to gather their assessment viz., 'agree', 'disagree' and 'don't know' with scores of three, two and one respectively.

Under 'basic needs', certain indicators such as fulfilment of essential needs such as food, shelter, work and money for essential expenses were included. Both the groups of women agreed that adequate shelter and food is an indicator of empowerment of women. But they disagreed with the statement on the fulfilment of essential needs such as water, clothing and sanitation and energy requirements, as essential for women empowerment.

Under 'resources', both the SHG and NSHG members agreed with all the statements, on good health, productive assets, minimum education, vocational skills and capital assistance as essential for empowerment.

Under 'health care', the response of SHG and non-SHG group members revealed that proper health care, ante and post-natal care with institutional support for delivery, small family size with adequate spacing of children and marriage after 21 years can be considered as the indicators of empowerment of women. Similarly, both the groups uniformly disagreed with the statement that family planning should be done by men.

Under education, the SHG and non-SHG women agreed that education up to school final (from primary to higher secondary education), polytechnic/industrial technical training and vocational education are necessary for women empowerment. On the other hand, while the SHG women agreed with higher education as necessary, the NSHG women disagreed.

The members of both sets of groups accepted all the statements under the heading 'decision-making' like selection of groom of her choice, number of children to be had, abortion, female infanticide, family planning, education of children, decisions related to farming, livestock, self employment and purchase/sale of property.

'Economic freedom' in the form of selection/rejection of occupation, spending their earnings, borrowing/repaying loans for domestic purposes, saving their wages/income in institutional sources besides buying materials for their family requirements were agreed to by both sets of the group members.

Under 'public participation', four statements, viz., participation in community level activities, women's group and gram sabha meetings and voting for a candidate/party of her choice, were agreed by both the group members. They expressed that participation of women in public welfare activities will contribute to empowerment. But they disagreed that contesting in election is an indicator. Because, women were compelled to contest in panchayat elections by the men in order to come to power through their women folk.

Freedom of mobility of women to any place and expression of their views was included as an indicator of women empowerment. Comparatively, both the self-help group and non-self-help group members agreed to the statements of articulating her views in family, group and community without fear or hesitation and send the girls/ women to distant places. Whereas, they disagreed with the availability of easy/quick means of mobility and travelling long distances without any support.

Psychological qualities comprise statement on confidence in self/ hope for progress, fearlessness and courage, uncomfortable with inequalities/unease at discrimination, protest against atrocities/ violence/harassment of women by men and desire for equalities of women with men. All these statements were agreed by the women groups who participated in the discussion.

Statements under 'government support' include reservation in local panchayat elections, free education for girls in school, welfare schemes for widows/their daughters, legal protection in varied spheres and reservation for women in employment. Both the SHG and non SHG group members agreed with all these statements.

Based on the ten indicators, discussed among the members of the women group, the scores were found out for each statement. The scores obtained by the indicators were put to chi-square test. It is concluded that basic needs and freedom of mobility and expression are not accepted as an indicator of women empowerment. On the other hand, health care, education, resource base, decision-making, economic freedom, public participation, psychological qualities and government support have been accepted to be the indicators of women empowerment.

D. Men's Perception on Women Empowerment

Members of youth clubs and groups in all the study villages were contacted in focus group situation, in order to elicit their views on women empowerment. Their response is given in the following paragraphs.

Men's groups were in support of girls' education, inter-caste marriage (with the permission of parents), registration of property in women's name, (initially as a safety for the property but subsequently, as a safeguard for women against the exigencies of men), expressed their concern against the vulgar exposure of women in the media, advocated reservation for women in panchayat, favoured legislations for crimes committed against women, and welcomed the idea of Self-Help Groups for women.

On the other hand, they were against men undergoing family planning, preferred boy baby over girls, opposed giving total freedom to women, blamed the bride's side for dowry and proposed punishment not only for the dowry takers but also for the dowry givers, disagreed with the commonly held view that women work hard and put in longer hours, advocated punishment not only for eve-teasers but also for provocative women, claimed that they give freedom of mobility to women but blamed the women that they do not avail it, expressed displeasure at the vulgar exposure of women and advocated stringent punishment not only for the film producers but also for the artists concerned, observed that women leaders are only a proxy to their powerful male spouses, refuted the claim that the men always subjugated the women and pointed out that not only the men but also the in-laws and women as responsible for hindering women empowerment.

The stand taken by men with respect to the multitude of women related issues is supportive in certain spheres but opposing in certain other spheres. Wherever they opposed, they justified it as 'in the interest of women, for the safety of women, for the future of women etc'. Secondly, men's fingers were pointed against girls, women and their in-laws for problems or issues such as dowry, eve-teasing, and registration of property which are traditionally considered to be more male-induced.

The men therefore love to hold their control over women but at the same time, concede whatever emerged in natural course with the changing times—such as education of girls, self-help group formation and social legislations. Men's desire to sustain the patriarchal system is evident from their response, though there is some change in the mindset of men in favour of women.

E. Findings from Case Studies

Case study respondents comprised Hindus, Muslims and Christians, Caste Hindus and dalits, illiterates and educated, the married and widows, poor, middle and upper income classes and those engaged in vocations ranging from teaching to illicit liquor brewing.

Except in one case (a graduate), others comprised school level educated as well as illiterates. Some women pursued higher education after marriage and underwent skill training.

Most of them were aware of recent social legislations. Many had contested Panchayat elections as Presidents and Ward members and had won.

All of them were employed as wage labourers, in self employment, owned small enterprises or were in low paid services.

Majority belonged to poor families. All of them were married, invariably at an young age. Arranged marriage, love marriage and forced marriage comprised the typology, their percentages in the descending order.

Most of them fought for women's problems and community issues. The forcibly married lady was unable to even fight for her own personal liberty and freedom. All but one woman studied was bold, enterprising and adventurous. Some had fought the police and were in prison too. Most of them were members of Self-Help Groups.

The spouses had similar level of education and economic base. In a majority of cases, their spouses supported them in their ventures. Some women ignored their resisting spouses quietly, while one continues to bear the suppression and tyranny.

Most of them believed that empowerment of women is not to be spoon-fed but should emerge from within or shape up with the available support.

Most of the women enjoyed parental support, except the one forcibly married. One *dalit* woman wage labourer could make one of their five sons an IAS Officer. A caste Hindu woman could come home from her farm alone even at midnight.

Some spouses had the habit of drinking, drug use and gambling. Such spouses indulged in wife beating and abuse.

Most of the women made decisions at home independently. The forcibly married woman's voting choice was also controlled by her drunkard husband and she was prevented from wearing a nighty, with verbal abuses and physical torture.

On the whole, the case studies revealed the presence of self empowered, valiant women in villages and the emergence of enterprising and empowered women from the areas studied. It also throws light on the plight of those who suffered in silence. Empowerment, therefore, need not always be a product of external intervention. Instead, a small segment in the rural belts studied, were found to be self-empowered through inheritance, opportunities and suitable environment.

8.3 Conclusion

Women living in the rural belts of Dindigul, a backward district in Tamil Nadu State, largely represent a poor, illiterate, unskilled and farm dependent lots. Most of these women continue to perform their traditional roles in maintaining the house, collecting firewood, cleaning the vessels, caring the sick/disabled, fetching water, and washing clothes. Transformation in the lives of rural women through transition in their traditional roles is tardy. However, on the decision making front, they have a better score. Respondents with their spouses jointly decided about the number of children, employment of women/girls, marriage, of sons/daughters, family planning, borrowing and lending and spending women's income. But then, the trend reversed in respect of access and control over resources. Whereas their spouses had greater access and control over productive assets, women had greater access and control over their ornaments. Majority were aware of the recent legislations dealing with gender issues concerning women and children. The status of women has thus been promising in some areas but perturbing in other areas.

Self assessment of their status showed that a section of women perceived their status as secondary to men, while another section perceived it as equal to men; a few felt it as superior to men. A substantial segment opined that they did not enjoy the freedom of mobility and articulation and, participation in community activities. Majority had come under the fold of self help groups and a small segment participated in the panchayat elections and many among them won it too. However, a large number felt that there was no gender discrimination and violence against women. Majority of the respondents realized that both men and women were the sources of problems confronting women. Women are thus gradually emerging from their traditional shell and have been joining the hitherto male dominated mainstream.

Highlighting the constituents and constraints of women empowerment, the women listed education, employment, freedom, and public participation as the constituents of women empowerment. On the other hand, social factors such as restrictive family, negative societal outlook, superstition and illiteracy and economic factors such as poverty and unemployment were identified as the deterrents of women empowerment. In order to remove these deterrents, they advocated building up of awareness and confidence, imparting of education and skills and provision of employment opportunities.

Serializing a set of factors which promoted women empowerment, Self-Help Group members informed that religion and community favoured women empowerment. Further, women hailing from nuclear, female headed and female dominant families and those brought up in urban locations were reported to be more empowered. Moreover, women who were young, educated, trained, skilled, employed, economically independent, mobile, organized, legally aware, politically active and of sociable type were reported to be more empowered. Locating the possible determinants of women empowerment, they identified basic needs fulfilment, resource base, education, health care, decision-making, economic freedom, public participation, freedom of mobility, psychological qualities and government support as the basic indicators.

Men's group was supportive to women's issues in certain spheres but opposed in others. While opposing, they justified everything by affirming that they were "in the interest of women, for the safety of women and for the security of women". The men found fault with girls, women and their in-laws for women-centered problems such as dowry, eve-teasing, female infanticide, foeticide and equal property rights. Whereas the men conceded whatever changes were inevitable and were emerging in the natural course (eg., education of girls, self help group formation), they still preferred to hold the reins of patriarchal system.

Case studies reveal the story of both the successful women who persistently struggled to come to the forefront in their communities as well as the sordid plight of women who continued to suffer in the hands of their husbands and the community. In particular, the study found the presence of women who were self empowered, with their inherited qualities and environmental support.

On the whole, findings of the study revealed that a solid base had been formed in the rural belts of the study area, through Self Help Groups which provide a congenial atmosphere for enlightening and empowering the rural women. Rural women who were, for long, treading on the traditional patriarchal track, have slowly but steadily switched over to the female-partnered empowerment track. The pace is slow, obviously because of their poor knowledge, skill and economic base. However, with a concerted drive towards empowerment through external intervention by Government, NGOs, Corporates, and colleges and universities, the pace of empowering rural women could be constantly accelerated.

Chapter 9

Policy Options for Empowerment Intervention

"There is not a single country in the world—not one, where men and women enjoy completely equal opportunities. That is why we must change our attitudes and policies. The aim must be to give each and every human being greater freedom to make choices about their own lives".

—Brundtland, Prime Minister of Norway, at the Fourth World Conference of Women, Beijing, 1995.

Neglected Majority

India is no exception to the presence of gender inequality. We are racing with the world in attaining human development and achieving Millennium Development Goals (MDG). Empowerment of women is a vital ingredient for the attainment of human development goals. Women and children together constitute 65.6 per cent of the India's total population (2001) and account for about 68 crores. Women, as an independent target group, account for 50 crores and represent 48.3 per cent of country's total population as per 2001 census. Rural women comprise more than 72 per cent of total women in the country.

The National Policy for Empowerment of Women (2001) envisages creating an environment through positive economic and social policies for the development of women to enable them to realize their full potential. It has, as its goal, building and strengthening partnerships with civil societies particularly women's organizations

(2001). It is therefore imperative that we devote our maximum attention for the empowerment of rural women. In the light of the present study, certain suggestions have been made which have built in policy implications to the Government and NGOs.

Educational Enrichment

Reducing the gender gap in secondary and higher education would be a focus area, claims the National Policy for Women Empowerment. Literacy status of females was lower (64.6%) than males (82.3%) as per 2001 census. Dropout rate was heavy among girls than boys. Plan of action under X five year plan envisages getting all children in school by 2003; making all children complete primary level by 2007 and reduce gender gaps in literacy and wage rates by at least 50 per cent by 2007. Hence, education of girls should be made compulsory.

Although government is providing free education up to school level, a sizeable number are still out of school. School enrollment figures for girls have been and continue to be lower than for boys at all stages and ages and the dropout rates are also higher for girls at every stage, from primary to high school. Male-female gap in literacy rate stands at 21.69 per cent as per 2001 census. The Gross enrollment ratio (GER) for girls stood at 85.2 in 1999-2000 for primary level but it remained at 49.7 at the middle level. Dropout rate for girls at primary and middle level stood at 42.3 and 58.0 in 1999-2000, more than for boys.

The scenario of literacy in the study area reveals that among the study respondents, two thirds of the respondents were illiterate. Among the literates, a large majority had only primary level of education, whereas among their spouses, 93 per cent were educated, with 77 per cent at secondary level. Women's illiteracy in the respondent households was ten times greater than that of their spouses. Literacy as a powerful tool in empowering women needs to be given special thrust.

In order to strengthen this component, a three pronged strategy is suggested by which the government can

➢ Provide additional incentives for higher education

- Impart compensatory education for dropouts, and
- Attempt compulsory enrollment for non-starters.

Gender Sensitization

Awareness about various legislations among the respondents of the study shows that about 51 to 71 per cent were aware of various existing and proposed legislations related to violence against women, sexual harassment at worksites and reservation in assemblies/parliaments. Though it is encouraging, this needs to be scaled up. Further, regarding the perception of women's status by women as well the men, it was found that 51 per cent of the respondents have rated women's status to be secondary to men.

Perception of rural youth on the various issues faced by women reveals that they supported women in certain spheres but opposed it in certain other spheres. Men's fingers were more pointed against girls, women and their in-laws for problems such as dowry, eve-teasing and property rights. Men therefore tended to resent rather than relish the empowerment of women. The process of empowerment of women therefore needs to draw its strength both from the men and women collectively.

Tenth Plan proposes to change social attitudes and community practices by active participation and involvement of both men and women. The men, especially youth and adolescent boys need to be gender sensitized across the rural areas. In order to trigger changes in societal attitude towards women and the girl child, as the X plan calls it, an integrated media campaign—covering electronic, print and film media, a series of awareness generation programmes and scores of interactive meet between youth and women could be planned in order to project a positive image of both women and the girl child among the men.

On the one hand, the women need to be educated about their legal rights while on the other hand, the men should be enlightened about the power and privileges women enjoy in legislations. The legal adviser proposed for each block, can play a pivotal role in this regard. Such an enlightenment programme would help change the gender biased attitude of men against women and facilitate a discrimination free social environment.

Skill Training

Providing gainful (high quality) employment to the addition to the labour force over the Tenth Plan period is part of the plan of Action for X Five Year Plan. The rural adolescent women are a source of vast potential of skills, talents and capabilities. Tapping these potentials would boost up their social and economic status as well as bolster the economy.

Among the study respondents, it was found that only 8 per cent possessed certain vocational skills of whom only half of them utilized their skills. Aspiration for skill acquisition among rural women and lack of opportunities for imparting skill training in the study areas were found to be low. In the process of empowering women, women need to be equipped with income generating skills.

In order to trigger such a process, Vocational Skill Training Centres may be started in every viable village cluster exclusively for girls and women.

These centres will have to impart short-term training in trades which are viable and could be utilized by the trainees productively in the vicinity. Such centres may be started in large villages, comprising a cluster of village panchayats and small towns nearby. Every centre may choose commonly acceptable trades as well as location-specific trades, unique to the respective regions and cultures. The government may fully subsidize these training programmes and offer a nominal stipend to the trainees, in order to net in all the willing girls and women under the canvas of these training centres.

Training Community Health Workers

Health scenario in the study area has several gaps and short comings. Forty per cent of the respondents have had from three to eight deliveries. Only about one third of them had availed Govt. hospital facilities. Nearly thirty per cent of the respondents had not adopted any birth control measures and about a fourth did not immunize their children fully. Nearly eighty per cent did not take post-natal care. Most of these owe to lack of health facilities and inadequacy of health personnel in their areas.

India's maternal mortality rates (MMR) in rural areas are one of the highest in the world. Nation-wide, only 40-50 per cent of women receive any ante-natal care. During 1998, MMR in India stood at 407 per one lakh live births. The Action Plan aims at reduction of MMR and IMR to 2 and 45 per cent per 1000 live births by 2007 and to one and 28 per cent respectively by 2012. While the sex ratio has increased for all ages, it has declined in the most crucial 0-6 age group, from 945 in 1991 to 927 in 2001 including in most advanced states like Punjab and Haryana. Therefore, economic growth alone does not bring about improvement in the status of women. Poor health and nutrition, female infanticide, foeticide, growing incidence of HIV/ AIDS among women are some of the serious threats to the health of women.

Women neglecting health care are not only among the unaffordable lots but also the ones living in remote and inaccessible areas. Hence the government may consider training of Community Health Volunteers through a 3 months' special intensive training programme (as designed under Rashtriya Sam Vikas Yojana sponsored by the Planning Commission, operational in select backward districts of the country). After training, they may be deployed in remote and inaccessible areas on a priority basis. These volunteers can be trained and posted for every 1000 population.

Legal Enlightenment

Half of the respondents have expressed that dowry problem has increased and 56 per cent informed that divorce rate has increased. Among problems facing the respondents, drunkard husband, gender discrimination, wife beating and separation were cited. In the case of children, they were subjected to eve-teasing. Of late, self-help groups have also been intervening in the domestic issues of members but without proper legal awareness.

National Policy for Empowerment of Women (2001) promotes to make the legal-judicial system more responsive and sensitive to women's needs, especially in cases of domestic violence and personal assault. In this regard, all the self-help groups may be provided with basic legal awareness on the vital legislations pertaining to women and children, dealing with dowry, female infanticide, foeticide, equal property, violence against women, eve-teasing and the like. Each federation of SHGs promoted by NGOs or Government or other change agents, comprising a reasonable number of SHGs (about 100) and encompassing the geographical area of a development block may be provided with a Legal Advisor, preferably a woman. All issues and cases emerging from the members within the jurisdiction may be referred to her, who will pursue all possible options in sorting out the issue starting from persuasion, counseling etc. till filing a suit, under the scheme of free legal aid to the poor. This would contribute to the minimization in gender-related crimes leading to formation of a base for women's dignified living.

Homogeneous Interest Groups

Self-Help Groups are a generic group, comprising both homogenous as well as heterogeneous population across castes, class, residence and other socio-economic groupings such as occupation and education. In these, the routines of a typical self-help group gets repeated cyclically viz., savings, credit, meetings, micro enterprises, exposures, exhibitions, awareness programmes, vocational training, participation in community activities and resolving gender issues keep repeating month after month. In order to make the concept of self help groups more strategic and vigorous, it is suggested that women can be organized in occupationally Homogenous Interest Groups (HIGs) for injecting greater dynamism. For instance, specific groups for landless agriculture labourers, agro-based industry workers, artisans, construction labourers and other non-farm activity workers could be grouped into interest specific exclusive groups. Such a grouping will enable the change agents to provide the following inputs:

- Organize activity-specific skill training programmes,
- Provide awareness to the members on relevant themes e.g. Minimum wages legislation to landless labourers, Plantation Labour Act to plantation workers,
- Impart skill training to the members in advanced tasks in the same trade, undertake efficiency-promoting and economy-intensive activities, and
- Take up economic promotional and welfare oriented activities.

Women's Bank

Liability position of the respondents revealed borrowers from institutional sources (banks, cooperatives and insurance companies) were at the minimum (8 to 11%). On the contrary, 85 to 86 per cent of the respondents had borrowed from private sources and self-help groups. This brings out the need for an exclusive institutional source supporting women's economic ventures.

National Policy for Women Empowerment envisages enhancing women's access to credit for consumption and production through establishment of new, and strengthening of existing micro-credit mechanisms and micro-finance institution. In this regard, Government may consider establishment of Women's Bank exclusively for transacting the SHG operations. Loans and grants allocated by Government for Self-Help Groups may be channelized through these banks. Such Women's Bank should be established at least one in each block. To be manned by all women staff, these banks can deal with the savings, credit, micro enterprise financing and loan scholarship to the children of SHG members, jewel loans, deposits and other financial transactions of self-help groups. In due course, these banks have the potential to grow on a par with the nationalized, commercial and cooperative banks.

Reduction of Wage Disparity

Poverty was identified as the prime obstacle in the empowerment of women. Disparity in the wages between male and female workers serves as the chief cause of low income of women which leads to their poverty. Recent Employment Generation programmes sponsored by the Govt. of India seeks to rectify this disparity.

Reduction of gender gaps in literacy and wage rates by at least 50 per cent by 2007 is part of the plan of Action by X Five Year Plan. The Government of India is adopting equal wages policy under the recently introduced National Rural Employment Guarantee Programme, besides certain other programmes introduced earlier. Similar approach may be followed in all the other sectors of the economy, particularly in the rural agriculture sector where, over three-fourths of the labour force is engaged. Non Government Organizations (NGOs) and Trade Unions have a greater role to play in this regard.

Higher Development Allocation

Government of India has scaled up its budget for women's component plan (WCP) from 25.5 per cent of gross budgetary support (GBS) in IX plan to 42.9 per cent in X plan, allocated to 15 women related ministries-departments. This highlights the increasing importance given to women. In recognition of the diversity of women's situations and in acknowledgement of the needs of specially disadvantaged groups, measures and programmes will be undertaken to provide them with special assistance. Select development programmes sponsored by Government of India and State Governments provide for up to 40 per cent of benefits for women. Experience reveals that when national indices of development show a rise, the benefits of these developments do not percolate in equal measure to men and women. Women often ended up receiving less than their commensurate share. Hence, Government may make it mandatory that all the grass-root level development programmes should allocate 50 per cent of the benefits for women.

Political Space

Space for women in politics has been less and has been monopolized by men. Women hold only 10.5 per cent of the seats in the world's parliaments. Women who constitute nearly half of India's total population, enjoy 33 per cent reservation in panchayats, but occupy only 26.6 per cent positions (2001) in reality. In Parliament, they represent only 8.5 per cent of the total members of parliament. However, their number is growing. The percentage of female cabinet ministers worldwide has doubled in the last decade from 3.4 in 1987 to 6.8 per cent in 1996.

Women's stake is thus improving, with more women becoming literate, employed, organized and utilizes their capabilities to their full capacity. Self-Help Groups have permeated into the nook and corners of our countryside and have promoted budding leaders. The trend of women shying away from public life and the practice of proxy leaders is gradually waning and instead, getting reversed too. The women of today are vying with each other (e.g. among different SHGs within one village) for contesting ward membership and panchayat presidentship.

The number of women in higher education has increased from 33.0 per cent in 1990-91 to 39.8 per cent in 1999-2000. The 73rd Amendment provided for 33.3 per cent to women, when the female literacy rate was 39.42 (1991 census). With 54.28 per cent female literacy in 2001 census, and over ten lakh self-help groups successfully operating in the country, government may revise the percentage of reservation for women. Tenth Five Year Plan proposes to provide equal access to participation and decision-making for women in social, political and economic life of the nation.

National Policy for Empowerment of women advocates women's equality in power sharing and active participation in decision-making, including decision-making in political process at all levels to ensure achievement of the goals of empowerment. Hence, it is suggested that the Government may increase the reservation for women from 33.3 per cent to 50 per cent at the ward level from the ensuing panchayat elections and to 40 per cent at the panchayat level for presidentship

Power to the Panchayats

Atrocities of drunkard husbands were cited as the second major problem faced by the respondents. Case studies on women (Annexure 'A') also revealed that women were tortured by their drunken husbands. These experiences underpin the need for eradication of alcoholism from the rural scene.

All forms of violence against women, physical and mental, whether at domestic or societal levels, including those arising from customs shall be dealt with effectively with a view to eliminate its incidence, affirms the National Women Empowerment Policy. However, National Women Empowerment Policy and Prohibition Policy of the government often lead to clash of interests. Reduction in alcoholism and decrease in domestic violence and women related crimes are in conformity with each other. Government may not be willing to forego the revenue by going dry. Hence, the option of opening liquor shops in the jurisdiction of a panchayat may be given to the respective panchayats in such a way that it has to be decided at the Gram Sabha meeting of every panchayat. Wherever the Gram Sabhas vehemently oppose, no shop should be allowed to be opened.

Hence, the power to decide the opening of liquor shops should be vested with the panchayats.

Caring for the Women Headed Families

Wife beating, alcoholism among husbands, and gender discrimination, result in the separation of women from their husbands. Consequently, the number of women headed families is on the rise. Invariably these women land in poverty. Poverty is claimed to be more feminized. The official country report for India presented at the Fourth World Conference on Women at Beijing (1995) observed that the percentage of poor among the women is disproportionately large, necessitating special attention for poor women. Women constitute nearly 70 per cent of the population living below the poverty line and are very often in situations of extreme poverty. Plan of Action proposed by X plan envisages reduction of poverty ratio by 5 percentage points by 2007 and by 12 percentage point by 2012.

National Women Empowerment Policy proposes to make poverty eradication programmes address the needs and problems of women in poverty. It says there will be improved implementation of programmes which are already women oriented with special targets for women. These groups include women in extreme poverty, destitute women, the disabled, widows, elderly women, single women in difficult circumstances, women headed households, etc., lists the Women Empowerment Policy. Households headed by females largely comprise widows, divorcees, separated and destitute and hence, their plight remains precarious. Government may, therefore, pay special attention to the families headed by women and living below poverty line, by extending them the same concessions and benefits on a par with the SCs/STs or by treating them as specially disadvantaged groups, warranting additional doses of support.

Suggestions made above relate to the various aspects of rural women's lives—social, health, educational, skill training, economic, political, legal, domestic violence, organizational, developmental and so on. When translated into action, these initiatives will ignite the process of bringing about drastic transformation in women's lives and form a solid base for empowering the rural women.

Chapter 10

Case Studies on Select Rural Women

1. Introduction

Case study was made on one select woman in each of the study villages, numbering 12. These women were identified for the case study, based on consultations with the respondents and Self-Help Groups in the respective study villages. Women who had struggled and succeeded or strained and suffered in their life were the criteria for selection of women for case studies.

Totally, 12 women were identified using an interview guide. Upon drafting, two cases whose life and work largely resembled the others among the remaining 10, were dropped for brevity. Women who were included in the study hailed from the following village panchayats of Dindigul district.

No.	*Name of the Case*	*Village Panchayat*	*Block*
1.	Ms. Jayalakshmi	Pithalaipatti	Athoor
2.	Ms. Kasthuri	Periapallapatti	Dindigul
3.	Ms. Pappathi	Periakottai	Dindigul
4.	Ms. Kalpana	Mattapparai	Nilakottai
5.	Ms. Pushpam	Nakkaluthu	Nilakottai
6.	Ms. Maheswari	Markampatti	Oddanchatram
7.	Ms. Amutha	Morepatti	Vadamadurai
8.	Ms. Thangamma	Puthur	Vadamadurai
9.	Ms. Bibi	Marambadi	Vedasandur
10.	Ms. Karupayee	Koovakkapatti	Vedasandur

2. Case Studies

2.1. A Fearless and Literate Farming Woman

"When a woman moves forward, the family moves, the society moves and the nation moves".

—*Swami Vivekananda.*

In Pithalaipatti, a village in Athoor block of Dindigul district, Ms. Jeyalakshmi (49), a graduate degree holder stands out from all other women. All the people here belong to Hindus. The dominant caste is *gounders* and *servai*. Jeyalakshmi belongs to the *servai*, a most backward community. Generally, servai community people living in this region are known to be bold and belligerent and hard working.

Jeyalakshmi's husband died after 18 years of married life, which was a great loss to her. Since then she has been heading the family. Being an educated lady, she did not lose hope after the loss of her husband, but kept doing farming, which her husband pursued earlier. She has a son (23) who has completed technical course in ITI (Industrial Training Institute). He is not interested in farming but wanted to start an industry with the help of his mother.

Jeyalakshmi, the third daughter to her parents, wanted to continue her studies even after marriage, but was refused by her husband. She comes from a rich family and so is her husband. They have about 25 acres of land and have cultivated coconut trees, which turn out a good yield and more income. There is none to maintain since her son avoids farming. She has been alone, and without any help from any others, has been managing all the operations. She is not in any SHG but is very bold and courageous.

She has been saving both in the bank and co-operatives. She termed insurance as a waste, as she will not be able to enjoy the fruits by herself. She has all the home gadgets like any typical urban family. Her way of dressing and style is different from all others in the village. She wears saree but has dressed her hair into a pop style. She travels even at night fearlessly like a man.

After getting his son settled, she wishes to spend her time in the field. She does not like wasting time and intends to spend in developing her farm. She says she will only guide her son but not interested in advising him, as he is a grown up adult.

One of the reasons for Jeyalakshmi's courage and development is her family background. All her relatives are well educated and employed. Her parents and family members never restrict her freedom as a girl child. There is no gender discrimination in her family but treat both the sexes equally. They repose faith in the children's ability to grow independently and be strong and self reliant in their life. Economic strength, family brought up and her personality composition are the major factors which have contributed to her empowerment.

2.2. A Progressive Petty Shop Woman

"Just as a bird could not fly with one wing only, a nation would not march forward if the women are left behind".

—Swami Vivekananda.

In Periyapallapatti village, the women have been neglected in the process of development, and only a secondary role is assigned to them. However, in the present case, Ms. Kasthuri played a dominant role and developed her family among the villagers. Ms. Kasthuri, born as the fifth child to her parents, belongs to a backward community in the Hindu religion. Born in an urban area of Madurai city, she hails from a nuclear family, and has a girl child of two years. She had studied up to twelfth standard.

Arranged to her close relative, she married at the age of 27. She lived in Tiruppur town (in Coimbatore district) working as a cloth merchant in a hosiery unit where her husband too was working. Poor wage and frequent joblessness drove them to their native village Periapallapatti, near Dindigul town. They lived in a house owned by her father, which had all the basic amenities.

They started a petty shop in the verandah of their house with a low investment of Rs. 15,000 obtained from her father as a loan. Kathuri's father, a retired employee with a monthly pension of Rs. 8,000 supported the family. He had given her 20 sovereigns of gold as dowry at the time of her marriage. Being new to this village, the couple did not get adequate patronage for their business. On an average, they were earning Rs. 50 to Rs. 75 per day. She informed that, till now, they possessed no other skills or capabilities. Kasthuri's husband, with lesser education, is an ignorant type and lacks motivation to earn money. By her sheer hard work and articulation power, she slowly gained more customers. However, there was not enough profit, as many of these locals purchased things from her shop on credit.

When she was in Tiruppur, she was a member of an SHG. She does all the domestic activities and takes care of the petty shop too. She takes all the major decisions and her decision is final. She was aware about the various legislations, bills and welfare programmes for women. She had undergone pre-sex selection diagnostic test through scanning, but she was not informed of the sex of the baby. She got a girl child, now two years old.

The status of her parent's family remains the same, whereas, her husband's family status has improved. Since she is the dominant member in the family, she enjoys full freedom in the family. But then, her husband has been opposing her participation in community activities, public meetings, strikes/*dharna*, visiting police stations, etc. She has been tactfully managing his opposition by participating in these forums moderately.

According to her, "empowerment lies in the hands of women". The women have to come forward on their own to take it up and enjoy the fruits. Empowerment lies in education, employment and freedom of women which should not violate others and disturb others. The major obstacle in empowering women is the dependence of women. "Initially I depended on my parents, now I depend on my husband and later, I have to depend on my children' said Kasturi. Under such a dependent atmosphere, how can women think of empowerment? She asked.

The yardsticks used in assessing women empowerment are character, and performance of women. The ideal characteristics are: education, hard work, decision-making ability, boldness, courage, and self-confidence. These characteristics, which existed in the respondent, helped her to exercise her rights against the odds and get through in life. However, her scarcely responsible husband who discourages her public participation and community initiatives, was reported to be the major obstacle in her getting empowered.

Kasthuri is different from many a women in her village—in her education, exposure, articulation, motivation, initiative, enterprise and public participation. Parents' support on the one hand and her husband's non-interest in family affairs, are perhaps the facilitating factors in as much as it may be an obstruction too. Such an atmosphere has perhaps, provided the required space for this woman to utilize her full potential.

2.3. A Bold Panchayat Member

> *"If you want me to tell you what a nation is like, or what a social organization is like, tell me the position of women in that country".*
>
> —*Pandit Jawaharlal Nehru*

Empowerment of women can be achieved only when women actively participate in the process. Pappathi (27) of Periyakottai belongs to Scheduled Caste and lives in a nuclear family. Born in a remote rural area, she was the first child in her family whose parents have three daughters and two sons. In spite of their poverty, she was educated up to 10th standard. She married her close relative, a repatriate from Sri Lanka through love marriage.

She has learnt tailoring and she is a practicing tailor. Her husband is a casual labourer. She has had two girl children and is in the family way. All her relatives are living closeby, in the same village. Her in-laws and all her relatives eagerly expect and pray that at least the third child should be a male. She foresees a hostile atmosphere in case she delivers the third girl baby.

Both her deliveries were at the Government hospital and she has had both ante-natal and post-natal care for her children, who were fully immunized. Smoking and drinking habit of her husband creates a lot of rift between them. She was the member of Panchayat earlier and is now in a Self-Help Group. Her two children were studying in 6th at Balwadi respectively. Her house is electrified, has all the home gadgets, but no gas connection.

She owns a house, some land, livestock and ornaments. She has borrowed about Rs. 12,000 from a bank to buy a sewing machine from which she was earning. She has a saving of about Rs. 20,000 in the bank. She has been provided with a free house by the government. Her husband took the contract of laying load in their village, which resulted in the loss of about Rs. 30,000. She helped him complete road laying work by pledging her jewels in the bank. Due to their hard work, they could bear the loss and manage to come up in life.

Slowly by hard work, they could build up certain comforts in their house. Envying that they must have made money from the contract, the village people complained to the police about his suspected corruption in the contract. The police investigated and raided their house, causing internal injuries to her husband while enquiring. Pappathi, however stood firm and bold and got her husband released.

Later, she successfully contested in the panchayat election with the support of her close relatives, SHG members and well wishers and became a ward member.

She performs all the domestic chores. Both of them take decisions on all major issues. Pappathi was aware of all the legislations, Bills, policies and programmes. She has been benefited by the Mahalir Thittam and IMRY/RMK.

She had adequate food and health care. But her husband disallows her freedom of mobility, wearing dresses and contesting elections. Without his permission, she cannot do anything. Whenever she dared to go against her husband, he thrashes her. Polyandry is rampant in her village. Hence, she is worried that her husband may leave her any time.

Despite his obstruction and beatings, she manages to participate in all the community activities, public meetings, visit government offices, police station, and articulate freely in the public. She has membership in local institutions. When her husband comes to know of these, he comes drunk and tortures her.

On her own effort, she cultivated paddy, grams and other vegetables in her farm. She had spent about Rs. 10,000 for contesting the election. She attends all the meetings and tries to be perfect in discharging her domestic duties and social responsibilities. She doesn't face any problem in the Panchayat, because it is a reserved area and the President too is a woman.

In her view, the educated women with greater awareness about the day to day activities could be termed as empowered women. She says that her family background and local community serves as the obstacle in her empowerment. Awareness can be made to remove these obstacles. Listing out their ideal characteristics, she said that an empowered woman should be educated, skilled and employed.

Ms. Pappathi possessed almost all the characteristics except education. She is a silver lining in her community and a model for her counterparts in a *dalit* community.

2.4. A Widow in Community Service

The women can stand on their own legs without the interference of any man and she can achieve her utmost effort. This is the case of Mrs. Kalpana in Mattaparai village who was educated up to +2 level and now employed as teacher in a private school.

Kalpana was married at an early age of 17 years. She had a happy married life and gave birth to three children—two girls and a boy.

After about 12 years, she could find a difference in her husband's mental behaviour, which had got changed and affected her deeply. Within a week's time, after this change, he became depressed and committed suicide by hanging himself. She could not recover from this shock and was choked in sorrow.

Her in-laws blamed Kalpana for his death, saying that he died unable to bear her torture. To the already grief stricken widow, this added fuel to the fire. Unable to tolerate, she came back to live with her mother.

Her mother had three children. She lost one son and was living with her elder son and daughter in-law. Her mother, who was working in an Anganwadi, received her daughter warmly and retained with her. After coming here, she joined the local primary school as a teacher. She also started a number of Self-Help Groups and thus became service minded.

As an animator of the Group, she started an income generating activity, selling sarees, garments etc. Though lives with her brothers, she gets along like a paying guest. Her remuneration from teaching and income from garment sales helps her to maintain herself and her children to their maximum satisfaction.

Now she realizes that her husband loved her very much. Even after his mental illness, he sincerely wanted her to take up some jobs and become aware of the day-today development. Since her children were young then, she stayed back. Due to her family compulsions, she now works, earns and achieves in her life, which her husband could not see.

Due to her hard work and self-confidence, she could come up in life and take care of her children. She is known to every body as a person doing social service among the poor and downtrodden. She is in search of a better job which would enable her to actively continue her social service work.

She informed that she was very calm, quite, and a reserved girl before her marriage. But after marriage, her husband enabled her to be bold, confident, courageous and articulate.

Listing out the possible attributes of empowerment, Kalpana pointed out education, self-confidence, courage, boldness, articulation, and freedom which would help women to empower. She stated that society and the in-laws are the major obstacles to empowerment and has still a long way to go in achieving her own freedom and empowerment.

2.5. A Determined Mother

Pushpam, from Nakkaloothu village a mother aged 50, from scheduled caste, is an illiterate, and married to another illiterate person in the early age of 18 years. Both of them eked out their livelihood by daily wages. The couple had five children—three girls and two boys. Since they were illiterates, they educated all their male and female children up to graduation level. All the children availed the scholarship, which minimized the burden of the parents to a large extent. They educated all their children by starving for two times and having food only once every day.

Their house did not have any facilities at the time of their schooling their children, But they struggled a lot. Their fourth boy was very studious, hard working and intelligent. This made the parents to educate him well. He came out with a gold medal in his graduation and post graduation and brought laurels to his college and pride to his parents.

With the aim of passing the Public Service Commission examination, he strived. After attempting twice, he passed the civil service examination and was appointed as the Sub Collector of Madurai district. Pushpam was so delighted and the entire village people felt joyous. Pushpam still continues to work as a labourer for daily wage with the objective of standing on her own legs. She got her son married from a rich family and they were living together in a joint family.

Though her family has all the necessary facilities, she still leads a simple life which brought her to this position. She had borrowed about Rs. 1 lakh for house construction and they have built a comfortable house in the village, with her own earnings.

She wanted to be a unique lady among the villagers. This has been achieved due to her hard work, and enthusiasm in the depth of her heart. Pushpam is a bold and courageous woman. She was having the characteristics of an empowered woman even at the early stages of her life. She wanted to be educated but due to her family situation, she was not able to get education.

According to her, education and employment would contribute to empowerment of women. Suppression by society is the main obstacle for women empowerment at each stage. These obstacles can be removed by education, social awareness, employment etc. She was very happy that she could achieve her goals and realize her dreams.

2.6. A Progressive Woman through Family Support

"Nations which do not respect women can never be great".

—Swami Vivekananda

Maheswari (38) of Markampatti village was born as the 6th child in her family in an urban area. She was married to a person living in a big family having three males and two females. Her husband was the third male member in his family. Earlier, she was living in a joint family but for the past one year, she has been living in a nuclear family. Her marriage was an arranged one, and she was given 10 sovereigns of jewels as dowry. Her husband was educated only up to 11th standard when she married him. But Maheswari had studied up to 12th standard. After marriage, she pursued her studies and completed her graduate degree with the help of her husband. Now she is employed as a Noon meal organizer and a coordinator in an NGO called World Vision. Her husband is running a lathe. She has the vocational skill of preparing bags, purses etc.

She gave birth to two male children who are now 17 and 12 years old respectively. They are studying in school. She lives in a rented house. She has constructed a house worth Rs. One lakh in Oddanchatram, a nearby town, by availing housing loan in her name. She has all basic facilities in her home. She leads a comfortable life. She delivered her children in private hospitals and had adopted family planning. She gave pre-natal and post-natal care to her children. Her husband has the habit of drinking.

She organized a SHG in her village and she is also a member of this group. She was heading *mahalir mandram* in her village, which has now been converted into a Self-Help Group. Maheswari is also functioning as a Recurring Deposit agent and canvassing among the people for depositing in Recurring account in the post office. She has independently saved Rs. 25,000 so far. She is the only salaried employee in her family and she is managing the house largely.

Her parents didn't give her freedom to move and she suffered a lot in her home as she was the sixth child. She had many a worries and did not have educational freedom. However, her husband gave her full freedom of mobility, articulation, dressing, and decision making. Her in-laws, co-brothers and co-sisters also gave her moral support to develop her in the community.

She has the full deciding power in the family and her husband, though an alcoholic doesn't harass or control her. She wants to continue her studies and has appeared for a number of government examinations. She now expects a good job with good salary. She is aware of all the legislations/bills and programmes.

She has undergone various EDP trainings, accounts keeping training and record maintenance training, leadership training offered by the NGO. She faced no gender discrimination at her home and she enjoys greater freedom. Whenever she visited government offices and her NGO, she invariably comes late in the evenings. But the family members, husband and children adjust themselves and supported her in her work.

She has often visited government offices, police stations, panchayat offices, participated in *dharna*, agitations, community activities, and meetings. She wanted to contest in election but the reservation decided, but the village leaders decided to allot it only for the women belonging to Gounder community. She has fought against Panchayat to get adequate water supply. Panchayat has allotted Rs. 1 lakh for construction of public toilets and toilets in the school largely due to the efforts taken up by Maheswari and her NGO.

She asserted that empowerment of women is not something that is offered by others but it should be acquired by the (women) themselves. Empowerment of women, according to her, can be achieved by education and employment. Women themselves are the obstacles in women empowerment, claimed Maheswari and advocated provision of education and awareness in order to remove these.

She outlined the yardsticks used to assess women empowerment which could be self-confidence, education, boldness and courage, good habits, good health, income etc. She wanted all the women to be empowered. She commented that 1/3rd reservation in Assembly/ Parliament is not sufficient because women deserve a greater share as they comprise half of the population.

She suggested that men and women should be equal and each other considered the better half. Since her husband is a supportive partner in her empowerment. She claims that she has achieved many a things and intends to achieve a lot more in future. She is not only an empowered woman but also wants to have many other women empowered.

2.7. From a Dependant to an Independent Panchayat Member

> *'If you want me to tell you what a nation is like, or what a social organization is like, tell me the position of women in that country".*
>
> —*Jawaharlal Nehru*

Amutha (39) from Morepatti village belongs to Hindu religion (Vellala Gounder Caste) and lives in a nuclear family. Her education was only up to fifth standard. She had been married at the early age of 15 years and her husband, a tailor, is her close relative. They have three children.

She is self-employed and manages a petty shop. She is leading a comfortable life. She delivered all her children at home and she has undergone the permanent method of family planning. Her husband has the habit of smoking and drinking. She contested the civic elections and was elected counselor, defeating a number of male contestants. She became popular since then.

She had borrowed about Rs. 50,000/-from a private money-lender for her election. Besides her official role in the Panchayat, she performs all her domestic duties. Both the husband and wife jointly decide about their family matters.

She is aware of the various legislations, policies and programmes of the Government out of her personal interest. She had not undergone any training programme. She entered into election, through her husband's influence but out of her hard work she is shining well. In the process of contesting and canvassing in the election, she had become bold and courageous.

She has a number of innovative ideas but her husband does not allow her to apply or give a trial in her work. Slowly, she has been allowed to do all her Panchayat responsibilities by herself without her husband's botheration. She wants her village and panchayat to be the best in the district.

Her panchayat president being a lady, both of them plan together with an young team of ward members. She had undertaken many developmental activities. So, the village people have been very much influenced by her work and are satisfied with her performance.

The counselor, in her own interest, had started Self-Help Groups in the village with the help of non-governmental organizations. Though educated up to only fifth standard, she has become aware of all the governmental activities with the help of her husband. Discrimination prevailed in their home between men and women and boy and girl. She has the freedom to decider about all aspects at her home.

Her concept of an empowered woman refers to the women who have savings in their account. Illiteracy and lack of skills and abilities serve as the obstacles to women empowerment but they have to be removed by training and continuous awareness. Employment, savings and skills could be considered as the yardstick to assess women empowerment.

2.8. A Woman in Fetters Thro' Forced Marriage

"In passing also, I would like to say that the first time Adam had a chance, he laid the blame on women".

—Nancy Astor (British Politician)

Women are the most vulnerable and weaker sections, which are considered secondary to men and are very much discriminated. This has been true in the life of the Thangamma (24) belonging to a backward caste in Hindu religion. She comes from a nuclear family, has had no education and has been married at the age of 15, when she was not fully aware of the marriage. In fact, since she was good looking and pretty, her husband kidnapped her from her home by drugging her.

She had to unwillingly marry him since he forcibly lived with her for two days. It was a force of circumstances and she had to live with him. All her dreams of marrying a charming person got shattered because her husband was a rustic farm labourer. Her parents were poverty stricken and illiterate. They could not and did not prevent their marriage. Nor could they afford to have their daughter with them in the event of disintegration of her family. Under these compulsive circumstances, Thangamma has been living an unwilling life everyday.

She had been working as a labourer. Her husband is also a labourer, but he rarely gets work because of his angry nature in the village. In this situation, she delivered five children—three daughters and two sons in the consecutive years, hoping that her children will take care of her during her old age. Her husband would never allow her to undergo family planning because he suspects that it would result in destroying her sexual urge. On her part, she was given the impression that undergoing family planning operation will lead to her death.

She feels that her future lies in her children's future. She wanted all her children to be educated and get employed. She lives in a hut with a single light (free service). Her husband doesn't provide the family with basic necessities. Thangamma purchases every thing from her earnings. His habit of smoking, pan chewing and drinking eats away whatever little he earns. He was earlier drinking but, as the village had the restriction to drinking, he stopped it. Since he was smoking, drinking and chewing pan without adequate earnings, his peer group teased him for his irresponsible behaviour. His friends had told him, before marriage that he will never be able to marry. Hence, he had kidnapped his wife only after such insults by his friends that nobody would give away their daughter and he would never as be married in this birth.

With all these difficulties, Thangamma has been running her family with her hard work and meagre earnings. Despite these, she has never borrowed nor does she have any savings, since she has to spend on all her five children and her wastrel husband. She does all the domestic activities besides her wage labour. All decisions are made by her husband authoritatively. Due to her ignorance and illiteracy, lack of awareness and lack of knowledge, she was not aware of any government programme, or legislation.

She had never experienced any freedom in her life. She has not been allowed even to wear a nighty by her husband. When only once in her life she wore a nighty, her husband abused her saying, that she was wearing such a dress in order to attract other men folk. She was very much depressed by this and since then she never wears any modern dresses. She doesn't have freedom to refuse his physical needs even when she is sick and unwilling. Nor does she have the freedom of voting in elections to candidates/parties of her choice; she must only listen to her husband's choice.

Even if she tries to violate, she would become nervous and reveal easily, the consequences of which be further torture. Hence, secret ballot system serves no purpose in Thangamma's case. She has been terrified and threatened so much by her husband that she would never dream of violating his commands and compulsions.

He has restricted her interactions with other women, not to talk of men, unless warranted and with only unsuspectable persons. He has not allowed her to join Self-Help Groups. Her husband shows clear discrimination between male and female children at home. But she was unable to pour out her feelings with the female Investigators, to come out of her shell and lead a free, fearless and independent life. Obviously she is afraid of dire consequences, from her husband since it would affect the future of her children.

According to her, empowerment of women means education, articulation and boldness. The obstacles to women empowerment are suppression, poverty and family situation. This can be removed by making them aware of the empowerment of women and create employment opportunities for them. Education, freedom of mobility, articulation ability, boldness, courage, employment, and savings constitute empowerment of women, according to Thangamma.

She wants all her girl children to be educated and wants that no other woman should ever face her hardships and torture. During the course of her suffering, she has gained some knowledge and managed some courage. She laments "what is the use of these at this stage? My entire youthhood is destroyed and I now look forward to the future of my children".

2.9. A Woman in Pursuit of Communal Harmony

Bibi from Marambadi village is a bold lady in this village. She is the only woman fighting against women's issues in this village. Every body in this village needs her help whenever there is a problem. She had contested in the last election, but could not spend much because of her poverty. She dislikes wastage of money. The other lady from a rich family won. She believes that she would win the next election, because of her social service and the ineffective role played by the incumbent members.

Her father is a retired teacher and her mother a housewife. She is the third child to her parents. Her brother and sister work as agriculture labourers. Bibi had studied ninth standard. Soon after her studies, Bibi married an illiterate person. Their marriage was a love marriage. Her husband gave more freedom to her. She had two children—a boy and a girl. Now her son had finished his twelfth standard and is employed in a private company. Her daughter is studying in eleventh standard at a local convent.

She participated in all the Panchayat meetings. Since her's was a love marriage, she fights for love marriages. Wherever there is a problem she also helps to solve certain problems and get injured or sick or need health care. When she contested the last year's election, although the local village people voted for her, the neighbouring village people supported the rich lady for monetary attractions. Bibi has been in the women's *sangam* for last two years. She got loan from the *sangam* and repaid it soon. Since others did not repay, she left the *sangam*.

Her husband encourages her community activities, but sometimes quarrels with her. Her son is against her public participation. Her husband brews and sells illicit liquor. She also helps him in the process of preparation. When her husband was arrested by police, she had got him on bail by arguing with the police at the station. When she was arrested by the police, and jailed for one night, her husband took her on bail. Since her imprisonment, she went to the court and won her case. Since then, she has stopped preparing illicit liquor.

Her father and other as well as her brothers and sisters were not bold. But her grand mother was very bold and she would punish all those indulging in mischief and misdeeds. Her parents had given more freedom and consulted her on each and every matter. Without her consent, nobody would do any thing. She thus got encouragement from parents as well as her people who supported her in her public activities. Except her illicit liquor activity, everybody had praise for her.

Though most of the people had good opinion, on her public service activities, a small segment did not like her due to her quarrelsome nature. In the midst of all these, Bibi has helping tendency. Her boldness is due to her heredity and family support. But economic status and education wise, she derived little strength. Her pursuit of an illegal activity, higher income from this trade, opportunities of interaction with people with varied background and confrontation with the police has also been a source of her strength.

2.10. A Woman in the Service of Community

> *'When a woman moves forward, the family moves, society moves, and the nation moves"?*
>
> —*Swami Vivekananda*

According to the saying of Swamiji, there is a woman in the village of Koovakkapatti who has developed not only herself but also her village.

All the people in Koovakkapatti village belong to Hindus. The dominant caste is *Maniakarar* and *Pillai*. The respondent of this case study belongs to the *Pillai*, a backward caste.

Karuppayee (38) hails from a nuclear family. Her husband (43) had education up to fifth standard and has been working as coolie. She has only one son (25), who is married and has two children—a boy and a girl.

The respondent was the fifth daughter to her parents which made her to limit her family size and work hard so as to come up in life. She had studied only up to sixth standard. Resident of the same village, she married a person belonging to the same caste, not familiar earlier.

The respondent was more eager to learn things but the parents, due to their poverty, stopped her from schooling. She got married at a very early age of 16 years, soon after her puberty, which made her more desperate. Fortunately, she had an understanding husband who took good care of her and made her life pleasant.

The great struggle she faced in her life made her to limit the number of children to just one, due to poor background. Her in-laws also insisted on her to have a small family. Her father gave 10 sovereigns of jewel as dowry during her marriage. Since she suffered harassment from her in-laws, she settled with her own family and started leading a happy life.

She felt very happy when was made the secretary of the local Self-Help Group organized by an NGO operating in this village from the nearby town. The group with 15 members has been successfully functioning for the past seven years. Before joining SHG she had borrowed Rs. 10,000 from a private money-lender at 120 per cent interest rate. After joining SHG, she got internal loan and repaid her private debt in full. She is now free from debt from private sources.

She was not having good articulation ability earlier. But after joining the SHG, being the secretary, she had to address the members in weekly meetings, and present the group proceedings in the block level coordination committee (BLCC) meeting held at the Block Development Office every month. She became more bold and courageous after joining SHG. She actively participated in strikes and agitations. She led the *dharna* at the Panchayat union office, Koovakkapatti demanding water facility to the village and then to the District Collector at Dindigul. The respondent, along with other members, fought for basic issues like street lights and also hand pumps.

As a result, the Panchayat took initiative to put up bore well at Alagapuri dam—two kms away from the village and pumped water to the overhead tank in this village. Now, the village has 24 hours water supply even during summer. Under her leadership and initiative, the members fought for site allotment to the SCs and got it registered in their names. The adage "Behind every man's success, there is a woman" should be changed in the case of Mrs. Karuppayee, as behind her success, there is a man—her husband, without whose cooperation and understanding, nothing can be done. He supported her in all the spheres and he helped her in every walk of her life.

3. Summary of Case Studies

Jayalakshmi, an educated, bold, modern, enterprising and enthusiastic widow, managed her husband's farm alone, fearlessly. From her farm, she comes home alone even at midnight as dreamt by Mahatma Gandhi. Good parental family background, discrimination free brought up, non-interfering son and her sportiveness have made Jayalakshmi in the present form, looked at as a model by her fellow women.

Empowerment of women lies in the hands of women themselves said *Kasturi* and added that dependence of women is the major obstacle in empowerment. Education, work experience, parental support, persistent efforts, public participation, awareness about social legislations and previous stint with Self-Help Groups and a non-interested (in families affairs) but a strict spouse made Kasturi to come up in life and stand out among other women.

Pappathi, a School educated *dalit*, from a poor family, with a suppressive husband said that the family background and local community are the major obstacles to women empowerment. With an alcoholic husband, two girl children and awaiting a male child for anxious relatives, she had undergone trials and tribulation against the local community, but stood firm, succeeded and became a ward member in the local panchayat. Surely, she is a silver lining for a scheduled caste.

Calm, quite and a reserved girl *Kalpana*, became bold, confident and an articulate lady after marriage, encouraged by her husband, who later committed suicide. Parental support, placement as a teacher, participation in SHG activities, income generating activities and her flair for social work made her into an independent and dignified woman, with courage and hard work.

Suppression by the society is the chief obstacle to women empowerment, said *Pushpam*, an illiterate *dalit* from a poor family. Married another illiterate early in her teens, they had five children but educated all of them, by starving and struggling, which fructified with one of her sons becoming an IAS. Despite this, she continued to work as an agriculture labourer and serves as a champion of poor women.

Empowerment of women is not something that is offered by others, but it should be acquired by the women themselves, said

Maheswari. With school final education, her job as a Noon Meal Organiser with an NGO, participation in SHG, and her public contact through small savings schemes, she was comfortable and allowed greater freedom by her husband, which was refused at her parental home. Allowed to pursue higher education, she has been awaiting better jobs through competitive examinations. Aware of various schemes and legislations, she has undergone skill training in series of trades and actively participates in all community activities; thanks to her husband.

Amutha with primary education married her close relative at 15. With three children, she planned her family and participated in civic elections successfully. Her husband was very supportive and they took joint decisions. She was very innovative but restricted not to be adventurous. Despite this, she successfully struggled for a multitude of basic amenities for the community. She was well aware of legislations and schemes. She has been gradually becoming independent of her husband and takes decisions at home too.

Thangamma, a pretty looking poor, illiterate, *dalit* girl was kidnapped by a rustic relative and forcibly married at 15. With five children, husband not working, but smoking, drugging (and formerly drinking too), she bore the entire domestic burden including paying for husbands habits. Despite this, he took all decisions, prevented any interaction with other males, restricted her dressing pattern, compelled her voting choice, prevented her to do family planning and participation in SHGs, and used her only as a sex object, an income raiser and a child bearer. He discriminated his daughters. She has thus been soaked in suppression.

Bibi was born bold, reportedly inheriting her grandma's boldness. Grown up in a democratic manner, she was wedded to an illiterate through love marriage. She assisted her husband in illicit brewing of country liquor and both had faced imprisonment. She had courageously fought with police, drunkards and rowdies. Member of Self-Help Group, she quit due to non-repayment of loan. She had taken up all public issues and vehemently fought for it. She successfully contested panchayat election as President in 2001 election and has been accomplishing tough tasks benefiting the community, including bridging the caste Hindus and *dalits*.

Karuppayee, from a poor family, primary school educated, married another poor, less educated husband at 16. With her entry in an SHG, participation in public activities and taking up community issues, she championed for public cause and achieved in plenty. The community salutes her and she says she owes it to her very supportive husband.

D. Case Studies

The case studies, made from among the sample village respondents revealed the presence of plethora of personalities in the poverty stricken families. Illiteracy, poverty, early marriage, and societal suppression constituted the features of women, with exceptions of an educated, and a rich woman among them.

Parental control, lack of skill, social restrictions, cultural compulsions and curtailment of freedom restrained some of the women from becoming progressive. Yet, there were women who had inherited boldness, democratic brought up, unfettered freedom, acquired courage, and determination which made them to be enthusiastic, enterprising, innovative, adventurous and aware.

Some successfully contested civic elections, a few participated in Self-Help Group activities, actively involved in social work, took up community and gender issues and fought for social justice and societal transformation. One woman was engaged in illicit liquor brewing and bravely fought with the police and anti socials. Emerging victorious on the public front, such women took decisions at home both jointly as well as independently.

A poor *dalit* mother who educated five of her sons and made one of them an IAS Officer, continued her agriculture labour. Widowed, abandoned and separated women continued their struggle to steer their life and succeed too. A forcibly married woman continued to suffer the tyranny of her torturous husband. She was treated as a sex object, an income raiser and a child bearer by her wastrel husband. There was a bold woman who manages her farm and frequents her home all alone even at midnight.

"Empowerment of women is not something that is offered by others, but should be acquired by the women themselves", said a woman. "Empowerment lies in the hands of the women themselves", asserted another. Dependence of women on all others is the major obstacle. "Suppressive husbands, restrictive community, poor family compound the process of curtailing the growth of women", noted the other.

Case studies of these women revealed the story of both the triumphant women as well as those who were in travails. The study has unearthed the fact that rural areas house women who were born or became empowered due more to their inherent strengths than through external intervention. An analysis of their assertiveness reveals that empowerment is not a product to be manufactured only through external inputs but it is a process which could be facilitated through fortification of factors supportive in their existing socio-cultural fabric.

Bibliography

Books

Adams, R. (1996). *Social Work and Empowerment*. London: Macmillan Press Ltd.

Banu. (2001). *Tribal Women Empowerment and Gender Issues*. New Delhi: Kanishka Publishers and Distributors.

Bernard, J. (1971). *Women and the Public Interest*. Chicago: Aldine.

Blumberg Re, *et al.*(Eds). (1995). *Engendering Wealth and Well Being: Empowerment for Global Change*. Boulder: West View Press.

David, N. & Loganathan (Eds). (1993). *Women and the Economy, Women Under Five Year Plans*. Madras: Department of Economics, Mother Teresa University.

Durkheim, E. (1987). *Suicide*. New York: Free Press.

Enerett, J. & Savara, M. (1994). *Women and Organizations in the Informal Sector*. Bombay: Himalaya Publishing House.

Fetterman, D.M. (2001). *Foundations of Empowerment Evaluation*. New Delhi: Sage Publications.

Francis, D. & Young, D. (1995). *Improving Work Groups: A Practical Manual for Team Building*. New Delhi: S. Chand & Company Ltd.

Giri, M.V. (1998). *Emancipation as Empowerment of Women*. New Delhi: Gyan Publishing House.

Goldthorpe, J.E. (1977). *The Sociology of the Third World—Disparity and Involvement*. London: Cambridge University Press.

Hall, C.M. (1992). *Women and Empowerment*. London: Hemisphere Publishing Corporation.

Indiresan, J. (2002). *Education for Women's Empowerment—Gender-Positive Initiatives in Pace-Setting Women's Colleges*. Delhi: Konark Publishers Pvt. Ltd.

Kalam A.A.P.J. & Rajan, Y.S. (2002). *India 2020—A Vision for the New Millennium*. New Delhi: Penguin Books India (P) Ltd.

Tomasevski, K. (1995). *From Vicious to Virtuous Circles? Gender and Micro-Enterprise Development*. Geneva: United Nations Research Institute for Social Development (UNRISD).

Kilby, P. (Ed.). (1971). *Entrepreneurship and Economic Development*. New York: The Free Press.

Kuppusamy, B. (1979). *Elements of Social Psychology*. New Delhi: Vikas Publishing House Pvt. Ltd.

Lalitha, N. & Nagarajan, B.S. (2002). *Self-Help Groups in Rural Development*. New Delhi: Dominant Publishers and Distributors.

Ministry of Information and Broadcasting (2003). *India 2003*. New Delhi: Publication Division, Govt. of India.

Narasimhan, S. (1999). *Empowering Women—An Alternative Strategy from Rural India*. New Delhi: Sage Publications.

National Policy for Empowerment of Women-2001. New Delhi: Department of Women and Child Development, Govt. of India.

Ninth Five Year Plan, (1997-2002). New Delhi: The Ministry of Information and Broadcasting, Govt. of India.

O' Connell Helen, (1993). *Women Organizing for a Fairer World*. UK: Oxford.

Oakley, P. G. & Masden, D. (1984). *Approaches to Participation in Rural Development*. Geneva: International Labour Organisation.

Páthak. (2003). *Empowerment and Social Governance*. New Delhi: Isha Books.

Pierson, T. (1995). *Dictionary of Social Work*. London: Collins Educational.

Purushothaman, S. (1998). *The Empowerment of Women in India: Grassroots Women's Networks and the State*. New Delhi: Sage Publications.

Ranjani, K. Murthy. (2001). *Building Women's Capacities-Interventions in Gender Transformation*. London: Sage Publications.

Rao, D.B. & Latha, D.P. (1998). *International Encyclopaedia of Women*. Volume 5, New Delhi: Discovery Publishing House.

Rath, N. (1996). *Women in Rural Society—A Quest for Development*. New Delhi: MD Publications Pvt. Ltd.

Sahay, S. (1998). *Women and Empowerment: Approaches and Strategies*. New Delhi: Discovery Publishing House.

Shanthi, K. (Ed.). (1998). *Empowerment of Women*. New Delhi: Anmol Publications Pvt. Ltd.

Srilatha. (1994). The Meaning of Women's Empowerment—New Concepts from Action in Gita Sen *et. al.* (Eds). *Population Policies Reconsidered—Health Empowerment and Right*. Cambridge: Harward University Press.

Stromquist, N.P. (1993). *Theoretical Basis for Empowerment. Paper Presented at International Seminar on Women's Education and Empowerment* Hamburg: UNESCO Institute of Education.

Tamil Nadu Corporation for Development of Women. (2001). *A Guide for Entrepreneurs Development*. Chennai: Mahalir Thittam Project.

Tapan, N. (2000). *Need for Women Empowerment*. New Delhi: Rawat Publications.

Tenth Five Year Plan (2002—2007). New Delhi: The Ministry of Information and Broadcasting, Govt. of India.

Wignaraja, P. (1990). *Women, Poverty and Resources*. New Delhi: Sage Publications India Pvt. Ltd.

Zimmerman, M.A. (2001). *Empowerment Theory*. New Delhi: Plenum.

Journals

Apte, J.S. (1995). Education and Women's Empowerment. *Indian Journal of Adult Education*, 56, July-September.

Bhasin, K. (1985). Education for Women's Empowerment—Some Reflections. *Adult Education and Development*, March, p.38.

Chandra, S.K. (1997). Women and Empowerment. *Indian Journal of Public Administration*, 43, July-September.

Clarke & John. (1992). Empowerment—A Theme for the 1990s. *Local Government Studies*, (Summer) 18, 2.

Das, A. (1998). Child Development and Women's Empowerment in India. *ICCW Journal*, 1 & 2, 3-26.

Dhar, U. & Mishra, P. (2001). Leadership Effectiveness. *Journal of Management Research*, 1, 254-266.

Giri, M.V. Empowerment of Women: An Overview. *Women's Link*, (July—Sep. 2003), 33-36.

Hall, C.M. (1990). Identity Empowerment through Clinical Sociology. *Clinical Sociology Review*, 8, 69-86.

Joshi, M. (2002). Women Organizations in the Uttaranchal Hills: Towards Social Empowerment. *Kurukshetra*, 50, 30-33.

Laxmi, R. K. & Gupta, A. (2002). NGOs in Micro Financing: Partners in Rural Development. *Kurukshetra*, 50, 26-30.

Laxmi, R. K. (2000). Micro-Finance—The New Development Paradigm for Poor Rural Women. *Kurukshetra*, 49, 22-25.

Laxmi, R. K. (2000). Self-Help Groups—Innovations in Financing the Poor. *Kurukshetra*, 49, 26-29, 32-34.

Lelithabhai, K.N. (1998). Empowering Women Through Panchayati Raj. *Kurukshetra*, 46, 9-12.

Mittal, S. (1999). SHGs and Micro Credit—Grassroots Finance in Tamil Nadu. *Social Welfare*, 45, 23-24.

Mor, D.P.S. (2001). Issues and Initiatives in Women's Empowerment. *Social Welfare*, 48, 22-27.

Murugan, K.R. & Dharmalingam, B. (2000). Self-Help Groups—New Women's Movement in Tamil Nadu. *Social Welfare*, 47, 9-12.

Nandal, S. Women's Empowerment Perspectives: A Critical Analysis. *Women's Link*, (July—Sep.2003), 28-32.

Nanavath, R. Empowering Women by the Women for the Women: The SEWA experience. *Women's Link,* (July—Sep 2003), 16-19.

Narasimhan, S. (1999). Empowering Rural Women—An Interview of Past State Initiatives. *Kurukshetra*, 47, 2-8.

Prasad, R.R. (2002). Participation and Empowerment—Rhetorics and Realities. *Kurukshetra,* 50, 4-11.

Purao, P. (2000). Poverty Alleviation and Empowerment Measures. *Social Welfare*, 47, 25-28.

Rao, K. M. C. & Krishna, B.V.V. (2001). Empowerment of Women Through Literacy—An Innovative Experiment. *Kurukshetra*, 50, 45-48.

Rao, D. V. (2001). Democratic Common Interest Groups Foster Empowerment in A.P. *Social Welfare*, 47, 27-33.

Rao, R. (2001). Kerala Model of Women's Empowerment. *Social Welfare*, 47, 34-35.

Rao, R. R. (2001). The Missing Women. *Social Welfare*, 48, 34.

Reddy, K. K. & Reddy, P. V. L. (2001). Globalisation, Agriculture and Women. *Social Action*, 51, 378-394.

Sharma, S.L. (2000). Empowerment without Antagonism: A Case for Reformulation of Women's Empowerment Approach. *Sociological Bulletin*, 49, 19-39.

Shashi, S. & Narayana. (1999). Gender Equality through Reservation in Decision-making Bodies. *Social Action*, 48, 147-159.

Singh, O.R. (2001). Education and Women's Empowerment. *Social Welfare*, 48, 35-36.

Sinha, A. (1999). Empowering Women for Food Security. *Social Welfare*, 46, 3-6.

Suriakanthi, A. (2000). Literacy—Essential for SHGs. *Social Welfare*, 47, 32-34.

Usha, R. (2004). Education and Empowerment of Women: Experience in India. *Indian Journal of Adult Education*, 65, 22-31.

Vijayanthi, K.N. (2000). Women's Empowerment through Self-Help Groups—A Participatory Approach. *Social Change*, 30, 64-87.

Index

Access and control 76
Age at marriage 101, 107, 113, 118, 123
Age group 2, 10, 58, 99, 102, 105, 107, 111, 113, 116, 118, 121, 123, 176, 192
Agro-based industry workers 193
Alcoholic husband 93, 174, 215
Alcoholism 34, 165, 196-97
Amenities, basic 54, 64, 65, 200, 216
Animal husbandry 13, 33
Ante-natal 62-63, 171, 192, 202
Anti-poverty programmes 16
Assessment of Empowerment 132, 134
Atrocities of drunkard husbands 196
Autonomy 25, 39, 43, 53, 87
Awareness about legislations 8
Awareness generation programmes 15, 190, 193

Backward caste 127, 177, 209, 213
Basic household amenities 172
Basic needs 8-9, 14
Birth
control measures 62-64, 171, 191
order 52, 54, 57-58, 96, 99, 105, 116, 121, 125-26, 175
Birth control 63
Birth order 58, 99, 105, 111, 116, 121, 125
Block level coordination committee 214
Bold Panchayat Member 202
Budget allocation 195
Budgeting processes 11

Canvassing 207, 209
Capacity-building programmes 179
Case studies 45, 50-51, 170, 184, 137, 196, 198-217
Cashew nut processing 8
CEDAW 11
Census of India 4, 6-7
Child
bearer 216-17
marriages 18
Christian Marriage Laws 15
Christian women 100, 106, 122, 175
Civic elections 144, 208, 216
activities 34, 43, 53, 91, 92, 166, 174, 186, 193, 201, 203, 207, 212, 216
based organizations 44
dalit 144, 146, 180, 203
health volunteers 192
participation 85, 91, 134-35
resources 28, 36
Service 204, 213
Community 55, 101, 106-07, 112, 117, 122, 127
Community Participation 91
Comparative status of women 131
Computer
programming 14
skills 127, 177
Constitutional safeguards 19
Contract labour 15
Crimes against women 163
CSWB 14-15, 18

Decision making 74, 151

Degree of freedom of movement 100
Department of Women and Child Development 12
Destitute women 18, 197
Devadasis 18
Development programmes 12, 166, 195
 beneficiary-oriented income-generating rural 29
 for women 12, 152, 188
 grassroots level 195
 integrated rural 35
Diagnostic
 design 45
 tests, regulation of 78
Disparity 5, 7-8, 194
Domestic
 expenditure of respondent households 70
 responsibilities 73
 violence 4, 11, 31, 33, 93, 174, 192, 196-97
Domination in family 129
Dowry 9, 15, 32, 79, 82, 137, 160, 162-63, 167, 174, 183-84, 187, 190, 192, 200
Drinking water, fetching of 73, 172
Dropout rate 189
Drunkard husband 82-83, 185, 192, 196

Economic Freedom, Relevance of 152
Economic indicators 31
Education
 basic 11
 component 95
 of girl children 160-61
 non-formal 13
 and Vocational and Life Skills 14, 126
 work for prevention of atrocities 15
Education 60-61, 99, 106, 111, 117, 122, 127, 128
Educational enrichment 189
Educational status of respondents 54
Employment 163
Employment
 articulation ability 175
 generation 194
 of women 76, 172, 185
 opportunities 16, 95, 157-58, 186, 211
 programme 13
Empowerment
 approaches to 30
 assessment of 134
 attributes of 166
 barriers to 140-41
 components of 29
 concept of 23-25, 133, 158, 159
 constituents and constraints 173
 definition of 24-28
 development and 39
 dimensions of 25, 136-139, 178
 economic 16, 18, 25-26, 37, 137, 139, 178
 educational 37, 138-39, 179
 factors influencing 144
 high level of 122, 176
 independent variables 96
 indicators of 30-32, 180-83
 measure 36-37
 measurement of 36-37
 obstacles to 166
 perception of men 183-84
 process of 28, 30, 36-38, 42, 46, 73, 141
 role of institutions 141, 179
 SHGs and 33-35
 spiral of 37-39
 status 144
 strategies of 35-36, 139
 theory of 28
 views of experts 177
 views of men 166
 yardsticks of 95-96
Empowerment women, characteristics 87-88
Entrepreneurship Development Programme 68

Environmental Indicators 31
Equal property rights 162
Eve teasing 5, 93, 164, 167, 173-74, 184, 187, 190, 192
Expenditure, domestic 70

Family
- budget 90-91
- planning 76, 150-51, 160-61, 167, 172, 181, 183, 185, 208, 210, 216
- type 57, 101, 107, 112, 117, 122

Farm-bound workers 102
Farming 151, 181, 199
Female
- infanticide 6, 32, 78, 151, 181, 187, 192
- literacy 7-8, 196

First World Conference on Women 11
Five year plans 20
Foeticide 187, 192
Food and Health Care 7
Freedom
- of articulation 43, 53, 164
- of interaction 160
- of mobility 32, 45, 103, 137, 139, 148, 153, 156, 167, 178, 181-83, 186, 203, 207, 211
- of movement 99-103
- of women 85, 90, 97-103, 104

Fuel wood 65, 73, 172
- collection of 73, 172

GEM 25, 36, 39
Gender
- based problems 82
- Development Index 1
- discrimination 92-93, 103-109
- disparity 5, 7, 25
- empowerment measure 25, 36, 39
- inequality 5, 188
- issues 82, 173-74
- role of 162
- sensitization 12, 15, 190

Girl children 4, 7, 10, 15, 20, 45, 55, 82, 160-62, 174, 190, 200-2, 211, 215
Girl children, education of 161
Governance 9
Government report 154
Greater dependence of women 46
Group interview schedule 51

Health awareness 34
Health Care 7
- Relevance of 150-51

Health hazards 8
High empowerment score 121-24, 175-77
Home gadgets 65-66, 172, 199, 202
Homogeneous interest groups 193
Hostels 14, 18
Household
- annual income 68, 102, 108, 113, 123
- latrines 17
- savings and liabilities 55

Human Development Index 1
Hunger free area programme 46
Husband
- educated 217
- supportive 217
- torturous 217
- unfaithful 163
- wastrel 210, 217

Hygiene 34, 138-39, 178

Ideal characteristics of empowered women 85, 87-88
Identity empowerment theory 29
Ill treatment 93, 174
Income generation activities 10, 12-13, 137, 139, 141, 150, 178
Income, household annual 48, 102, 108, 113, 118, 123
- of respondents 102, 108, 113, 118, 124

Independent variables and women empowerment 96
Indicator of Empowerment 90-94, 180
Infant mortality 4-6
Information and mass education 16
Inter-caste marriages 79, 161-62, 167, 183

JGSY 16
Joint families 101, 107, 112, 117, 123, 170, 205-06

Leadership skills 54, 67
Legal
awareness 32, 145-46, 180, 192
protection 141, 144, 182
enlightenment 192
Legislation 165
Level of
empowerment of women 32, 101, 175
freedom 85, 97, 99, 100, 103
Liabilities 71
Liquor shops 196-97
Literacy
programme 33
skill 175
level 5,7
status of females 189
Livestock 76-77, 151, 172, 181, 202
Living index 103, 109, 119, 124, 177

Maharashtra Rural Credit Programme 34
Maintenance of house 73, 172
Malnutrition 7
Marital status 59-69, 101, 107, 112, 118, 123, 127
of women 101
Marriage
arranged 60, 128, 184
early 34, 162, 164, 217
forced 184, 209
love 60, 79-80, 128-29, 173, 184, 202, 212, 216
system 79
Mass education 16
Maternal
death 4, 6
mortality rates 6-7, 191
Maternity 62
Media exposure 164
Ministry of Rural Development Programmes 16-17
Ministry of Social Justice & Empowerment 12
MMR 6-7, 191-92

NABARD 22
National Commission for Women 17, 19
National Credit Fund for Women 18
National Initiatives for Women Empowerment 12
National Policies
employment of women 188-97
empowerment of women 20, 188-89, 192, 194, 196
National Rural Employment Guarantee Programme 194
National Women Empowerment Policy 196-97
Nativity 58
Non-farm
activity workers 193
labour 66-67, 102, 107, 113, 118, 123, 171, 177
Non-government organizations (NGOs) 12, 18, 22, 29, 35, 42-43, 48, 68, 140-41, 144, 147, 148, 158, 169, 171, 177, 179, 206-07, 209
Role of 141
Nuclear families 57-58, 101, 107, 112, 145, 170, 200, 202, 206, 208-09, 213

Occupation 66, 102, 107, 113, 118, 123, 128
Oxfam 36

Pacific Centre for Women and Development 26
Panchayat elections 78, 153, 173, 182, 186, 196, 203
Panchayat Raj 19
Parental control 217
Parliamentary Committee 19
Participation in elections 78
Patriarchal ideology, challenges 26-27

Perception of men 80-81, 187-188
Perception on women empowerment 183
Petty shop 200-01, 208
Place of birth 99, 106, 111, 117, 121
Plantation
  programmes 34
  workers 193
Political participation of women 44-45
Political space 195
Polygamy 161-62
Poverty alleviation programmes 35
Power and influence 95, 114-119
Power to panchayats 196
Predominance of rural women 77
Pre-sex selection diagnostic test 201
Primary health center 6
Problem solvers, independent 28
Problems of women 80
Programme implementation 5
Property, equal rights 162
Psychological
  barrier 141, 179
  empowerment 25, 36, 38
  qualities 154, 156, 181-83, 186
Punishment 163-64, 167, 183

Rape 4, 9, 15, 18, 137
Rashtriya Mahila Kosh 18
Registration of property 163
Religion 55, 100, 106, 112, 117, 122, 127
Religion exercises 100
Reproductive rights 138-39, 178
Reservation 9, 21, 78, 138-39, 141, 144, 158, 160, 164-65, 173, 179, 182, 190, 195-96, 207-08
Reservation for women 164
Resources 149
Restructured Centrally Sponsored Rural Sanitation Programme 17
Rights of Women 11
Rural
  adolescent women 191
  development 12-13, 16, 22, 35
  women 2, 4-5, 8, 33, 42, 45-46, 53-55, 77, 84, 122, 131, 169, 175-76, 187-88, 197-98
  process of empowering 53, 144, 179
  status of 42, 54, 131, 169

Safety of women 91, 167, 183, 187
Sanitation 18, 139, 149, 178, 181
Savings 71
Scheme for women in difficult circumstances 16
School drop-outs 14
Self employed women 29
Self employment
  infrastructure 77, 172
  programmes 67
Self-help group 5, 10, 21-23, 33-34, 45-46, 49-51, 71-73, 75-77, 103, 108, 114, 116, 124, 147-48, 165, 167-68, 171-72, 182-84, 192-95, 215-16
  indicators sheet for 51
  members of 46, 50, 77, 153, 184
  participation in 114
Self-reliant women 13
Servai community people 199
Sex preference 162
Sex ratio 2, 4, 6, 47, 49, 192
  juvenile 6
Sexual harassment 9, 17-18, 78, 93, 173-74, 190
SHA women 181
Shying women 195
Single women 197
Skill
  acquisition 68, 191
  basic 22
  entrepreneurship 37
  generating 191
  leadership 67
  possessed typing 127
  training 191
  upgradation 16
  vocational 79
Smoking, habit of 208, 210

Social
- customs 31, 55, 79
- empowerment scale 32
- evils 34, 137, 139, 178
- mobilization 22
- indicators 31
- justice 12, 19, 32, 217

Social Welfare Board 18
Societal suppression 217
Socio-economic background 170
Standard of living 103, 109, 114, 116, 124
Status of women 2, 131, 157, 172-73, 177
- economic 2
- educational 2
- health 3
- political 3
- men's response 132

Strategies and barriers to women empowerment 139
Suppressive husbands 215, 218
Swami Vivekananda 199-200, 206, 213
Swarozgaris 16

Tamil Nadu Women Development Corporation and District Social Welfare Officer 46
Third world countries 24
Torture 33, 203-04, 211
Trade unions 158, 194
Trafficking in women, prevention and combating 17
Training 191
Training-cum-Production Centres for Women 14
Tribal women 18
Triumphant women 218

UNDP 39
UNIFEM 10-11, 23, 37
United Nations 3
United Nations Development Fund for Women 15, 23
Unmarried women 17, 107, 123, 176
Unskilled women 106, 112, 117, 122, 176

Village development assembly 34
Village sanitary complexes 17
Violence against women 4-5, 9, 93-4, 109-114
Vocational
- skill 100, 106, 112, 117, 122, 206
- training for adult women 14

Voluntary agencies 145
Vulgar exposure of women 164, 167, 183

Wage disparity 194
Widow remarriage 137, 162
Women and child development 12
Women empowerment
- and methods, obstacles to 89
- bottlenecks obstructing 42
- component 158
- comprised 138, 178
- concept of 85-86
- constituents of 41, 87, 175, 186
- defined 26
- factors influencing 119-24
- indicator of 147, 149, 181
- obstacles to 89
- policy 197
- process of 42, 44, 132, 141, 144, 146, 177, 179-80, 190

Women headed families 197
Women Study Centres 15
Women welfare programmes 44, 53
Women's bank 194
Women's convention 11
Women's empowerment year 16
Women's freedom 76
Women's problems 130
Women's work participation 8
Work Participation 8
World Conference on Women 31

Youth
- clubs 48-50, 169, 183
- groups 161